PRAISE FOR A QUEST FOR V

"For years I have had a personal rule: read anything that David Lorimer writes. I have benefited from David's insights for decades. *A Quest for Wisdom* is his latest and most profound contribution, a summing up of accumulated wisdom. Lorimer is a rare cultural treasure. I hope your quest for wisdom includes this great book."

—Larry Dossey, MD
Author: *One Mind: How Our Individual Mind Is Part of Greater Consciousness and Why It Matters*

"What a blessing David Lorimer's work has been for many fellow seekers over these past several decades. Reading, assimilating, and reviewing countless works at the frontiers of science, philosophy, and spirituality, he has provided his readers year after year with a unique gift, opening up to them horizons that without his intercession might have remained unexplored. Especially important, he combines a wide-ranging, agile intellect with a spiritual foundation that has long grounded his inquiries and deepened his insights. David has made an enduring contribution to our intellectual and spiritual life that I hope will ripple out into the broader culture."

—**Richard Tarnas**, Professor of Philosophy and Psychology, California Institute of Integral Studies, author of *The Passion of the Western Mind* and *Cosmos and Psyche*

"What a wonderful read this collection of essays is from David Lorimer, who has been a curator of seminal thinkers for nearly four decades. Well organised, broad ranging, and filled with penetrating insights, this book is a tour of great minds by a great mind. Highly recommended."

—**Christopher Bache, PhD**, author of *LSD and the Mind of the Universe*

"The range of David Lorimer's writing is extraordinary. Yet every one of these scholarly essays has a freshness and vigour that inspires the reader from the first sentence to the last. Lorimer's contribution to the understanding of the spiritual side of our existence is increasingly widely appreciated. He is a wise and humane guide."

—**Alexander McCall Smith, CBE**, best-selling author and Emeritus Professor of Medical Law, University of Edinburgh

"Events of the last few decades have revealed an alarming decline of wisdom from the mainstream discussion, calling into question any claims of human progress. Enter David Lorimer with his voluminous knowledge of modern science and spirituality, and his heartfelt reflections on an optimistic reverence for life. This book is a gift to humanity, perfectly attuned to the apparent challenges that will energise our awakening into lives rich with purpose and meaning!"

—**Eben Alexander, MD**, neurosurgeon and author of *Living in a Mindful Universe, Proof of Heaven*, and *The Map of Heaven*

"David Lorimer's far-ranging enquiries have taken him through many realms of science, spirituality and philosophy. He has read more books on these subjects than anyone I know, and knows most of the leading thinkers in these fields. This book brings together some of his reflections, previously scattered in various publications—it is an invaluable resource and a perfect bedside book."

—**Rupert Sheldrake, PhD**, biologist and
author of *The Science Delusion*

"David Lorimer is just the sort of thinker that is today all too rare: hugely well read, unstuffy, and interested in philosophy in the best sense. In the course of these essays, spanning forty years, he asks most of the big questions about the nature and meaning of life, with an accent on a spiritual understanding, and drawing on a wide range of sources. They are a delight to read; and on this 'quest for wisdom', there is many a nugget already there to reward the seeker along the way."

—**Dr Iain McGilchrist**, neuroscientist and philosopher,
author of *The Master and his Emissary*

"For the last 40 years, David Lorimer has made an immense contribution to the emerging spiritual worldview of our culture. This book is a marvellously rich and varied collection of his writings, pervaded with a rare combination of acute intellectual insight, spiritual depth and encyclopaedic knowledge. It's a joy to read, showing how a spiritual perspective can illuminate every aspect of our lives and our culture."

—**Steve Taylor, PhD**, author of
Spiritual Science and *The Leap*

"Seated within the Scots "generalist" intellectual tradition of rounded knowledge, David Lorimer braids a guiding thread of philosophy, psychology and politics. Like Jung, he understands the ways in which the outer life of the times draws its drive and meaning from inner spiritual currents. Neither does he flinch from searching out empirical evidence of that psychospiritual reality. These are grounding essays of the past half century that transcend the hustling bustle of a frenzied world."

—**Professor Alastair McIntosh**, author of
Soil and Soul and *Poacher's Pilgrimage*

"The quest is of paramount importance, the substance of it as presented in this book is fascinating and meaningful—and the book as a whole is great and even essential reading in our critical times."

—**Ervin Laszlo, PhD,** Founder, Club of Budapest,
Author, *The Wisdom Principles: A Handbook for our Time*

"There is too much information and a lot of knowledge in our contemporary world, but sadly very little wisdom. David Lorimer's book helps to fill that void. A *Quest for Wisdom* distils the profound thoughts and insights of many philosophers and prophets of our time. It is a handy guide to navigate through the confusions and illusions of the modern materialistic paradigm and shows us the way leading to a more holistic culture. A *Quest for Wisdom* is a most accessible and deeply inspiring book. If you are searching for meaning in your life then this book will certainly prove to be a wonderful companion in that search."

—**Satish Kumar**, Editor Emeritus, Resurgence & Ecologist

"I am delighted to follow David Lorimer's search over decades for Truth, Love and Beauty—usual epithets of the One which remains a Mystery beyond description—without restrictions of the West or the East, or of science and religion, modern and ancient, or of this and that. It is amazing to learn about the number of books he has read, reviewed and assimilated. Each essay in the book is worth staying with and pondering, questioning and learning from. Every searcher will find this book stimulating, encouraging, delightful and full of insights in their journey towards eternal wisdom which of necessity includes taking care of our world with compassion and kindness. I highly recommend David's book A *Quest for Wisdom* but with a caution: find a quiet place and enough time because if you pick up this book you won't be able to put it down."

—**Ravi Ravindra, PhD**, Emeritus Professor of Physics
and Comparative Religion, Dalhousie University

"These wise and wonderful essays offer a penetrating survey of human thought from Heraclitus, Anaxagoras and Plato to Albert Schweitzer, Carl Jung and Peter Deunov. Reading them is a revelatory experience in itself. The brilliance, intelligence and lucidity with which complex ideas are explored and evaluated for their contribution to the enlightenment of humanity is extraordinary; the commitment to this task from the age of 21 prodigious. The critique of materialist science that has cut us off from the universe and dispensed with both God and the soul is both timely and necessary. But most of all, these essays reflect the ideas and values which have informed the author's lifelong quest for wisdom: ideas and values that he has imbibed and assimilated from great teachers and which are totally missing in today's world. They can be summed up by the words Reverence for Life. A truly outstanding gift to us from a man who lives the role of philosopher-king in an era sorely in need of one."

—**Anne Baring**, author of *The Dream of the Cosmos: A Quest for the Soul*

"When I was taking my first steps in philosophy at Winchester College, David Lorimer stressed to me the importance of taking into account lived human experience alongside abstract argumentation; if readers of this book benefit from his humaneness as much as I did, they will be lucky indeed."

—**Benjamin Morison, DPhil**, Chair of Classical Philosophy, Princeton University, former scholar, Winchester College

"A gifted, original and inspirational teacher, David Lorimer is also a writer who compels the attention—and whose passionate quest for wisdom comes through on every page."

—**Harry Bingham**, best-selling author, and Chairman, Jericho Writers, former scholar, Winchester College

"Deep Dave—that's what they called David Lorimer at school. But when I met him, it wasn't so much his *deepness* that struck me, though, certainly, as soon as we did finally start talking, our conversation went down to the deepest profundities of life, as if we were two swimmers. What struck me was how *easy* the swimming felt. He was such a wonderfully kind and clear-eyed guide. His interest in ideas, his affection for the thinkers, his lucidity—they light the way. And reading these marvellous essays brought back how influential he has been. I read first his fascinating pieces on Swedenborg and Beinsa Douno, but then I wanted to read about *everyone* that David has enjoyed. I shall! This is a book that I shall swim in often!"

—Andrew Clover, writer, teacher, actor, director,
comedian and former scholar, Winchester College

"Written in eloquent prose that makes reading a pleasure, this volume of essays by David Lorimer is exceptional in breadth and depth as the author explores some of the deepest and most troubling concerns for the world today. The three sections, Philosophy, Spirituality and Meaning, Consciousness, Death and Transformation, Taking Responsibility—Ethics and Society, between them cover the most pressing existential questions that face humanity: why are we here, what lies beyond birth and death, and how can our lives individually and together fulfil the spiritual potential of humankind. Modernity is challenged by a global crisis largely of our own making and the author, with both compassion and scholarship, shows how the solution lies in our hands. Starting with Swedenborg, Lorimer draws with wonderful clarity on some of the great spiritual exemplars in recent history, to which he adds his own sensitive and thoughtful reflections. Notwithstanding the worst excesses of the human species, this book offers a profound message of hope for the future—never more needed than at the present time."

—Dr Andrew Powell, Founding Chair, Spirituality and Psychiatry
Special Interest Group, Royal College of Psychiatrists, UK,
author of The Ways of the Soul, Conversations with the Soul

"I very much like the idea of someone publishing a collection of the thoughts and explorations of their lifetime, and this one is rich in its coverage and depth. The references, the topics and the arguments show David Lorimer's passage through time, shifting and deepening, with love, Divine Love appearing everywhere. Fascinating, full of wonderful quotes, and worth taking slowly."

—Prof David Cadman, Harmony Adviser to The Prince's
Foundation and author of Love and the Divine Feminine

A QUEST FOR WISDOM

A QUEST FOR WISDOM
Inspiring Purpose on the Path of Life

David Lorimer

AEON

First published in 2021 by
Aeon Books
PO Box 76401
London W5 9RG

British Library Cataloguing in Publication Data

A C.I.P. for this book is available from the British Library

ISBN-13: 978-1-91350-476-2

Typeset by Medlar Publishing Solutions Pvt Ltd, India
Printed in Great Britain

www.aeonbooks.co.uk

*For my daughter Charlotte,
the next writer in the family.
And my son George, a tower of
strength to his many friends.*

CONTENTS

FOREWORD

I first met David Lorimer at the University of St Andrews in October 1970. He was studying economics, French, and German; I was studying theology, and we both took the compulsory philosophy course in our second year. We were nineteen years old; bright-eyed, questioning, uncertain about our futures and the future of the world, naively seeking answers to perennial questions. We had long—sometimes night-long—conversations, rambling and earnest but also entertaining—about books, ideas, potential girlfriends, gossip, wine, snippets of information we had picked up in lectures. He was a considerable athlete; I played rugby. We were Children of the Sixties.

I had taken what is now called a "gap year" between school and university, had spent some months in Ceylon (as Sri Lanka was then), travelled a bit in Europe, and mainly lived alone in my family's cottage by the sea on the south coast of the Isle of Arran. Reading, walking, talking with friends—with the vast sky and glimmering sea always present.

By the time I went up to St Andrews I was already interested in parapsychology, spiritualism, and, broadly, the Western mystical tradition. I had had an out-of-body experience in 1969 which made me profoundly conscious of the possibility of universal "one-ness", which David writes about in this book. In retrospect, it may be that such topics were an initial shared interest; what is certain is that David has devoted his life to pursuing them, which is why this book is appropriately titled *A Quest for Wisdom*.

After St Andrews, I studied law in Dundee and Edinburgh, arriving in the latter university in 1976 and being elected to the "exclusive" Speculative Society the same year. As David mentions in his Introduction, the "Spec" is a literary and debating society, founded in 1764 and little changed in its order of business and its candle-lit, fire-lit debating chamber since then.

David arrived in Edinburgh in 1978 and I proposed him for membership. Admission is by ballot, and on the night on which our petition was being voted the members were unusually boisterous and obstreperous, questioning the validity of the application on spurious grounds and requiring the president of the night, Duncan Menzies, to exercise all his considerable skills of advocacy to order an unprecedented recount. It is not surprising that Mr Menzies is now a Senator of the College of Justice and Privy Councillor, as the Right Hon. Lord Menzies.

What a loss it would have been to the Spec had David not been elected. The three essays he delivered in the Society's Hall—*The Absurd and the Mysterious, Tao and the Path Towards Integration*, and *Voltaire and Russell: the Crusade Against Dogma and Fanaticism*, all included in this book—amply display his erudition, breadth of reading, and intellectual depth. At least to those who managed to stay awake, given the lateness of the hour and the effects of quantities of claret.

David introduced me, and in many cases gave me, many books which have brought me joy and influenced my thought—Gerard Manley Hopkins, Arnold Toynbee, John Moriarty, Sir James Frazer (I managed the 800-page abridged edition of *The Golden Bough*; typically, David has the entire twelve volume canon). My contributions were meagre by comparison, although I did introduce him to Colin Wilson's sixth-form synthesis of existential thought, *The Outsider*, and to the poetry of Ted Hughes. I gave him a membership of the Poetry Book Society for his twenty-first birthday.

Our further careers led David briefly to banking, then teaching, then to devoting himself to philosophical research and spiritual development. I qualified as a solicitor but immediately knew I was not sufficiently committed to the job and set up my plate as a literary agent— I had always aspired to be a writer. In the early 1980s I found my calling writing about Scotch whisky, and in this I am happy to say, I am now pre-eminent.

David Lorimer is a true intellectual in the respected European sense—the British are ambivalent about intellectuals. Over the past forty years he has devoted himself full-time to his search for meaning with intellectual honesty and rigour—not only does he read the books, he understands and reviews them. He has the ability to synthesise and clarify complex ideas from this vast array of sources, and then to draw his own conclusions in the essays which comprise this book.

David now lives in France, but we have kept up over the years—me limping along behind, like Jack Kerouac following Alan Ginsberg and Dean Moriarty, who "... burn, burn, burn like fabulous Roman candles exploding across the skies". David is, and deserves to be, a star.

I have to admit that some of the essays are beyond me, where they require a greater familiarity with authors, concepts, and ideas than I possess to follow David's tightly constructed arguments. But others are glorious revelations—eureka moments, epiphanies—connecting and explaining previously dimly conceived hunches and beliefs.

As I say, the book is truly one person's quest for wisdom over nearly half a century. A highly intelligent, open-minded, extraordinarily well-read person. His is a fascinating quest, from which we can all benefit.

I certainly have.

Charles MacLean
Edinburgh

Charles MacLean has been researching and writing about Scotch whisky for forty years and has published seventeen books on the subject. He was the founding editor of *Whisky Magazine*, sits on a number of judging panels and advises whisky companies on a variety of matters, travelling extensively on their behalf. He was elected Master of the Quaich (the industry's highest accolade) in 2012 and was inducted into the Whisky Hall of Fame in 2016. *The Times* describes him as "Scotland's leading whisky expert".

www.whiskymax.co.uk

PREFACE

Dr Peter Fenwick

David and I first met back in the early 1980s. I had been asked to be Chair of the Scientific and Medical Network and David was its new Director. I asked him why he wanted to take on the Network and he told me that although his father had wanted him to remain a merchant banker and then a conventional public school teacher, David wanted to do something much more spiritual. When it looked as if he was putting his spiritual development ahead of family interests, he was warned that they would disinherit him. David told me this without any rancour or criticism, just accepting that this was the way things were. I could see straight away that I was in the presence of a very unusual person and this became more and more apparent as I got to know him.

Throughout the last 30 years he has produced outstanding programmes for the Network and helped develop Network membership as a web of mutual support and friendship. But his interests extend far beyond the Network. The Inspiring Purpose character and values programme he created for children in Scotland is remarkable. Up to 20,000 children take the course every year and the programme has now expanded beyond the UK into the Commonwealth. David is the modern example of a renaissance man, highly intelligent and pushing forward each area that he touches. His capacity for hard work is phenomenal and his amazing memory even more so. *The Quest for Wisdom* contains 20 pages of references and I can guarantee that David will not only have read them all, but would probably be able to quote accurately from any one of them. He has reviewed up to 200 books a year since 1986 as editor of the Network journal *Paradigm Explorer*. His knowledge of music is vast and he has a deep understanding of the underlying spiritual meaning of many of Bach's preludes and fugues.

The Bulgarian sage Peter Deunov has always been central in David's philosophy. The three words love, wisdom and truth, which are central to the teachings of Deunov, play an equally large role in David's life. This book of essays begins with Victor Frankl and his search for meaning, something which David's own life clearly demonstrates. His deep spirituality is expressed in everything he does—and in every page of his book. But even more importantly he is also a communicator, able not only to convey the essence of a particular philosophical teaching, but also to spark the interest he feels himself in his readers. This book will naturally have a ready-made readership in anyone with an interest in this field. But perhaps more surprisingly, it has the power to interest and even to captivate those for whom the areas of spirituality and philosophy have never held much fascination.

Dr Peter Fenwick is a neuropsychiatrist who is Emeritus President of the Scientific and Medical Network and a world authority on death and dying, about which he has written many books with his wife Elizabeth.

FORMATIVE BACKGROUND

By his labours he has given to our nation many a poem in wood and stone which will continue to impress on the minds of men the sense of another and greater world which surrounds us, and which will lift the thoughts of generations yet unborn to that house of God not made with hands, eternal in the heavens. The workmen die, the dreamers pass away, but the dreams, the idealism, the vision, and the work remain. The dust must return to the earth, but the spirit shall return to God who gave it.

—Tribute to Sir Robert Lorimer KBE at
St Giles Cathedral, September 1929

When I discovered this tribute to my architect grandfather only recently in some family papers at Gibliston in Fife (where I was brought up and which Sir Robert bought in 1916), I was impressed by the phrase referring to "the sense of another and greater world which surrounds us" as this has been a central theme of my own work, though not in stone, but rather in terms of sculpting words. I had read the penultimate sentence during a visit to the Scottish National Archives on the occasion of a conference we organised in 2014 for the 150th anniversary of Sir Robert's birth, and was intensely moved by "The workmen die, the dreamers pass away, but the dreams, the idealism, the vision and the work remain." I wrote it down in my diary at the time, as the dreamers and idealists have important work to do in every human culture. Dr Albert Schweitzer, who features prominently in this volume, wrote that just as a fruit tree produces fruit every year that is the same and yet different, so the perennial truths of human wisdom need to be reborn and expressed anew in every generation. As I wrote of Aldous Huxley when re-reviewing his final book *The Human Situation*, he was a realistic idealist or an idealistic realist—a position which I also espouse.

The earliest of these essays was written forty years ago, and the reader will find in some instances reflections of the time which have to some extent been overtaken by events. There is also, inevitably, a certain amount of repetition, but often in different contexts, although I have carried out some editing in this respect. The essays are divided into three sections: philosophy, spirituality, and meaning; consciousness and death; and ethics and society. They range widely over existential, philosophical, and ethical issues, also with respect to our different levels of identity.

I read very little outside the syllabus during my time at Eton College, although in my last half I did read a book called *They Saw the Future: The Story of Fulfilled Prophecy*, by Justin Glass, which also began to make sense of a number of impressive psychic experiences that my mother had related. My time was principally devoted to athletics, squash, and fives, and as a result, I represented the school in all three sports. When I went on to St Andrews University, I represented the university in athletics, cross-country, and squash, and also ran 3,000 m steeplechase for Scotland in 1972, the same year I won the British Universities Championship at Meadowbank in Edinburgh—one of my first exhilarating experiences of the tartan track that had hosted the Commonwealth Games two years previously.

At St Andrews, I mainly read French and economics, although I also read German, and, crucially, philosophy in my second year. At that time, it was compulsory for arts undergraduates to spend a year studying philosophy, about which I knew next to nothing. There were compulsory courses on logic and metaphysics, including Plato, Aristotle, and the British empiricists of the eighteenth century. At the same time, I was reading Voltaire and Rousseau, and had a brilliant teacher of French poetry in Ian Higgins. It was while studying Baudelaire's poem *Correspondances* with him that I discovered Swedenborg. In twentieth-century literature, we read Camus and Sartre, which gave me an entry into existentialism. The two philosophy courses I found most engaging were Leslie Stevenson on *Seven Theories of Human Nature* and Penny Palmer on the history of existentialism. Stevenson covered Plato, Christianity, Marx, Freud, Sartre, Skinner, and Lorenz (looking this up on the internet reveals that the book has since sold over 250,000 copies). Each thinker or system was covered in terms of basic ideas about human nature, what is wrong with it, and how to put this right—hence it was a consideration of metaphysics and ethics. It was my first proper introduction to Karl Marx's materialist political theory, B. F. Skinner's behaviourism, and Konrad Lorenz's work on aggression, both animal and human.

Penny Palmer opened up new avenues beyond Camus and Sartre to include Kierkegaard, Nietzsche, Marcel, Husserl, Heidegger, and others. I remember one exam question asking us to explain the meaning of Kierkegaard's "teleological suspension of the ethical" in relation to the sacrifice by Abraham of his son Isaac. You really had to have read the text in order even to understand the question. My friend the whisky writer Charlie Maclean and I had a couple of personal sessions with Penny, and of course these were prolonged far into the night on many occasions—I'm sure you know the feeling of the conversation being so interesting that you don't want it to end despite the fact that it is already 2 am. There is a deep sense of shared quest to plumb the depths of the human condition.

For me, as for many others of my generation, a pivotal and intensely engaging intellectual experience was reading Colin Wilson's book *The Outsider*, which had become a runaway bestseller on its publication in 1956 when the author was only twenty-five. The book was the same title as the English edition of Albert Camus's *L'Etranger*, but was a *tour de force* of scope and erudition, especially for one so young. It introduced me to a galaxy of new thinkers beyond Camus and Sartre, and in particular T. S. Eliot, T. E. Hulme, T. E. Lawrence, William Blake, W. B. Yeats, William James, Hermann Hesse, Leo Tolstoy, Fyodor Dostoevsky, and George Fox. I followed this up with his second volume *Religion and the Rebel*, where I encountered A. N. Whitehead, Edmund Husserl, Jakob Boehme (I already knew about Swedenborg, Pascal, and Goethe), Nicholas Ferrar, William Law, John Henry Newman, Rainer Maria Rilke, Ludwig Wittgenstein, Ramakrishna, George Gurdjieff, P. D. Ouspensky, Oswald Spengler, C. G. Jung, Arnold Toynbee, and Bernard Shaw.

This was all heady stuff, and I set out to read as much as I could of the original work of these authors. They seemed to me to be addressing the really important philosophical questions relating to the nature of freedom and the importance of intentionality, our true identity and the way to seek it out. When I had completed my first book, *Survival*, in late 1982, I sent it off to Eileen Campbell at Routledge, whom I had met at the 1981 Mystics and Scientists conference and who had invited me to send her the manuscript. She sent this on to Colin Wilson as the publisher's reader, and he came back with an incredibly enthusiastic recommendation. I have unfortunately lost the original, but it kindly contained the phrase "destined to become a classic in its field". After the book was published and on one of my regular visits to Cornwall, I was invited to spend the night at Colin's house, and I remember enjoying the bottle of Mercurey Rouge 1977 in the course of our fascinating conversation. At the time, he had over 25,000 books spread all around the house and in his garage, and offered me £10 if I could locate a space where he could put another bookshelf! He also tested me on whether I had read all his books, and gave me a couple that I had not read, including his biography of Wilhelm Reich.

I graduated in 1974, and, on the strength of my French and economics, was employed in the international loans department of City merchant bankers Morgan Grenfell. It soon became apparent that this was not to be my career path, although I did work there until the summer of 1976. During that time, I continued to read widely while commuting on the train and I remember one occasion when my colleague Quentin Davies—now Lord Davies of Stamford—saw a volume of Bertrand Russell on my desk, having tracked my other books over the previous few weeks, and remarked, "I agree, life's too short for trash!" One key book I read at the time and discussed with my very supportive honorary grandmother Barbara Hayward (almost all my grandparents had died before I was born) was *Testimony of Light* by Helen Greaves. This was ostensibly a post-mortem account of the experiences of Helen's nun friend Frances Banks and contained the essential idea of a life blueprint agreed to by the soul before incarnation, similar to the process of choosing lives described by Plato in the 10th book of the *Republic*. It is our task and challenge not to forget this blueprint (in Plotinus, the fall is one into ignorance, forgetfulness, and density) and to try to live our lives in alignment with it. It is my experience that, at certain critical moments, there is a strong sense of this blueprint in the way that our lives unfold.

In 1975, I met an important mentor in the Rev Dr Norman Cockburn. He was born in Edinburgh in 1907 and became a canon at Saint Mary's

Cathedral while studying for his PhD at the University on the Platonic Church Father Origen. Norman had an immense library, also extending into his garage, ranging over the huge variety of disciplines. He most generously gave me his sets of C. G. Jung's Collected Works (20 volumes), *The Golden Bough* (12 volumes) and other works by Sir J. G. Frazer, *A Study of History* (12 volumes) by Arnold Toynbee, James Hastings's 12 volume *Encyclopaedia of Religion and Ethics*, the *Catholic Encyclopaedia*, the complete works of Emanuel Swedenborg and Rudolf Steiner, *The Sacred Books of the East* (50 volumes) an almost complete set of the journals and proceedings of the Society for Psychical Research along with other works by Oswald Spengler (*The Decline of the West*), Nicholas Berdyaev, Vladimir Solovyev, and John Macmurray.

At the time, I was considering becoming ordained, either in the Swedenborg Church or the Church of England (I remember my mother saying, rather to my indignation, when we first visited Canterbury in 1966 that I might make a good bishop!). Norman advised me to stay within the mainstream, so I arranged to spend a weekend at St Stephen's House in Oxford. There I had an interview with the admissions tutor, John Cobb, who told me to my astonishment that if I studied theology for three years, I would probably lose my faith in the process! Suffice to say, by the end of the weekend I had decided against this path. During one of my visits to Norman in New Malden, I asked him what he thought were the most important principles in life. Almost without hesitation, he replied Love and Freedom. I have found this to be very good advice on the path of life.

In the meantime, I visited my old university friend Robert Bogdan, who was teaching at Charterhouse. This seemed to me an intrinsically worthwhile and congenial way of life, which had the advantage of long holidays that would give me an opportunity for study and writing. So I got in touch with Cambridge and secured a place more than a year in advance for the Postgraduate Certificate in Education in the academic year 1977–78. It was now the very hot summer of 1976, with temperatures over 90° and no air conditioning in the offices. While I was a student, in the summer of 1971, I was lucky enough to have a job at Moet & Chandon in Epernay showing visitors around their champagne cellars, and drinking champagne with them either in a salon or in the garden. I learned a lot about champagne in particular, and wine in general. So I decided to write to Patrick Forbes, the managing director in London, on the off chance that there might be an opening for

September. He replied synchronistically that someone had just withdrawn and that they would be delighted if I could come out and work during September and October. This sign was all I needed, so I resigned from the bank the following day.

I spent August in Scotland putting a part of my music collection onto cassette tapes and choosing what amounted to four boxes of books that I had resolved to read over the following year. These included many of the authors mentioned above, including Radhakrishnan, Jung, Spengler, Toynbee's abridged *Study of History* (still over 1,000 pages), Frazer's *Golden Bough* (almost as long) and a large number of books on philosophy, psychology, theology, spirituality, consciousness, and comparative religion. I arrived in Epernay at the end of August, just in time for the vintage beginning on September 1, the earliest since 1893. It was a glorious autumn, and I was also able to read during the day when I was not giving a tour, as well as in the evening.

At the end of October, I drove through eastern France to Heidelberg, where I was initially hosted by Fritz and Gordon, two friends of my old school friend Martin Powell, who had studied at the university there. I had saved up enough money not to have to work until after Christmas, so I spent the time reading in the library and attending lectures on a number of topics. In the evening, the bells from all the churches in the city chimed at once, a magical feeling. I read late into the night in my lodgings in nearby Schwetzingen, which also had a castle, but nothing like as romantic and beautiful as Heidelberg. I had wanted to go there ever since the city was featured in my first German textbook, *Deutsches Leben*. I spent Christmas in Scotland, and on my return managed to find a job delivering furniture to US military bases with my flatmate Harald from Poland. The most amusing incident occurred when, having received an enormous consignment of china eggs, we had to take part of the stock over to Nuremberg and were stopped by the police as they reckoned that we might be overweight. I suggested to Harald that we should jump out, but the police told us to get in again as we were part of the weight. In the event, we were fined for being overweight on the back axle and warned that we were liable to be fined again if stopped by another police patrol before reaching our destination. Luckily, we weren't.

I returned to Epernay at the beginning of April 1977 and worked there until the end of May, moving down to Cognac to work for Hennessy during June. At the end of my stay, my university friend

Alex Field, who was working for Martell, paid a visit and we were allowed to enter the *"Paradise"* area and lower test tubes into three barrels of ancient cognac—we chose 1815 as the oldest, 1864 as the year of my grandfather's birth, and 1920, the year of Alex's father's birth. It has to be said that the 1920 brandy was the best, although it is always fascinating to taste old wines and spirits. I also had this opportunity at Moet, where I tasted 1911, 1914, 1928, and, during the visit of a representative from Andre Simon, 1878. They had hoped to dig out some 1876, but there was none to be found, so they went for 1878, and apparently had to open forty bottles in order to find two that were remotely drinkable.

I spent a very stimulating year in Cambridge, and carried out my teaching practice at Tonbridge. There I took transcendental meditation after listening to a lecture by Peter Russell, and also had my intellectual and artistic horizons broadened by my friend Henry Dyson, who introduced me to the work of Martin Buber and the artist Thetis Blacker. During the Lent term, I had an interview at Fettes College in Edinburgh with my old head, Tony Chenevix-Trench, who appointed me for the autumn of 1978. I lived in School House on the top floor of the building, where the rooms were 127 steps up and only accessible through the boys' washroom. However, there was a magnificent view over the skyline of Edinburgh, and east down towards north Berwick. It was during this period that I was elected a member of the Speculative Society, founded in 1764 and about which I write in relation to three of the essays in this collection.

During the Easter holidays of 1980, I went to have lunch with Ian and Esther Higgins, and I bought a copy of the *Times Educational Supplement*, something I never did. I leafed through the advertisements for modern languages, and fell upon an appointment at Winchester College for French and German. It was one of those blueprint moments and I knew immediately that I would get the job, despite some intermittent uncertainty during the appointment process. Auspiciously, on my way to the interview with the headmaster, John Thorn, I passed through the cathedral where Bach's fugue in D major, BWV 533 was being played on the cathedral organ—I thought this a very good omen, which indeed it turned out to be. Years later, when visiting my former colleague David Conner, now Dean of Windsor, I heard this same piece again being played in St George's Chapel as he was escorting me to the gate—I had not heard it before or since.

By the summer of 1981, I had decided to write two books, the first of which was *Survival—Body, Mind and Death in the Light of Psychic Experience*, which I more or less completed in St Andrews during the eight-week summer holiday of 1982. I typed it directly on a manual typewriter, then retyped it onto a clean copy at two pages a day until I had a manuscript of 240 pages—I made hardly any changes between the first and second versions. It was very exciting when the published copy dropped through my letterbox in June 1984. As you can appreciate, writing a book is hugely easier with our current technology, which also allows a cut-and-paste process as well as the simple correction of mistakes before anything is printed out. In addition, I am dictating this piece, as with all my writing.

Winchester was a hugely stimulating environment, both in terms of pupils and dons. I was enormously aware of the history and pedigree of a school founded in 1382, and regularly walked around the cloister where many distinguished Wykehamists were commemorated. I also used to meditate in the Chantry in the centre of the cloister and would often work peacefully in School, a magnificent building designed by Sir Christopher Wren where hardly any other colleagues were to be found. During my time there, I got to know many of the cleverest scholars in the school and held regular discussion groups by candlelight on Friday evening in my dining room at 6 Kingsgate Street. Three of them stand out: the first was Christopher Gray, who collected almost one language O Level from scratch per term, and whom I was deputed to teach German (he later learned Polish, Romanian, Czech, Slovak, and Lithuanian). I lent him many books, including Jung's *Psychological Types*, which he read at the age of sixteen. He took the top First in Greats in his year at Oxford, and another First in theology before becoming ordained and working in a poor area of Liverpool, where he was tragically murdered by one of his parishioners in 1996, at the age of only thirty-two. Obituaries appeared in all the major broadsheets.

The second was the author Harry Bingham, son of the distinguished judge Lord Bingham of Cornhill, KG, who held the posts of both Lord Chief Justice and Master of the Rolls. Harry arrived in Winchester as a scholar at the same time and I initially taught him German. Then in his third year he was in my Div (general studies class) where boys had to write fortnightly essays on the books we were reading. Harry's essays were uniformly brilliant and incredibly well written. I remember writing at the bottom on one of these essays that he wrote as well as Aldous Huxley, and that I hoped he would become a writer. He read PPE at Oxford and achieved a Congratulatory First, moving on to become a merchant banker. However, he took a sabbatical to look after his wife in his late twenties, and took the opportunity of writing his first novel, *Money Matters*, receiving, as I understand it, a six-figure advance for this and his next two books—so he became a writer after all. Indeed, he now coaches people on how to write.

The third person was Ben Morison. My friend and colleague Simon Eliot told me that Ben had written a six-page essay at the age of fourteen entitled *Does God Exist?* Could he come round and discuss the essay? I read it in advance and remember Ben turning up in his gown on my doorstep for tea on a rainy afternoon. He had considered the various philosophical proofs of the existence of God, and had concluded that God did not exist. I put the point that God is not just a concept, but that the divine can be directly experienced in mystical states—so I lent him my copy of William James's famous Gifford Lectures, *Varieties of Religious Experience*. Ben became a regular at my discussion groups until I left Winchester in 1986. I saw him again in Paris in 1988, when he was studying piano with the widow of Olivier Messiaen. We lost touch, until I looked him up in the Old Wykehamist Roll, only to find that his address was Exeter College, Oxford. I immediately rang him up and found that he was a philosophy don and senior tutor, having chosen this path over that of a concert pianist. As it happened, I was planning to come to Oxford only a fortnight later, so he kindly invited me to stay as his guest in college, and it turned out that he was also the wine steward, a further congenial link. Ben now teaches at Princeton, but I believe he is still an atheist …

In 1985 I discovered via Omraam Mikhael Aivanhov the work of Beinsa Douno (Peter Deunov), as I describe in one of my prefaces below. Even now, and notwithstanding my own modest publications (see bibliography), he is very little known when one considers that he is arguably among the greatest spiritual teachers who have ever lived. He left an extraordinary spiritual and musical legacy, as I explain in *Prophet for Our Times*. I was attracted by the way in which he combined the Greek and Christian heritage of the West, as well as his focus on five key principles—Love, Wisdom, Truth, Justice, and Virtue—rather than on a series of creedal propositions to which one is obliged to assent.

The incorporation of physically based spiritual exercises and the Paneurhythmy sacred dance was also attractive by contrast with the neglect
and even denigration of the body within the Western Christian tradition.

It was around this time that I began to think of moving on from
Winchester, and had the opportunity of becoming either Director of
Wrekin Trust—an adult spiritual education charity founded by one of
my mentors and friends Sir George Trevelyan, or Director of the Scientific and Medical Network. I chose the Network and left Winchester,
moving to Gloucestershire to live in a house belonging to my friend
Serge Beddington-Behrens. Another Winchester scholar, Andrew
Clover, helped with the move involving a huge number of books onto
shelves with bricks in between. Just out of curiosity, as I was writing
this, I looked him up on the internet and found that he had become a
famous writer, actor, and comedian …

I have been working with the Network ever since, and have just completed my 100th issue as editor of what began as a plain newsletter and
has become a fully-fledged review called *Paradigm Explorer*. One of the
aspects I have strongly developed over the years is the book review
section. I write long reviews of between forty and fifty books a year
and shorter accounts of a further 150, all of which adds up over the
years. More than 5,000 books were entered into the Network database
between 1996 and 2014. These cover science and philosophy of science,
medicine and health, philosophy and spirituality, psychology and consciousness studies, ecology and futures studies, and a general section
for other areas including politics. It has been an immense privilege to
be in a position where I am learning all the time across a considerable
range of disciplines, distilling many essential insights in the process—
which I aim to pass on to readers, but which also form part of my own
intellectual and spiritual development, along with our programme of
conferences—especially Mystics and Scientists and Beyond the Brain.
As such, I regard myself as a curator who has been creatively exhibiting
and communicating a selection of important works for my readers.

The structure and content of this volume is self-explanatory, and
I have written short introductions to each piece to put them in context.
Many of the people I have written about have been inspiring beacons
on my own path and I hope that you can likewise draw some inspiration for your own journey through life.

Many of the essays were written without the extensive academic
apparatus of footnotes, and where there were such notes I have removed

them. However, readers will find a comprehensive bibliography at the end of the book, including details of my other publications.

I am dedicating this book with immense love to my daughter Charlotte, who is just embarking on her own career as a writer, podcaster, and curator, which I expect to surpass my own by a considerable margin; also to my son George, whose life will not be a literary one but rather one dedicated to acting and the performing arts, cooking, and, in his spare time, to our common passion for golf.

I'd also like to thank my wife Marianne for kindly typing up so many of the essays—our life together with our dogs and horses is such a blessing!

St Colombe sur l'Hers, France, January 2020.

PHILOSOPHY, SPIRITUALITY
AND MEANING

Victor Frankl and the Human Search for Meaning

Man's Search for Meaning *is one of the few books I have reread more than once. The first part is an extraordinary existential narrative of the author's experience in Auschwitz, while the second draws out some of the implications that Frankl developed in his career as a psychiatrist. I recently reread* Beyond Reductionism, *the book that emerged from the symposium of the same name held in 1968 at Alpbach in the Austrian Alps. The last chapter on reductionism and nihilism is by Frankl and discusses what he calls nothing-but-ness and its association with the emergence of an existential vacuum leading to widespread "noogenic neurosis", especially among young people. The search for meaning in life remains an essential aspect of our human situation, including, as he points out, meaning in suffering and also in self transcendence, which goes well beyond hedonistic will to pleasure and the pursuit of happiness.*

Partly as a result of reading this book, I made a point of going to the former concentration camp at Buchenwald when I spent the summer of 1983 in Leipzig. On the same trip to Weimar, I visited Goethe's house and spent a couple of hours in Buchenwald, where I collected two symbolic items—a bent rusty nail and a short piece of barbed wire. I did wonder how I might explain this if challenged at the border by the East German police. There I had an intensely moving experience. I was in a small building where anatomical

3

experiments were carried out on prisoners; it was also the site of the incinera-tor. There was a small room with wood panelling where people had perhaps spent their last minutes, and I wondered if there might be any inscriptions. Low on a wall, I discovered three French words in capital letters, etched with a pin: CROIRE, ESPERER, PRIER (BELIEVE, HOPE, PRAY). I was aghast, and just at that moment a man came in. I told him what I had found and he said: ACH, GLAUBEN, HOFFEN, BETEN. I should naturally have expected a response in German, as I was after all in Germany—but I was nevertheless taken aback, and have never forgotten that moment.

Journey to an unknown destination

Victor Frankl was one of some 1,500 people travelling through sev-eral days and nights towards an unknown destination, supposedly a munitions factory, where they would be employed as forced labour by the Nazis. At length the train seemed to shunt into a siding, and some passengers were able to look out, only to be confronted with a sign which froze them with horror—Auschwitz. In an initial parade of prisoners, some were selected for the right-hand side, which meant work, while others were syphoned off to the left side—immediate gas-sing and incineration; the survivors were able to see the smoke rising from the incinerators. They were herded into sheds where they had to give up all their belongings and clothes, and then have their heads shaved, after which they were scarcely able to recognise themselves. They were stripped literally to their naked and apparently insignif-icant existence, and realised that their whole former lives had to be struck out. At this point many were unexpectedly overcome by a grim sense of humour as they huddled into the showers—at least it was real water coming out …

None of the prisoners could previously have experienced such a lim-iting set of external circumstances: they must all have been compelled to face up to the question posed by Erich Fromm: "If I am what I have, and what I have is lost, who then am I?" They had only their own and their fellow prisoners' inner resources to draw on—their being rather than their possessions. Much of their energy was devoted to the simple struggle for survival: it was imperative to seem fit for work if one was to avoid the gas chamber. It was a struggle which had to be renewed daily, without knowing whether the present situation was going to per-sist indefinitely—"with the end of uncertainty came the uncertainty of the end" as Frankl himself put it. Each day had to be lived through without peering into an apparently hopeless future. It was not necessarily those with most physical strength who survived, but rather those who were anchored in some deeper meaning which allowed them to retain a sense of dignity and freedom. Some fixed for themselves imaginary dates of release, projecting, for instance, that they would be out by Easter. When the day finally arrived, it frequently occurred that the prisoner in question ostensibly contracted some illness as a result of which he died within a few days. Frankl comments that it seemed that such men had made an inner bargain with themselves; they could put up with anything for a limited period, but beyond this their will to live withered, resulting in death.

Life in the raw

Frankl approvingly quotes the following words of Nietzsche: "He who has a why to live can bear almost any how." Obviously the defeatist assertion, "I have nothing to expect from life any more" is scarcely a recipe for survival in a concentration camp. "What was really needed," says Frankl, "was a fundamental change in our attitude towards life. We had to learn ourselves and, furthermore, we had to teach the despairing men, that it did not really matter what we expected from life, but rather what life expected from us. We needed to stop asking about the meaning of life, and instead think of ourselves as those who were being questioned by life—daily and hourly." He contends that the right answer lies not in talk and meditation, but rather in attitude and conduct, in realising one's responsibility to fulfil the tasks placed on one's path. For the prisoners such a change of attitude involved perceiving or discovering a meaning in their response to circumstances; in one case this became clear when a woman compared her situation in camp with her past life, and realised that her free state had been one of spiritual inertia—"In my former life I was spoiled and did not take spiritual accomplishments seriously ... I am grateful that fate has hit me so hard." Without her apparently appalling experience, she would never have gained an insight which she clearly felt to be of great significance. A contributor to the anthology of letters written mostly by imprisoned German citizens—"Dying we Live"—makes a comment with similar implications to the effect that no time of a man's life is lost except that which he allows to flow past him unthinkingly and foolishly.

Frankl's experiences in Auschwitz are both the starting point and the key to his philosophy and psychotherapy.

Like Jung, Frankl finds modern man disoriented, living in what he calls "an existential vacuum", which he defines as "a total lack, or loss, of an ultimate meaning to one's existence that would make life worthwhile. The consequent void, the state of inner emptiness, is at present one of the major challenges of psychiatry." He attributes this to the dual loss of "instinctual security", a pre-moral automatic response to life, and of religious traditions which laid down clear guidelines for conduct, implicitly backed by an absolute divine guarantee. Associated with this existential vacuum are four so-called collective neuroses which Frankl considers to be typical of the modern Western outlook: first, an ephemeral attitude to life, involving a provisional day-to-day living devoid of any wider or deeper perspective; second, a fatalism which leads man to consider himself the plaything of external or internal forces, the first implying a resigned apathy towards events, and the second some form of behaviourism or psychological determinism—this second feature reinforces the ephemeral attitude by regarding any kind of planning for the future as superfluous; third, the prevalence of collectivist or conformist thinking, with the individual's desire to remain inconspicuously submerged in the mass: and fourth, fanaticism, which has the pernicious effect of politicising humans instead of humanising politics—the individual's only value is in service towards the cause, perhaps to the extent of dying for it; the cause almost certainly involves the brutal sacrifice of other individuals who do not happen to share the obsessive sympathies of the fanatic himself.

A further more topical problem, namely unemployment neurosis, brings us back to the existential vacuum; this neurosis is seen by Frankl in a more diluted form as "Sunday Neurosis", when the rush of the week is suspended, and people may be thrown back onto their own resources. Retirement provokes a similar set of questions, questions which we are frequently too "busy" to answer. Unlike Sartre, Frankl does not contend that man must *invent* his own meaning and justification, but rather that such meaning must be *discovered* by the individual—"What is demanded of man is not, as some philosophers teach, to endure the meaninglessness of life; but rather to bear his incapacity to grasp its unconditional meaningfulness in rational terms. *Logos is deeper than logic*" (my italics).

The will to meaning

The mind cannot do the job single-handed, but requires the assistance and commitment of the will. Frankl goes further than his Viennese predecessors Freud and Adler by contending that the "will to meaning" is primary, and that the will to pleasure (or pleasure principle) and the will to power (or money) are "substitutes for a frustrated will to meaning". He directs his main critique towards the pleasure principle, or the pursuit of happiness for its own sake, by asserting that happiness must ensue and not be pursued "for it is the very pursuit of happiness that thwarts happiness". In other words, happiness is derivative, a side-effect or result of having done something. Besides, gratification of needs, drives, and instincts does not necessarily lead to fulfilment and integration: Frankl differentiates his view from psychoanalysis by saying that he "considers man as a being whose main concern consists in fulfilling a meaning and in actualising values, rather than in the mere gratification and satisfaction of drives and instincts"—animals can achieve as much. For Frankl, going beyond gratification means going beyond self-actualisation, which he maintains is derivative in a similar way to happiness in that it cannot be pursued in itself. Man should realise that his task is the realisation of values and the fulfilment of meaning potentials which are to be found in the world, rather than within himself or within his psyche as a closed system. These values reveal a gap between what one is and what one might be, a gap which creates a tension which can never be fully resolved; more importantly they are a beacon which draws us ahead rather than a drive which pushes us from behind.

Transience and human values

The gap between being and becoming is inherent in the human condition; even if it is momentarily bridged, time brings us back to earth. Hesse talks of peace of mind in this way—"There is such a thing as peace, but there is no peace that dwells in us eternally and never leaves us. There is only a peace which must be won time and time again by unceasing struggle, that must be won each day anew." Frankl singles out three factors which make it impossible for us to achieve personal fulfilment—pain, death, and guilt, or, in other words suffering, mortality, and fallibility, all of which impose severe limitations on us;

but they constitute the context within which we are constrained to operate, and in the face of which we must strive to achieve our values and
ideals. Frankl rejects the idea of asking any question about the general
meaning of life, which he equates with asking the chess player what
is the best chess move; he must ask the questioner to specify the context. Hermann Hesse makes a similar statement—"I hold that I am not
responsible for the meaning, fullness or meaninglessness of life, but
that I am responsible for what I do with my own unique life." It is the
context that determines the nature of the values and meaning which can
be fulfilled at any given time.

Frankl divides these values into three categories: creative values associated with art and work; experiential values where a person discovers
meaning in the contemplation of a beautiful object or in love; and thirdly
attitudinal values where a meaning and purpose is discerned in suffering. Frankl has comparatively little to say about the meaning of creative
values, which involve the greatest degree of active participation, but
deals at length with the other two categories, superficially more passive in character, but which are ignored by those who equate value and
identity with their jobs. Before discussing these in more detail we must
elaborate on the postulates of what Frankl terms "logotherapy".

Logotherapy is a form of therapy which aims to confront a person
with, and reorientate them towards, the meaning of their life. As well as
asserting that there is a will to meaning and that suffering has a meaning,
it holds that we have freedom of will, and can decide how to interpret
our life. This freedom of will has to be exercised in the face of instincts,
inherited disposition, and environment—factors which have all been
used to exonerate us from responsible conduct. Frankl contends that in
our century, while the influence of such factors is undeniable, "Man alone
is not determined by his origins; his behaviour cannot be calculated from
the type. The reckoning will not come out even; there will always be a
remainder. This remainder is in the freedom of man to escape the conditioning factors of type." He goes on to argue that we only become human
to the extent that we rise above the type. This freedom in turn entails
responsibility for choosing one's attitude or course of action. One might
object that the transitory nature of life makes the exercise of such responsibility pointless, since death marks the end of our efforts.

Frankl does not at this point invoke a future existence as a criterion
of meaning, but pursues the same line as Goethe who stated, "I feel pity
for those persons who make so much ado about the transience of all

things and lose themselves in the contemplation of earthly vanity. Why, we are here for the very purpose of making the transitory imperishable, and this can only be done if we know how to appreciate both conditions." Frankl sees the past as the storehouse of achieved potentialities where "nothing is irrevocably lost but everything irrevocably stored". Thus he maintains that the transience of existence is far from rendering it meaningless; but equally he warns that this very transience constitutes our responsibility: "for everything hinges on our realising the essentially transitory potentialities". Our responsibility is to these present potentialities, and only to the past to the extent that reinterpretation might make it more meaningful in the present context. It is a daunting ethical challenge.

The meaning of love

"Hell", says Dostoevsky's Father Zossima, "is the inability to love." Frankl first discovered the full meaning of love as an experiential value when, one morning at Auschwitz, he was trudging out towards the railway line. A casual remark by a fellow prisoner turned his thought towards his wife—

> For the first time in my life I saw the truth ... that love is the ultimate and highest goal to which man can aspire ... the salvation of man is in and through love ... I understood how a man who has nothing left in this world may still know bliss, be it only for a brief moment, in the contemplation of his beloved. In a position of utter desolation, when a man cannot express himself in positive action, when his only achievement may consist in enduring his sufferings in the right way—an honourable way—in such a position man can, through loving contemplation of the image he carries of his beloved, achieve fulfilment.

He talks of the grace, enchantment and miracle of love which throws open a whole universe of values—"In his surrender to the Thou, the lover experiences an inner enrichment which goes beyond that Thou; for him the whole cosmos broadens and deepens in worth, glowing in the radiance of those values which only the lover sees."

Love also enables the loving person to grasp the uniqueness of the loved person, who becomes *ipso facto* irreplaceable, and thus completely differentiated from others. Love enriches our experience, even if it is unrequited, by deepening our sense of values, and through the fulfilment of reaching beyond ourselves to the core of another human being. The historian Arnold Toynbee makes a similar point in his *Experiences*: "Love gives life a purpose and meaning and value that cannot be found, in human life at any rate, so long as it is lived for its own sake. The absolute value of love makes life worthwhile, and so makes man's strange and difficult situation acceptable. Love cannot save from death, but it can fulfil life's purpose; and, in so far as life's purpose has been fulfilled, its fulfilment cannot be undone by death when death puts an end to life itself."

Toynbee not only attributes to love the same potential of fulfilling a purpose beyond self-interest, but also maintains that the value of the fulfilment achieved cannot be destroyed for the person who has experienced it. Frankl asserts that

> Suffering and trouble belong to life as much as fate and death. None of these can be subtracted from life without destroying its meaning. To subtract trouble, death, fate and suffering from life would mean stripping life of its form and shape. Only under the hammer blows of fate, in the white heat of suffering, does life gain shape and form.

It is easy to discern the patterns of Frankl's own experience behind these words; the conditions implied have already been discussed above with reference to Auschwitz. They represent such a constriction of circumstances, such a curtailment of the opportunities to act or experience positive values, that the only freedom left is the freedom to take a stand against them. Even in this condition, which is only genuine if unavoidable, "the conditions do not determine me, but I determine whether I yield to them or brave them"; the suffering becomes a task, an opportunity for attitudinal values such as courage or compassion to be actualised. In his *Markings* Dag Hammarskjöld maintains that we already know all we need to know about the next demand of life—"that its sole measure is our own strength": an assertion that we cannot be defeated by life, and should not worry about whether we will find ourselves able to rise to the occasion.

Sometimes the realisation of attitudinal values occurs in retrospect, when the value of a particular experience is reinterpreted. Frankl claims that the greatness of a life can be measured by the greatness of a moment, that it is the peaks, as in mountain ranges, which determine the meaningfulness of life, and that a single moment can retroactively flood an entire life with meaning. While he was still in Auschwitz Frankl himself had the experience of visualising himself in a warm comfortable lecture hall talking about the psychology of the concentration camp. It enabled him to rise above his immediate suffering and confer some retrospective meaning on the horrors of the present. One case which he is fond of citing himself concerns a retired doctor whose wife had recently died; the man was devastated, and paid Frankl a visit. He was asked what would have happened if he had died before his wife: he immediately realised that his wife would have had to endure the suffering which he himself was now going through: the fact that he had spared her this conferred value on the suffering of his bereavement. This change of attitude was accompanied by the emergence of meaning.

For Martin Buber "Existence will remain meaningless for you if you yourself do not penetrate into it with active love, and if you do not in this way discover its meaning for yourself. Everything is waiting to be hallowed by you: it is waiting for this meaning to be disclosed and realised by you." One is looking for what he calls the "hidden significance" of the situation. Buber confines himself to Frankl's sphere of "experiential values". Frankl's contribution includes but goes beyond this sphere, as a result of the insights which he gained from his experiences in Auschwitz. He rejects psychoanalytical determinism; he regards as illusory the direct pursuit of happiness, and the actualisation of the self through various forms of gratification. As Maslow also realised, self-actualisation is only attainable through surrender and transcendence of the self; a man must be prepared to lose his soul in order to find it. And even when there are no opportunities to realise creative or experiential values, man still retains the freedom to choose his attitude towards present circumstances, however unfathomable the questions posed by life may seem. "There is no predicament", said Goethe, "that we cannot ennoble either by doing or enduring."

The Absurd and the Mysterious

E *ssay delivered to the Edinburgh Speculative Society in 1982. This is one of three essays originally delivered to the Speculative Society founded in 1764 during the Scottish Enlightenment for the improvement of literary composition and public speaking, and whose members have included many distinguished judges as well as Sir Walter Scott, Robert Louis Stevenson, the first Earl Russell and Benjamin Constant. The halls have been in the same location in the Old Quad of Edinburgh University since 1832, which means that my great-grandfather, the jurist and moral philosopher James Lorimer, sat on the same benches under the same candlelight from 1844 to 1846. All this explains the style of the introduction, where the essayist reads from a lectern with a candle illuminating his script for either side. At the end of the essay, members have a chance to criticise it, and, in the case of the most undistinguished efforts, vote for it to be consigned to the Society's fire. I am relieved to report that this essay—and the others in this volume—were voted into the archive although it was never clear that this was more than a box file.*

This essay builds on the first one in its reference to Viktor Frankl, but has its origins in my study at St Andrews University of twentieth-century French literature, including the work of Jean-Paul Sartre (I did plough through his 700-page Being and Nothingness*) and Albert Camus. Following my reading of* La Peste (The Plague) *with its reflections on evil and fate by the central* *character Dr Rieux, I remember thinking as an atheist for a few weeks, but later arrived at the view that the Divine can be experienced and lived. This does not make physical and moral evil any less tragic, but it does provide a deeper existential context, as this essay suggests.*

Mr President, you may well have been wondering, over the past week, whether your essayist had the remotest idea of what he intended to talk about, having submitted such a comprehensive, not to say incomprehensible title. Would he appear in the Society's halls at all? Would he follow the shameless example of his great-grandfather Professor James Lorimer by failing to deliver an essay on a pretentious-sounding title (*The Comparative Merits of Goethe and Schiller as Dramatists*)? Would he read the first silent essay, leaving members on the benches to deduce its arcane qualities from the cryptic expression on his face?

Not so. But the title requires some amplification. I propose to examine the genesis and development of currents of thought which have led to widespread proclamations, in our century, of the purposelessness of man and the meaninglessness of life; then to analyse the roles of intellect and intuition, the nature of consciousness and its relation to perception of meaning in life; and finally to suggest that experiences of beauty, love, and mystical union point the way to our true identity and fulfilment, beyond the partial vision of the absurd man.

Absurdity—one interpretation of life

The original connotation of the word absurd was musical, meaning out of harmony, an analogy which seems particularly apposite when considering our current relation to life and the environment. "Man", writes Henri-Frederic Amiel, "is only what he becomes—profound truth; but he becomes only what he is—truth still more profound—What am I? Terrible question. There lies the abyss." What, then, is our true relation to the universe? Does the absurd man have the final answer?

At the end of the eleventh century Omar Khayyam wrote:

> *Into the universe and why not knowing*
> *Nor whence, like water willy-nilly flowing*
> *And out of it like wind upon the waste*
> *I know not whither, willy-nilly blowing.*

Nearly nine centuries later, this view was echoed by Bertrand Russell—
"Brief and powerless is Man's life; on him and all his race the slow, sure

doom falls pitiless and dark. Blind to good and evil, reckless of destruction, omnipotent matter rolls on its relentless way"—or T. S. Eliot—"men and bits of paper, whirled by the cold wind, which blows before and after time". Both views depict human impotence in the face of a hostile and implacable universe, to which we seem to be totally unrelated and unconnected. Einstein expressed a similar vein of thought, but with an important if hesitant qualification—"Strange is our situation here on earth. Each of us comes for a short visit, not knowing why, yet sometimes seeming to divine a purpose." He remained a metaphysical agnostic and felt that it is enough "to contemplate the mystery of conscious life perpetrating itself through all eternity, to reflect upon the marvellous structure of the universe which we can dimly perceive, and to try humbly to comprehend even an infinitesimal part of the intelligence manifested in nature".

It will be noted that, at this point, Einstein is writing of his experiences on an intellectual level. Elsewhere he hints at his idea of divining a purpose and states, "The most beautiful thing we can experience is the mysterious. It is the source of all true art and science. He to whom this emotion is a stranger, who can no longer stand rapt in awe, is as good as dead: his eyes are closed." Here Einstein is describing a more intense apprehension, although he seems to be subsuming two distinct terms under one category. In the first sentence he writes of the creative insight of intuition, the stage at which the idea is grasped as a whole before being expressed in thought or art; while in the second part he refers to the sense of awe, akin to Pascal's uncomprehending fear in the face of "the eternal silence of this infinite space". Pascal, like Einstein and Russell, draws the conclusion that man should not seek his dignity in relation to physical space, as it contains him and swallows him up like a point, whereas in thought he can claim to contain the universe. The themes of awe and intuition will be elaborated at a later stage. We must now consider the spectacle presented by the mystery of the universe.

Mystery and flux

The material universe is in a state of constant flux—"the boundless realm of unending change: naught may endure except mutability" says Shelley. Rudolf Otto, in his *Idea of the Holy*, pictures the reaction of early man faced with the ceaseless transformation and perplexing unpredictability of the universe as one of "daemonic dread" in the presence of what he terms the *"mysterium tremendum"*, something both alien and overwhelming. Unlike his modern counterpart, ancient zoological classification culminates with the elephant; people could not even conceive of dominating nature, owing to their physical insignificance, and to the fact that their consciousness is still largely identified with, and thus projected onto, natural phenomena; such identification eventually develops into a fully-fledged animism, a pattern of controlling powers, some hostile, some benevolent, but all to some extent arbitrary and magical. Even at this stage, however, the emerging human mind attempts to impose some coherence on the universe.

The concept of change is nowhere more developed than in Chinese thought, where it is expounded in terms of complementary and related polarities, the primary ones being yang and yin. In their original sense they represented the light and dark sides of a mountain, but have become the models of other polarities such as masculine/feminine, good/evil, heaven/earth, creative/receptive, expansion/contraction, growth/decay, unity (yang is symbolised by an unbroken line) and division (yin being symbolised by a broken line). The process is never static, but is always moving between one polarity and the other.

Some Greeks reached a similar formulation. Anaxagoras claimed that the categories of coming into being and passing away were incorrect, and that, given the eternity of matter, the terms "mingling and separation" were more appropriate. Thoughts of polarity are found in Herakleitos—"It is the cold things that become warm, and what is warm that cools; what is wet dries, and the parched is moistened." Is such a process aimless? Schweitzer would appear to think so, at least on the sensory level—"What is glorious in the universe is united with what is full of horror. What is full of meaning is united with what is senseless. The spirit of the universe is at once creative and destructive, and therefore it remains to us a riddle." Perhaps Toynbee is right when he comments that we now have more knowledge of the universe, but no more understanding of it. However, Herakleitos would argue that the process of flux carried symbolic significance for the one who sought self-knowledge and regarded the human mind as a microcosm—"Men do not know", he writes, "that what is drawn in different directions harmonises with itself. The harmonious structure of the world depends on opposite tension, like that of the bow and the lyre." Herakleitos thus confers meaning on the flux by relating it to harmony, which both requires and transcends the polarities.

The next step was taken by Parmenides in Greek thought and by Lao Tse and Chuang Tsu in China. Lao Tse defines insight as knowing constancy behind the phenomena, while Chuang Tsu writes—"At the still point at the centre of the circle, one can see the infinite in all things." (It is interesting to note that Eliot refers to this still point in his *Four Quartets*, and Blake claims that if the doors of perception were cleansed, everything would appear as it is—infinite). Parmenides stated that the only true thing was the "One", which was both infinite and indivisible, like the Tao. He considered the senses deceptive and thus the appearance of transformation illusory, and Herakleitos's conception of opposites and harmony superfluous. He was concerned to anchor the becoming of the transitory world in constant underlying being. The insights of Herakleitos and Parmenides were developed by Plato, who considered that reality was eternal and timeless, culminating in the idea of the Good, and that no phenomena in the world were permanent. The philosopher, therefore, should strive to emerge from the cave and make contact with genuine reality.

From Christianity to mechanism

The Christian conception of the creation, fall, redemption, and salvation systemises still further the interpretation of the "mysterium tremendum". The creation myth explains the origin of life, the fall the origin of death, suffering, and evil, while faith in redemption through Christ promises a reconciliation between humanity and God and defines the purpose of human life. In time, the security of tradition provided a bulwark of metaphysical certainty against any ideas of a hostile and senseless universe, and allowed the development of a new framework beyond instinct.

Until the mid-sixteenth century the medieval church fulfilled the functions of religion defined by Toynbee as "enabling people to cope with the difficulty of being human by giving them spiritually satisfying answers to the fundamental questions about the mystery of the universe and of man's role in it, and by giving practical precepts for living in the universe". The publication in 1543 of Copernicus's heliocentric theory was a landmark and constituted the first major scientific challenge to the authority of the Church, which held the geocentric view. Since then, the allegedly immutable truths of religion have been beating a somewhat undignified retreat, or, as with the thought of Teilhard de Chardin, adapting themselves to new formulations.

The psychological consequence of this has been what Jung calls the degeneration of the spirit into intellect. Spirit, he explains, is higher than intellect, as it contains feeling as well. Thus human needs could no longer be met from one source: the intellect evolved by means of science, while the feelings and intuition remained largely undeveloped by science, whose nature is to deal with quantities rather than qualities, with facts rather than values. The rational endeavoured to satisfy the whole spectrum of human needs, something which it could only attempt within its own map or mode of reality, as Lawrence LeShan puts it—the sensory mode. Thus, with the help of the critical, analytical method, it was obliged to reduce humans to fit inside its own terms of reference. This initiated a process of disintegration, and humanity began to founder on the shifting sands of doubt and uncertainty.

The disintegrative process was extremely complex, so that it is only possible to venture a few general considerations as to its outline. Descartes shifted the focus of philosophy from God to the human, and introduced the principle of universal doubt. This naturally led to intellectual and religious scepticism and removed the absolute basis for ethics and moral principles, which were ultimately expressed in terms of the material satisfaction of the greatest number, a goal of comfort and happiness—which Einstein considered fit only for a herd of cattle.

The rise of capitalism and technology went hand in hand with that of liberalism and democracy, against the background of Newton's and Kepler's work on physics and astronomy. Although both men were deists, as well as alchemists, and saw in their discoveries a confirmation of the argument from design, the overall effect of their findings was to reinforce the materialistic and mechanistic theory of the universe. God was denied by Nietzsche's Zarathustra, dismissed by Laplace and his nebular hypothesis, and the Clockmaker argument seemed to receive its death blow from Darwin. Human origins went back much further than 4004 BC, and there was no need to distinguish humans from the rest of the animal kingdom.

The mechanistic interpretation resulted in various forms of determinism: Marxist dialectical materialism with man as a puppet in the class struggle; authoritarianism in the field of ideas, producing an uneasy conformism and a prevalence of collective thought; technology's prowess paradoxically enabling humans to regain their sense of insignificance; psychoanalysis claiming that we are dominated by the subconscious, and behaviourism asserting that we are impelled by our instincts.

Existential angst

And yet not one of these theories has removed man's feelings of anxiety, insecurity, and uncertainty, which have grown apace since the shattering of the illusion of progress by the First World War. These sentiments were the central preoccupation of thinkers such as Kierkegaard, Heidegger, Sartre, Fromm and Watts. Despite the rumblings of the will-to-power and the triumphs of technology, we have remained acutely aware of our finiteness and contingency, and we do all we can to divert our attention away from fundamental problems. "At the bottom of the modern man, writes Amiel, "there is always a great thirst for self-forgetfulness, self-distraction. He has a secret horror of all that makes him feel his own smallness: the eternal, the infinite, perfection therefore terrify him." He is a civilised parrot "distracted from distraction by distraction" as Eliot would put it, intoxicated by the drug of ceaseless activity and restless pursuit of pleasure. We have lost contact with our inner centre, which is a vacuum, we have substituted nothingness for God, and we are engulfed by an anxiety which Eliot poignantly expresses in *Murder in the Cathedral*—"We are afraid in a fear we cannot know, which we cannot face, which none understands. And our hearts are torn from us, our brains unskinned like the layers of an onion, our selves are lost in a final fear which none understands." So we stand alone, reeling and gaping into the beckoning fathomless abyss, which we find both without and within.

It is this sentiment which has produced the literature of the absurd, rejection of the world, sardonic and despairing humour. Starting from the Euclidian understanding of Ivan Karamazov, who respectfully returns God his entrance ticket, we arrive at the passionless Meursault of Camus's *Etranger*, the nausea of Sartre's Roquentin, and the disgust of Beckett's tramps. The absurd, asserts Camus in *The Myth of Sisyphus*, is essentially a divorce. The world is perceived as hostile and strange, dense and irreducible, while humans feel contingent and superfluous; but Camus describes a "nostalgia for unity", an appetite for the absolute which he discovers within himself. For him, the crux of the dilemma is the contradiction of the internal and the external, a conflict which led Sartre to conclude that "man is a useless passion". Camus writes—"My reasoning wants to be faithful to the evidence which aroused it. That evidence is the absurd. It is a divorce between the mind that desires and the world that disappoints, my nostalgia for unity, this fragmented universe, and the contradiction which binds them together." In this contention Camus makes a false connection between evidence and reason. The evidence is a series of phenomena or experiences interpreted by the mind. His mind imposes its own pattern on the phenomena—in this case an inference of the absurd nature of the human situation. The absurd is not evidence but inference.

Yet, in an earlier essay, without apparently suspecting any inconsistency, Camus wrote—"Every time that it seemed to me that I had grasped the deep meaning of the universe, it is its simplicity that has always overwhelmed me." The key words here are "simplicity" and "overwhelmed". The word simplicity borders on unity, while "overwhelmed" suggests that the individuality was merged in something greater than itself. It seems to me that Camus is intuitively answering his own question here—the divorce is overcome through a different mode of perception and understanding.

For Camus, there is nothing beyond reason. Any abdication of reason, any leap of faith is regarded as philosophical suicide, as an escape from the struggle between mind and life. This yearning for unity can never be fulfilled, so that values can only be founded on what Bertrand Russell calls "unyielding despair". It is revolt, contends Camus, which restores majesty to life in spite of the certainty of a crushing fate. Sisyphus overcomes this through courage and scorn, while maintaining that the struggle to the heights is enough to fill the human heart. But is it? Camus realises that humans must create their own meaning, but he can discern no connection with any underlying reality.

Settling for less

Few people choose the Stoic path of Camus and Russell. Most people are content to aim at material security or allow their identities to be taken over by work, nationalism or communism. Material security is based on self-fulfilment through the pleasure principle, and must, as such, remain an illusion. Either the satisfaction of desires will lead to further cravings, as the Buddha argued, or else the indulging in pleasures will culminate in a feeling of satiety which becomes awareness of the futility of such an ephemeral pursuit. Erich Fromm poses the ultimate question in this way—"If I am what I have, and what I have is lost, who then am I?" The one whose being is invested in possessions or pleasures is prey to an inner emptiness.

Those who opt for nationalism or communism are endeavouring to fulfil themselves in something larger than the ego. In the former case, as Reinhold Niebuhr shows in his *Moral Man and Immoral Society*, personal egoism is transmuted into collective egoism which can be more dangerous and just as divisive, while constituting a serious threat to world peace; this is a reversion to the Hellenistic city-state mentality and prevents us from taking a wider view of the interests of humanity. Communism is a form of Christian heresy which has itself become the opium of the people. It started with the aspiration of the fulfilment of each person in the collective interest but has finished, ironically, by reducing the individual to a function of society, a mere cog, as alienated as before the birth of Marx. The transcendence offered by nationalism and communism depersonalises individuals and leaves them without the necessary depth of identity and experience. The future is not eternity, and the collective embraces only one human dimension.

Ways of knowing

The root of our problem, as hinted at earlier in this essay, is the inability of reason, by itself, to confer the sense of fulfilment which we seek. Science has developed the critical, analytical, rational faculty at the expense of the synthetic unitive, intuitive faculty. The functions of the left hemisphere of the brain have evolved without regard for the functions of the right hemisphere. Yang has been invading the territory of yin, contemplation has been dissolved in action, the whole lost in the parts.

A Red Indian chief once expressed his views on whites to Jung— "We don't understand the whites; they are always wanting something, always restless, always looking for something. What is it? We don't know. We can't understand them. We think they are all crazy." The trouble is that white man himself does not know what he is looking for, although he has a dim apprehension that it must lie beyond reason.

"The last resort of reason", says Pascal, "is to realise that there is an infinity of things which are beyond it." "Life", writes Radhakrishnan, "is much more exultant and mysterious than our intellects can comprehend. Russell's philosophy does not prove the failure of man, but only the inadequacy of our intellect." In his recent Gifford Lectures, Ninian Smart drew a distinction between sensory knowledge, and knowledge which requires a deeper participation by the individual, for which he coined the term "gnowledge", referring to the Gnostic tradition. This distinction has naturally been drawn by other thinkers. Russell himself in *Mysticism and Logic* distinguishes between insight and discursive analytical knowledge, between the convincing intuition of the new and its formulation in words as a result of reflection on inarticulate experience. Sir Arthur Eddington, in his *The Nature of the Physical World*, differentiates between the symbolic, codified knowledge of the scientist and what he calls the intimate knowledge of the artist and the mystic. Nikolai Berdyaev distinguishes philosophical mysticism grounded in personal spiritual experience from rational theology based on discursive reason, and elaborated in abstractions which relate only to the intellect and are therefore vulnerable to purely intellectual attacks. Radhakrishnan is right in considering such conceptual substitutes for ineffable experience inadequate. Even if the intellect arrives at the idea of unity, such an idea is merely a postulate, an act of faith at best. Only in spiritual encounters can the self be wholly integrated and experience through intuition the idea of the whole, and through intellect an appreciation of the parts. "Intelligence can never penetrate the mystery," claims Simone Weil, "but it, and it alone, can judge the suitability of the words which express it."

Intentionality

Taking into account the complementary functions of intellect/reason and intuition, Whitehead proposes two different ways of perceiving—immediacy-perception, and meaning-perception. Both are essential to a balanced appreciation of the whole and the parts, and are to be understood within the framework of a third concept—prehension. This term was coined by Whitehead in order to indicate the active and grasping nature of consciousness in perception, an idea originating in the phenomenology of Husserl, and commonly referred to as intentionality. If consciousness is the link between subject and object, then intentionality is what gives structure to this consciousness, which in turn confers meaning on the experience. In other words, intentionality of consciousness is responsible for investing existence with meaning. In its negative aspect, time is extended and consciousness wallows in torpid listlessness or drifts aimlessly on a sea of boredom like Beckett's tramps in *Waiting for Godot*. Like Eliot's Hollow Men, they have no inner resources and condemn themselves, through passivity and indecision, to an eternity of listless suspense. In its positive aspect, time is contracted and intentionality focused so that the self feels fused in the experience, thus losing awareness of its apparently inherent separation and isolation.

Intentionality is closely related to the level of vitality expressed through consciousness. If the level of vitality is high, then a higher level of interest will be brought to bear on one's experience. In his book *A Geography of Consciousness*, William Arkle calls this "interest energy", which creates its own virtuous circle of feedback: the more interest we bring to an activity, the more interesting we will find it. The converse clearly applies, and Rollo May, in his Book *Love and Will*, indicates the danger of undirected response in even more arresting terms— "The human being cannot live in a condition of emptiness for long: if he is not growing towards something, he does not merely stagnate; the pent-up potentialities turn to morbidity and despair, and eventually into destructive action." The validity of his thesis is only too apparent, and highlights the danger of the vicious circle. Amiel goes one stage further by relating vitality, happiness, and health when he remarks— "Happiness gives energy which is the basis of health. So that to make someone happy is to augment his store of being, double the intensity of his life, ennoble and transfigure him." Strong words, perhaps, but words that confirm and extend the thesis of Arkle and May.

If intentionality is related to our level of vitality, vitality in turn is related to our perception of meaning in life. Time and separateness are most clearly transcended in experiences of intense happiness, which imply active participation in reality, rather than passive resignation to it. Schumacher, in his *Guide for the Perplexed*, outlines four levels of being in mineral, plant, animal, and man. Each stage represents a greater degree of consciousness, activity, and complexity, and inversely a lesser degree of determinism. Thus he argues that "Human beings are highly predictable as physico-chemical systems, less predictable as living bodies, much less so as conscious beings, and hardly at all as self-aware persons." Thus freedom develops in proportion to self-awareness, which implies an active, intense grasping of reality and challenges us to rise above simple passive filtering of perception.

But to return to the problem of transcending time and separateness. A few seconds of intense happiness can flood a whole life with meaning and give a person the resources to cope with the humdrum and negative aspects of life. "The greatness of a life, argues Victor Frankl in his book *The Doctor and the Soul*, can be measured by the greatness of a moment: the height of the mountain range is not given by the height of some valley, but by that of the tallest peak. In life too, the peaks decide the meaningfulness of life." The occasion may be response to a person, through compassion or love, response to music or art, or response to the beauty and mystery of nature, all of which are hints of the final transcendence of the mystic in God.

Transcendence

Martin Buber also stresses the need for participation in the perception of meaning in life—"Existence will remain meaningless for you", he says, "if you yourself discover its meaning for yourself. Everything is waiting to be hallowed by you: it is waiting for this meaning to be disclosed and realised by you." In addition to interest and vitality, Buber introduces love as a factor in the perception of meaning—"Where there is no love, says St. John of the Cross, pour love in, and you will draw love out." The important words used by Buber are "discover" and "disclose". He does not say invent, as Camus and Sartre might, but infers that meaning is latent and can be perceived. "Hell", comments Dostoevsky through Father Zossima, "is the inability to love." Love creates its own significance and is one level of interpenetration of being, where isolation merges into a fuller identity.

Naturally, the ecstatic experience should be differentiated from a continuing heightened state, and it is these ecstatic experiences which contain the most intense significance. Krishnamurti contends that love is its own eternity and that the question about the meaning of life is only put by those who do not love. He says that in the moment of experience there is neither the observer nor the observed—there is just the experiencing. This experience of tenderness leaves an indelible stamp on the person, and is of almost limitless value. Russell describes this in the prologue of his autobiography, although, one should add, it does not shake his atheistic foundations. "I have sought love ... because it brings ecstasy so great that I would often have sacrificed all the rest of life for a few hours of this joy." Further on he expresses himself in terms of the mystical union of love, but is careful to make it clear that the saints and poets have imagined rather than experienced this. The etymology of the word ecstasy—standing outside oneself—implies the very transcendence which we are treating.

In his *Four Quartets* Eliot describes a similar state of ecstasy induced by listening to music—"music heard so deeply that it is not heard at all, but you are the music while the music lasts". Absorption in the music is so complete that one is aware of nothing else—only the intertwining of harmony and fugue, discords melting into resolutions, and the occasional magical phrase, the essence of which, as described by Proust, is so tantalisingly elusive. As Schweitzer points out in his book on Bach, the world depicted is not the external universe but an inner reality which is perceived and expressed by the artist. In its highest and most serene manifestations, such as in certain fugues of the "Well Tempered Clavier" the emotions experience overflows into transfigured peace. Amiel expounds his reaction to music in a characteristically terse style— "If music carries us to heaven, it is because music is harmony, harmony is perfection, perfection is our dream, and our dream is heaven." He writes elsewhere that harmony seeks nothing outside itself, a comment which applies also to contentment. I have taken the response to music as an example, but the beauty of other art forms can elicit similar reactions.

The transcendence of space and time (or should one say space-time) is well documented in relation to nature, and many experiences have been recorded and classified by Sir Alister Hardy's Religious Experience Research Unit in Oxford. The experience of at-one-ment dissolves the sense of alienation from nature, so that the observer is caught up as part of reality. He feels an impression of expansion, lightness, exhilaration, he is in harmony with his surroundings so that the ego is the centre of the universe, but the centre is everywhere. In terms similar to William James in *The Varieties of Religious Experience*, Radhakrishnan expresses it thus—"There is a mode of consciousness which is distinct from the perceptual, imaginative or intellectual, and which carries with it completeness of self, and an intuition of all pervading unity and harmony." This is frequently accompanied by what a correspondent described as "an amazing knowingness rather than knowledgeableness", and by an assurance of purpose and meaning, of certainty and security, of peace and serenity.

In his poem on Tintern Abbey, Wordsworth expresses his reaction to such an experience of this "blessed mood ... in which the burthen of the mystery, in which the heavy and the weary weight of this unintelligible world is lightened … and with an eye made quiet by the power of harmony, and the deeper power of joy, we see into the life of things". Further on he continues—

> And I have felt a presence which disturbs me with the joy
> Of something far more deeply interfused
> Whose dwelling is the light of setting suns,
> And the round ocean and the living air,
> And the blue sky and in the mind of man;
> A motion and a spirit that impels
> All thinking things, all objects of all thought,
> And rolls through all things.

Similar impressions are conveyed in *The Prelude*, and in *Intimations of Immortality*. It is fascinating to note how close Wordsworth comes to Herakleitos's definition of Wisdom—"It is to know the thought by which all things are steered through all things" he writes.

Union

If moments such as these are ineffable and hard to put into words, the problem applies *a fortiori* to those who attempt to describe the mystical union with God. "Words are vessels filled with experience which overflows the vessels" writes Erich Fromm. The glimpses are of a level of being beyond becoming and transformation, and one in which the whole soul is immersed. The union can only be expressed symbolically, such as in Plotinus who describes the coincidence of two circles of being. The *Tao Te Ching* puts the problem succinctly—"Those who talk do not know, those who know do not talk." Here one is in the realm of Eddington's intimate knowledge, of Berdyaev's philosophical mysticism, since the ineffable experience is entirely valid for the individual concerned and cannot, by definition, be shared or passed on. Perhaps it is most effectively summed up in the words of the Mandukya Upanishad—"In union with Atman is the supreme proof of his reality. He is the end of evolution, and non-duality. He is peace and love."

The mystics who glimpse such a state in this life do so only as the crowning moment of years of striving and discipline. The mystic is, according to Evelyn Underhill, the pioneer of life on its age-long voyage to the One; and shows us, in his attainment, the meaning and value of that life. Such mystics are a challenge to mankind to follow the same self-authenticating path which transcends the petty limitations of the empirical self.

Life, says Victor Frankl, is not so much a question of self-actualisation as self-transcendence. Attempts at self-actualisation through self-indulgence and self-centredness are chimerical and afford only the most fleeting satisfaction. These result only in further restlessness and separation or even the boredom of extended time, the vertigo of meaninglessness: the absurd man scarcely sees more than a chink of light. Genuine fulfilment, plenitude of being and integrated identity stem from a quickening of intentionality, vitality and compassion in each individual, and perhaps from the occasional flash, in silent sensitivity, of our inherent continuity and harmony with the whole of reality. This self-transcendence should not remain sterile—the transient mystical blossom should mature into the fruit of compassionate concern.

> *The sage*, says the Tao te Ching, *never tries to store things up.*
> *The more he does for others, the more he has.*
> *The more he gives to others, the greater his abundance.*

John Moriarty Memorial Lecture—
Rhythmica Mythica: Separation and Union, Exile and Homecoming

Clifden, Connemara, September 27, 2008

Rereading this lecture brings back strong memories not only of the brilliant and larger-than-life John Moriarty but also of the occasion on the West Coast of Ireland where we danced to the fiddle played by two sisters who were also doctors and walked along the rugged cliffs and wild sea of Connemara. John was the first member of his family to go to university and lectured for a few years at the University of Manitoba before returning to Ireland and spending the rest of his life as a writer and gardener. Readers will appreciate how his perception is shaped by his immersion in natural rhythms that prioritises a different way of knowing.

John did not live to read the work of my friend Iain McGilchrist, whose tour de force The Master and his Emissary—the divided brain and the making of the Western world *was published in 2009. However, he would have cheered at its central message of complementary ways of knowing represented by the right and left hemispheres. Later in this essay I discuss exactly this theme, also taken up in the Galileo Commission project of the Scientific and Medical Network, where Iain wrote the introduction to the Report (www. galileocommission.org). For Iain, the master hemisphere is the right, with its creative and holistic mode of perception, while the left—often called the dominant hemisphere—needs to operate in tandem with the right rather than independently claiming exclusive access to knowledge. Pursuing this process has the potential to rebalance our skewed and stress-ridden culture* (www.iainmcgilchrist.com).

Bach 1st prelude, Rosalyn Tureck

It's a great privilege to be invited to give the inaugural John Moriarty Memorial Lecture here at the Clifden Arts Festival, which I know John supported for so many years. Many of you in the audience will have special memories and associations with John, entranced as you must have been by his extraordinary eloquence, sympathetic intelligence, and warmth of personality. It is given to few people in a generation to live their lives so rooted in place, myth, story, and literature, plumbing the depths and scaling the heights of human existence and potential. John was such a man. I first met him with Marie Hughes in Dublin—and it is a delight to see her here today.

On another occasion, I arrived at a castle outside Dublin in the torrential rain for a TV programme hosted by John about life, the universe, and everything. We sat round a vast fireplace with six-foot logs, drinking Guinness along with our conversation. John's introduction set the scene for a relaxed evening on camera. A few years later, I invited him to speak at a Mystics and Scientists conference on the Sun, where he struck up a friendship with the Indian philosopher and mystic, Ravi Ravindra, with whom I spoke only this week, reminding him of the conference. John's title was typically enigmatic: *Ancient Egypt: Sun-Day and the Ever-Present Sacred.* He spoke about the long and dangerous night journey undertaken by the sun god, who eventually re-emerges into the light. It is a journey which we all make, more or less consciously: the initiation represented by birth and death, death and rebirth, separation and reunion, exile and returning home—*Nostos.*

John draws on the insights and experiences of many literary companions, among them D. H. Lawrence, William Wordsworth, Sir Thomas Browne, Herman Melville, W. B. Yeats, Meister Eckhart, Friedrich Nietzsche, Jakob Boehme, Gerard Manley Hopkins, Rainer Maria Rilke, St John of the Cross; but most of all, Jesus, who was for him the pivotal point of human evolution.

The archaeology of the mind

I begin with D. H. Lawrence (*Bach—Morimur—Partita No 3, Hilliard Ensemble*)—John quoted this often: "The abyss like the underworld is full of malefic powers injurious to man. For the abyss, like the underworld, represents the superseded powers of creation. The old nature of man must yield, give way to a new nature. In yielding, it passes away down to Hades, and there lives on, undying and malefic, superseded, yet malevolent—potent in the underworld. Hence every new conquest of life means a harrowing of hell."

So any advance in consciousness has to entail an advance in depth. Elsewhere, John quotes Lawrence as saying that man's consciousness has many layers, with the lowest layers continuing to be crudely active centuries after the cultured consciousness of the nation has passed to higher planes. In reverting to these original levels, we can do so either through degeneration and decadence or, as John would suggest, "by deliberate return in order to get back to the roots again, for a new start". This is what John himself tried to do.

He found parallel insights in the words of Gerard Manley Hopkins:

> *O the mind, mind has mountains, cliffs of fall*
> *frightful, sheer, no-man-fathomed. Hold them cheap*
> *May who ne'er hung there.*

"The unfathomable immensities of inwardness", as he put it.
  Or Rilke:

> "However vast the outer space may be, yet with all its siderial distances it hardly bears comparison with the dimensions, with the depth dimensions of our inner being, which does not even need the spaciousness of the universe to be within itself almost unfathomable."

Lawrence encapsulates in some of his last poems this process of separation or fall and return.

> *Only man can fall from God*
> *Only man.*

No animal, no beast nor creeping thing
no cobra, no hyena nor scorpion nor hideous white ant
can slip entirely through the fingers of the hands of God
into the abyss of self-knowledge,
knowledge of the self apart from God.

For the knowledge of the self apart from God
is an abyss down which the soul can slip
writhing and twisting in all the revolutions
of the unfinished plunge
of self-awareness, now apart from God, falling
fathomless, fathomless, self-conscious wriggling
writhing deeper and deeper into all the minutiae of self-knowledge,
downwards, exhaustive,
yet never, never coming to the bottom, for there is no bottom;
zigzagging down like the fizzle from a finished rocket
the frizzling falling fire that cannot go out, dropping wearily,
neither can it reached the depth
for the depth is bottomless,
so it wriggles its way even further down, further down
at last in sheer horror of not being able to leave off
knowing itself, knowing itself apart from God, falling.

And in *The Hands of God* he says:
It is a fearful thing to fall into the hands of the living God.
But it is a much more fearful thing to fall out of them.

And the return:

Pax
All that matters is to be at one with the living God
to be a creature in the house of the God of life …

In search of identity

We have an identity crisis in the modern world: we don't know who we are or where we're going. A jet pilot once relayed this message back to base: I'm lost but I'm making record time. We too are lost, even if we are making record time. We suffer from excluded soul, which John regarded as the great calamity of our age. C. G. Jung, rarely quoted by

John, wrote about "modern man in search of a soul", remarking that all his patients in the second half of life were searching for this hidden dimension within themselves.

The God of economic growth tells us that to be is to have and to consume. We have consumed the Earth herself—half the resources ever used have been expended in the last fifty years. Yet, as Wordsworth said nearly 200 years ago: "The world is too much with us. Getting and spending we lay waste our powers." Possessions cannot fill the void within our identity; only the presence of being and love as renewal can.

Or, as John would put it, we have fallen out of our story and need to find a new one. Not only a new story, but also a new way of seeing and being, of relating as a part to the whole, as individuals to society, as cells to the body.

The journey of life begins with separation. As John expressed it, "To exist separately is to have amputated ourselves from the whole. To be is to be amputated." This is what Plotinus called the fall from unity into separation.

The human journey is a story, and the story a journey in itself. The story that John embraced was much vaster than the terms of reference of his personality. Being human is both dangerous and what he described as a tremendous opportunity, which also happens to be a reflection of Tibetan Buddhism. The human incarnation is a priceless possibility. John consciously widened his sympathies and excavated his being to participate in the universal process of life and transformation. To be is to have the potential to become something else, a potential which we don't always fulfil, in spite of life's invitations and initiations.

Here is a passage from *Benedictus*, the final book by the late John O'Donohue, a fellow Irish writer.

> *May I have the courage today*
> *To live the life that I would love.*
> *To postpone my dream no longer*
> *But to do at last what I came here for*
> *And waste my heart on fear no more.*

We too easily retreat into fear, we batten down the hatches in the name of security, which is the mere shadow of peace. Peace is something much more profound that can only emerge from our inner resources, from the very essence of our being rooted as it is in the Divine Ground.

Helen Keller wrote that "life is either a daring adventure, or nothing". This quotation appears on our Learning for Life website and is often cited by young people working on the values poster project. When they discover the nature of Helen Keller's challenges in life, they are amazed and realise how much they take for granted. Their lives are by and large blessed by comparison, but they have few deeper criteria against which to measure their situation. Anne Frank, author of the famous *Diary*, is another such model, and is often written about as an inspirational figure. We need these external reference points in order better to understand and appreciate our own situation.

Open to life

How can we remain open to life? Children are fully engaged, fully open as they grow and unfold. The primordial movement of life can be seen in plants and trees. The daffodil emerges in the spring from the dark earth, just as we come out of the darkness of the womb. It pushes up, breaks ground, and unfolds the beauty of its flower as a gesture of life— like this, the first movement of Peter Deunov's paneurhythmy. The sap rising in the tree performs the same gesture, but on a larger scale: beech, oak, ash, cherry with its exquisite blossom, a symbol of transience celebrated in Japanese culture every year.

The storms of life can take their toll. Recently, two of our oak trees shed very large branches. Detached from the source of life, they die, but the tree lives on and the logs are consumed. Part of us may die, but our essence lives on. Moreover, if a tree loses a particularly large branch, it puts out new branches and leaves on that side, especially if facing the sun. Can we heal the wounds left by the amputation of a branch? Are we able to put out new branches? I once saw a chestnut tree in Sweden in May, just a stump, but it had one twelve-foot branch jutting out horizontally. This was full of the leaves of new life, with its white candles pointing skywards to heaven.

Closer to home, in our park, there is an ancient cherry tree propped up by a sturdy telegraph post as if by a walking stick. It has needed support for as long as I can remember. However, just like the other tree, it blossoms in springtime and shows the first autumn leaves. My mother died over the summer, and it was her wish that half of her ashes be scattered beneath this venerable tree where she had found refuge.

Her wishes were written down thirty-one years ago, and I found them on a sheet of paper in a drawer on the exact anniversary—September 21, the day of the equinox.

Trees can be a lifeline. Victor Frankl tells the story of a fellow inmate whose death he witnessed in Auschwitz. He writes:

> This young woman knew that she would die in the next few days. But when I talked to her she was cheerful in spite all this knowledge. "I'm grateful that fate has hit me so hard," she told me. "In my former life I was spoiled and did not take spiritual accomplishments seriously." Pointing through the window of the hut, she said, "This tree here is the only friend I have in my loneliness." Through that window she could just see one branch of a chestnut tree, and on the branch were two blossoms. "I often talk to this tree," she said to me. I was startled and didn't quite know how to take her words. Was she delirious? Did she have occasional hallucinations? Anxiously I asked her if the tree replied. "Yes." And what did it say to her? She answered, "It said to me, I am here—I am here, I am life, eternal life."

Hermann Hesse writes:

> *A tree says:*
> *I live out the secret of my seed to the very end,*
> *I trust that God is in me.*
> *Out of this trust I live.*

We too have to live out of trust as the secrets of our seeds come gradually to fruition.

In the autumn, trees shed their leaves. They are stripped bare as the sap withdraws from the light branches and descends once again into the dark roots to rest after the activity of spring blossom and summer fruit. We too can be stripped, laid bare, exposed to the icy wind and lashing rain. However, as Shelley remembered, if winter comes, can spring be far behind? Death leads to rebirth, decay to new life. In "Serious Sounds", John reminds us that baptism is into death as a nativity into newness of life. "To be baptised in Christ is to be baptised into chrysalis Christ, it is to be baptised into a principle of transformation, into a principle of metamorphosis, it is to be baptised into life disposed to further faring, into this life supposed to follow the Christian faring." This is the direction of T. S. Eliot in "East Coker" in his *Four Quartets*:

> *Old men ought to be explorers*
> *Here and there does not matter*
> *We must be still and still moving*
> *Into another intensity*
> *For a further union, a deeper communion*
> *Through the dark cold and the empty desolation,*
> *The wave cry, the wind cry, the vast waters*
> *Of the petrel and porpoise. In my end is my beginning.*

Ernest Hemingway, on the other hand, once ruefully suggested that as we grow older, we do not grow wiser, we grow careful. There is always a danger that we retreat into ourselves instead of boldly engaging in a continuous transformative process which is life itself.

Surrender

To die is to surrender, to let go. The tree lets go of its leaves. We let go of the past, even finally of the body. The Benedictine monk David Steindl-Rast explains: "Letting go is a real death, a real dying; it costs us an enormous amount of energy, the price, as it were, which life exacts from us over and over again for being truly alive. For this seems to be one of the basic laws of life: we have only what we give up."

Goethe once said that once you have understood the cyclical nature of the universe, you will encounter it everywhere.

> *Des Menschen Seele*
> *Gleicht dem Wasser*
> *Vom Himmel kommt es*
> *Zum Himmel steigt es*
> *Und wieder nieder muss es*
> *Zur Erde muss es,*
> *Ewig wechselnd.*

[The human soul resembles water. It comes from heaven and rises back to heaven and must descend again to earth, eternally transforming.]

Und so lang du das nicht hast,
Dieses: stirb und werde!
Bist du nur ein trüber Gast
Auf der dunklen Erde

[So long as you do not have this: die and become! You are only a dull guest on the dark earth. This verse was often quoted by my mentor Sir George Trevelyan.]

In his remarkable book *Time and the Soul*, Jacob Needleman explains: "When the eternal and the temporal meet, the result is what has been named in all cultures as the *cycle of time*. The timeless and the temporal meet in the reality of rhythm and recurrence." We all know this from our own experience but we are nevertheless perplexed by the problem of time. The soul's answer, for Needleman, "is the experience of timeless being". But we are frequently in too much of a hurry to remember this and make time for the silence and stillness that open us to inner connection and meaning. Here we discover what the Indians call the Self, the Atman, the Christ within. Needleman continues: "The experience of meaning occurs only when the Self touches the self, when the soul touches the ego ... the Self is everything that the ego pretends to be, and the Self has the time that the ego searches for in vain. When these two worlds meet, only then can the ego breathe freely and let go and accept that it is secondary and, yes, mortal." For John, things are more dramatic in that our mortality is sometimes a wonderful, sometimes a dreadful way of experiencing our immortality. And he adds: "I know that Time is Eternity living tremendously, living dangerously."

Silver-branch perception

John spent much of his life working in gardens, being in silent solitude in these beautiful temples. This enabled him to venture into the rhythms and language of nature, to attain a new way of seeing which got the rational mind out of the way. As Proust suggested, to see a new world we need new eyes. John arrived at an important insight about the nature of sympathetic knowing. To know sympathetically is to know by identity, by becoming one with the thing that is known; this is the knowledge of the mystics rather than knowledge of the scientists. The mystic knows by union, the scientist by detachment and mathematical or philosophical abstraction. Darwin and Descartes knew nothing of this sympathetic knowing. Darwin described his mind as a machine grinding out the facts, regretting the loss of his aesthetic sensitivity. Descartes was one of the fathers of a mechaniistic outlook that reduced everything to the workings of a machine, first clockwork, then telegraph exchanges, and now computers. Eventually, the human being is also understood merely as a machine. However, the machine has no inwardness, no depth dimension. The machine can be measured, while the human being is unfathomable.

For the next year, we will hear a great deal about Darwin, but much less about his more interesting contemporary Alfred Russel Wallace. The year 2009 is the 200th anniversary of Darwin's birth and the 150th anniversary of the publication of *The Origin of Species*. He and Wallace (1823–1913) presented a joint paper to the Linnean Society of London in July 1858. Part of the reason that we hear so little of Wallace is that he was also a spiritualist interested in the evolution of consciousness and the hidden dimensions of the human mind. Most other scientists around him were materialists, like T. H. Huxley, who derided his interest. However, there were other open-minded scientists like Sir William Crookes, Sir William Barrett, and Sir Oliver Lodge who were among the founders of the Society for Psychical Research.

One of the results of the Enlightenment with its deification of Reason was the loss of a symbolic understanding of nature or what other thinkers call the desacralisation of nature. Emanuel Swedenborg was perhaps one of the last thinkers in the eighteenth century to espouse a doctrine of correspondences between the inner and outer meaning of things. This literal interpretation of nature corresponds to an analogous fundamentalist interpretation of scripture. The symbolic depth of sayings in St John's Gospel such as "I am the way, the truth, and the life" is lost in favour of a literal interpretation that encourages an exclusive attitude to salvation and therefore an intolerance of other spiritual paths. It is a tragedy that the mystical gospel is interpreted literally in this way.

Darwin inherits this literalistic tradition, which is why John asks the question: "How much of what is in the bills of Galapagos finches did Darwin see or not see, and if he saw but a little of what is there, what does this mean for his account of how life has evolved?" Reaching into the depth of things, John comments that "Beyond its furthest reaching words are unexplained and possibly unexplainable abysses of being. The universe in other words isn't fully penetrable to human intelligence." This leads John to ask the question whether Wordsworth while still a boy in his boat on Derwent Water saw further into things than Darwin. This is not to diminish the value of scientific insight, but rather to indicate its limitations. Perhaps poetry can see more deeply than science. Two voyages, two modes of perception, which should coexist in a state of mutual respect. The rational and the intuitive are complementary rather than mutually exclusive. One of my favourite passages in *What the Curlew Said* is the conversation with Jimmy Phead who remarks, "I've come to dh'end of thinking John, but I shtill haven't found dh'answer."

The loss of sympathetic knowing is also a loss of soul, an eclipse of the feminine, a repudiation of intuition. John's diagnosis is that we will have to go beyond cognition and the Kantian categories of our under-standing. The next big revolution in science, he insists, will be episte-mological. That is, it will entail the very notion of knowledge itself, of how we know. As John puts it: 'Our efforts towards full comprehension frustrated, we will be forced to return from the object to the subject, from the things, including the universe that we have been enquiring into, to the enquiring mind." This is a monumental step. For the last three centuries in the West, we have been looking outwards, analysing everything objectively, indeed in the case of behaviourism, removing the subject altogether. There is a story about two behaviourist psycholo-gists, man and wife, who have just made love. One says to the other: that was all right for you, how was it for me? This sounds like the the-atre of the absurd. However, there is a serious underlying point, namely that consciousness and mind are prior to science; the subject is prior to the object. In the last fifteen years, the study of consciousness has become central, and there is a growing realisation that we need to look inwards as well as outwards, situating science within consciousness and not consciousness within science.

John was concerned with how to recover an innocence of perception which he observed in nature—what he called "silver-branch percep-tion". He writes about herons, which intrigue him: "Watching one, I'd fall into his fishing-silence, his fishing-stillness, and soon I would know that our knowing mind is the big obstruction between us and things, between us indeed and our own being." This is a profound observa-tion, and one which can arise in our own still contemplation of nature. Most of us value this knowing mind, and the thought that it might be an obstacle to knowing truth comes as a great surprise. Likewise, the call of the curlew is an opening in the world "But it is an opening not into somewhere beyond the world, rather is it an opening into a mode or mood, mostly unvisited, of the world itself." John continues: "Sitting silently over long hours in the oak wood in Ballinafad, I have come to know that all elsewheres, supernatural and natural, are where we are."

John sought to mirror the mountains with as much calm candour as a Connemara lake:

> *Perception not mastered by a conception.*
> *Perception not distorted by a conception.*
> *Perception not watermarked by $e=mc^2$*—the quest for paradisal perception.

Emptiness

The Western mind is cumulative, acquisitive. This is the opposite of the Taoist mentality which encourages us to subtract rather than add until we have reached the stillness of inactivity where, it is said, "By this very inactivity everything can be activated." This includes the subtraction of the self and of desire, getting out of one's own way and, as John expressed it, "out of God's way, and God's way is the way of the lily of the field, doing in not doing". The nearest many of us get to this is the experience of flow or effortless activity where we find that trying harder makes things worse. Timing is of the essence as those of you who frequently split logs or hit golf or tennis balls will know.

Sir George Trevelyan used to quote this wonderful poem by T. E. Brown, which expresses the same message:

> *If thou couldst empty all thyself of self*
> *Like to a shell dishabited*
> *Then might He find thee on an ocean shelf*
> *And say: this is not dead,*
> *And fill thee with Himself instead*
> *But thou art so replete with very thou*
> *And hast such shrewd activity*
> *That when He comes He'll say: 'It is enow*
> *Unto itself. T'were better let it be*
> *It is so small and full, and has no need of Me.'*

This is echoed by John, quoting Meister Eckhart: God expects but one thing of you and that is, that you should empty yourself in so far as you are a created human being so that God can be God in you. The personal gives way to the impersonal, or rather to the transpersonal (even universal), or what Emerson called the Oversoul. The individual and collective are two poles of our being, neither of which is complete in itself. We are both individuals and integral parts of the collective. What happens in the one is reflected in the other, so that even our own personal experiences are in a sense collective.

Our natural state is one of self-centredness but, as the Buddha realised 2,500 years ago, this leads to suffering, *dukkha*. We need to move our centre to what the Indians call the Self, but this is not a comfortable process and is one often brought about by suffering, an experience that John describes as being "cataclysmed into no-thing-ness that I didn't recognise yet to be divine, to be the Divine *Urgrund* that grounds all things." Equally, it can be brought about by love, as the historian Arnold Toynbee observed: on the one hand, "Self-centredness is just another name for being alive, and power is one of the consequences of self-centredness, because all living creatures are competing with each other for exploiting the universe; and this competition is a conflict of power." All this is only too evident on the world stage today. This striving for power is counterbalanced by love. Toynbee again: "Love, as we know it by direct experience in living creatures on this planet, is also present as a spiritual presence behind the universe. Love is the only spiritual power that can overcome the self-centredness that is inherent in being alive. This love that is a form of self-denial is also the only true self-fulfilment." In losing ourselves, we find ourselves.

Albert Schweitzer puts it like this: "Whenever my life devotes itself in any way to life, my finite will-to-live experiences union with the infinite will in which all life is one, and I enjoy a feeling of refreshment which prevents me from pining away in the desert of life." This is what he calls ethical mysticism, union with the Divine through sacrificial service, a process which he himself exemplified in his life.

John quotes the twelfth-century mystic Marguerite Porete—another one burned at the stake—that the peace of the soul is to lose herself through God just as the river which has done its work can relax in the arms of the sea. Her work is over and she can lose herself in what she has totally become: Love. The next stage is what she calls "falling into a trance of a nothingness", when the soul no longer lives in the life of grace, nor in the life of the spirit, but a glorious life of Divinity. For Christ, this passage involved Gethsemane, "the place or the olive press" where we are karmically pressed, karmically squeezed. The Bulgarian mystic Peter Deunov refers to the outer pressures and inner tensions of life events as means of transformation. John uses the powerful metaphor of karmic canyon Christianity, which Christ dared to cross in his harrowing of hell. One of his points is that this process is not accomplished once and for all, but has to be achieved both individually and collectively anew. Can we be redeemed? John sometimes doubts it, since the hammerhead shark within us will not and cannot be redeemed. However, we have to hope that we can be redeemed and act on that hope, as John himself suggested: "Christ in the Karmic Canyon is the evolutionary transition from the Earth as Earth to the Earth as Buddh Gaia," the Earth as Divine and enlightened. And Jesus has crossed the Torrent into what John calls deinanthropological self-awareness, the next stage of evolution. *Wach auf from Cantata No. 110 by Bach.*

Homecoming

Buddh Gaia is also *Nostos*, homecoming, Paradise Regained. The exquisite last movement of Peter Deunov's Sunbeams is *Raia*—Paradise, with his nostalgically evocative and sublime music that reminds us of our deepest identity grounded in the Divine. He knew this, Orpheus knew this, Pythagoras knew this, not in a detached way but by identity and union. *Nostos* is also a journey to the land of the dead, taking leave of the world. As it says on my family headstone: I have seen the works of the Lord, now it is your turn to behold them and rejoice. And here we come back to D. H. Lawrence.

Sleep

Sleep is the shadow of death, but not only that
Sleep is a hint of lovely oblivion.
When I am gone, completely lapsed and gone
and healed from all this ache of being.

Forget

To be able to forget is to be able to yield
to God who dwells in deep oblivion.
Only in sheer oblivion are we with God.
For when we know in full, we have left off knowing. [We are out of the way]

Know-All

Man knows nothing
till he knows how not-to-know.
And the greatest of teachers will tell you:
the end of all knowledge is oblivion
sweet, dark oblivion, when I cease
even from myself, and am consummated.

Shadows

And if, in the changing phases of man's life
I fall in sickness and in misery
my wrists seem broken my heart seems dead
my strength is gone, and my life
is only the leavings of a life:
and still, among it all, snatches of lovely oblivion, and snatches of renewal
odd, wintry flowers upon the withered stem, yet new, strange flowers
such as my life has not brought forth before, new blossoms of me—
then I must go that still
I am in the hands of the unknown God,
he is breaking it down to his own oblivion
to send me forth a new morning, a new man.

This is not ultimately about physical death, but rather mystical death, death to the sense of separation inherent in human existence, removing the obstacle of the self, the I am which we think we are. In truth, it is not we who live our lives, but life that lives through us, that same life which we see all around us and most of all in the eyes of our fellow human beings. Not only life, but also light and love; to be, to know, to feel.

John has gone home, he has taken his leave from us. He has made his night journey to Buddh Gaia, he has gone through the door, he has subtracted himself from what he was, he has extracted himself from the body that finally turned against him and he has fallen into the hands of the living God. It is a journey which we will all make, even if we fall presently into distraction and forgetfulness, preferring not to remember this fact. Although we see him no more, we sense him powerfully in his work, which will reverberate down the generations. We can truly celebrate John, celebrate his work, celebrate his presence in our hearts. He lived precariously, but magnificently, on the grandest archetypal scale, actualising his deepest potential and thereby inviting us to do the same.

First movement (God has done a great thing, from Bach's Cantata 110— May our mouth be full of laughter)

The Principles of Love and Wisdom in Swedenborg and Beinsa Douno (Peter Deunov)

*A*s I explain below, my first acquaintance with Swedenborg arose from a note to a French poem I was studying in my last year at university. When I came to London in the summer of 1974, I immediately joined the Swedenborg Society and was soon co-opted onto its council as by far the youngest member. I then set about an extensive reading of his main works, including Divine Love and Wisdom *on which I draw here. My first encounter with Beinsa Douno came more than ten years later in April 1985 and I soon became aware of the parallels between their central principles of love and wisdom; also their direct access to invisible spiritual dimensions so surprising in our materialistic age but which nevertheless give an indication that we live in a multidimensional reality. I became president of the Swedenborg Society in 2000, so this is my first presidential address—the other two are printed elsewhere in this volume.*

You are all familiar, possibly more so than I am, with the life and work of Emanuel Swedenborg, but may well be wondering who Beinsa Douno is and how his ideas are related to those of Swedenborg. My answer is partly autobiographical and partly historical.

My own first encounter with Swedenborg came in 1973 via a footnote to the famous poem *Correspondances* by Charles Baudelaire. I had read elsewhere of his influence on other writers such as Blake and Balzac, but I was sufficiently intrigued by the footnote to borrow a biography of Swedenborg from St Andrews University library. It lay unread on my bedside table for some weeks, then one evening I dipped into it and was hooked. I was immediately struck by the fact that a scientist had become a mystic without sacrificing his reason and common sense. Indeed, the same level-headed quality is apparent in both Swedenborg's scientific and mystical writings. D. T. Suzuki points out that this may be a disadvantage when extraordinary claims are made about his visionary experiences and are conveyed in the same sober prose style. However, for me this was part of his appeal.

In 1985 I read a book by Omraam Mikhael Aivanhov called *Cosmic Moral Laws*. This set me off reading his other work and, in Volume One of his collected works I read an article about his teacher, Peter Deunov, whose spiritual name was Beinsa Douno. This impressed me enormously, so I acquired a few volumes of his original work in French plus the entire back numbers of a periodical called *Le Grain de Blé* going back to 1958. I ploughed through all this work and was amazed by the scope, power, and depth of his teaching. I resolved to learn Bulgarian so that I could read some of his work in the original—consisting of 150 volumes, mostly untranslated. As luck would have it, I found a Bulgarian woman living in my local village in Gloucestershire and began twice-weekly lessons with her. I then went to Bulgaria in 1989 and met a number of Beinsa Douno's disciples as well as attending the summer camp in the Rila Mountains. It was there that I encountered Vessela Nestorova, then nearly eighty, who told me that Beinsa Douno had suggested to her that she read the work of Swedenborg as it would enable her better to understand his teaching. I began to see a pattern falling into place.

Bulgaria was the source of two previous spiritual impulses. The first was Orphism, and legends claim that Orpheus had lived in the Rhodope Mountains. Orphism and Pythagoreanism exerted a seminal influence on Western mystical philosophy, transmitted as they were through Plato and via neo-Platonism into Christianity. Then in the tenth century the teaching of the Bogomils (meaning dear to God) came to Bulgaria. This sets great store by the mystical Gospel of John, and corresponded in Southern France to the Cathar movement. It was a very pure religion, claiming to represent an original form of Christianity. I would like to read you a short Bogomil prayer:

Cleanse me my God,
purify me inwardly and outwardly.
Purify body, soul and spirit
so that the seeds of light may grow within me
and make me into a flaming torch.
I should like to be my own flame
so as to transform
everything in and around me
into light.

A little biography: Beinsa Douno was born in 1864, the son of an Orthodox bishop who was active in the liberation of the country from the
Ottoman Empire, which came about in 1878. He studied theology
and medicine at Methodist universities on the East Coast of America
between 1888 and 1895 before returning to Bulgaria. He subsequently
had a period of retreat before beginning his teaching mission in 1900.
From 1905 to 1926 he was based in Sofia, although he was interned in
Varna during the First World War. He began systematic teaching in 1914,
and delivered over 4,000 talks and lectures until his passing in 1944.

From the 1920s he began to take his followers for summer camps
in the mountains, where he gave many of his most inspiring lectures
and introduced an ecological dimension to his mystical spirituality. The
Isgrev Centre (meaning sunrise) was built during this period. Beinsa
Douno was also a musician. He composed over 200 songs as well as
the music for his sacred dance movements called Paneurythmy. His
new prophetic vision of Christianity did not endear him to the Church
authorities, but then there is always a tension between the prophet and
the priest, between the spirit and the letter, between essence and form,
esoteric and exoteric.

The three key principles

I come now to the kernel of his teaching, the three principles of love,
wisdom, and truth (I translate the Bulgarian word *razumno* as noetic):

The first principle on which the whole of existence is based is love. It brings
the impulse to life, it is the compass, the stimulus within the human
soul. The second principle is wisdom which brings knowledge and light

to the mind thus enabling human beings to use the forces of nature in a noetic way. The third principle is truth—it frees the human soul from bondage and encourages her to learn, work well and make efforts towards self-sacrifice. There is nothing greater that these three principles, there is no straighter or surer path. In these three principles lies the salvation of the world.

The principles need to be applied, or else they lose their power:

Love in the heart brings purity, thanks to which the capacities latent in human beings will develop, enabling them to achieve all their noble desires. Wisdom in the mind brings light, which helps us study the laws of nature. Truth within the soul, shining within the soul brings freedom from every weakness and vice. Love eliminates hatred, violence, murder. Wisdom eliminates ignorance, error, darkness. Truth eliminates lies, slavery, sin.

He was once asked about the essence of his teaching: (quoted from Chapter 13 of *The Master Speaks*)

The essence of the divine teaching is love, wisdom and truth, and I know you will ask what are they? I say to you eat the kernel, taste truth but do not stumble over the shells; do not ask for proofs. So here is the answer to your question—love is that without which no life can exist. Wisdom is that without which no movement can exist. Truth is that without which no limit exists. Love is the beginning of life, truth is the end of life. These are the two limits of the great reality in life. That which moves in between and gives form to things is wisdom. Wisdom cannot act if there is no beginning and no end. Between these, wisdom acts—in the space between the beginning and end which fills all eternity without ever filling it fully. In this space wisdom moves and reveals what love and truth are and wisdom says "I that move between the beginning and the end", I say to you love is the beginning of all creation. Truth is the ultimate limit of creation, its highest goal. And beyond truth? Beyond truth there is nothing. It is not possible to go beyond truth. Everything that has been created after moving and moving will finally stop at truth. It might move for millions and billions of years but when it arrives at truth there it will stop. You must choose, whether you will adhere to the laws of truth and live according to them, or you will turn into dust and ashes. You asked "tell me the truth" (and this is the key phrase)

Truth cannot be told. It must be lived. Truth is the fruit of the entire life, it includes that in which God reveals Himself; it includes all eternity which is composed of thousands and millions of eternities for there are eternities which are limited and there are eternities which are limitless. So remember if with your love you cannot pass back from the beginning to the end and enter into Truth, and if with your truth you cannot pass back from the end to the beginning you will never comprehend what life is. You must unite the beginning and the end. If you cannot do this you can do nothing and comprehend nothing. And what can unite the beginning and the end? Only Wisdom.

Parallels

Turning now to Swedenborg's *The Divine Love and Wisdom* we read in the first part that "Love is the life of man" but that people are quite unaware that love is their very life: "No one knows what the life of man is unless he knows it is love."

In Beinsa Douno we read: "The source of life is Love. If people do not understand love, they do not understand life. Life is the fruit of Love. Life cannot manifest itself without love. There is no life without Love."

The second heading in Swedenborg reads that God is Love itself, because He is Life itself. The Divine Love appears as a sun giving forth heat (corresponding to love) and light, in its essence wisdom. Thus Love and Wisdom are joined in the Divine. The following heading explains that God is not in space, although He is Omnipresent, a concept which can only be grasped spiritually. Beinsa Douno also describes God as the sun of life or the sun as the expression of God.

Now compare the following: (from Chapter 7 of *The Master Speaks*)

There is One who manifests himself as love, wisdom and as truth. There is one! All of living nature speaks of this One, of this great One who fills everything, all of creation, all works, all solar systems and is nevertheless, still unrevealed.

God cannot reveal Himself (Douno used the word "Himself" in his time) *completely even in all eternity. It does not contain all the forms in which he might reveal Himself. Of Himself, the Absolute, the Unattainable has no form. He is nothing but this nothing contains everything within Itself. He limits Himself without becoming limited. He diminishes himself without becoming diminished. He creates and is never exhausted.*

He reveals Himself in everything but He Himself is not in that which is revealed. He sustains everything from within and from without but participates in nothing. We compare God with Light and reason, the Logos, but God is neither Light nor reason; Light and reason—these are the manifest forms of God. The great unknown reveals Himself as light without shadows, life without interruption, love without change, knowledge without errors, freedom without limitations. And when we say that God is love, we understand that love is one manifestation of God, therefore wherever there is love, wherever there is goodness which is the fruit of love, God is revealed. When we speak of God as love we have in mind that Being from whom all life in the universe proceeds and who unites all living souls in one whole without being changed.

A difference between Swedenborg and Beinsa Douno can be seen here: while Swedenborg sees God as Man existing in Himself, He is beyond all form for Beinsa Douno. For Swedenborg, love is the *esse* or essence and wisdom the *existere* or manifestation, while for Beinsa Douno the *esse* is beyond form and both Love and Wisdom are manifestations of the formless Absolute. For Swedenborg, love needs to be in wisdom in order to exist as such, although he states elsewhere that the Divine Essence itself is Love and Wisdom.

For Beinsa Douno, Christ is the manifestation of God: (Chapter 21 of *The Master Speaks*)

There is only one Christ, the Living Christ who is the manifestation of God, the manifestation of love. Christ is God revealing Himself to the world. As a manifestation of God, Christ cannot be separated from Him, cannot be considered apart from Him, cannot be considered apart from God, and when I speak of Christ I do not mean an abstract principle but rather an actual incarnation of love. Love is the greatest reality and not an abstraction. It has form, content and meaning. So again as soon as the Absolute becomes manifest there has to be a form, and we understand Christ in the cosmic sense as the form, or the manifestation, or the Divine principle—as love.

In Beinsa Douno Truth is the third principle leading to freedom or liberation, as we have seen. More specifically, the application of Love and Wisdom together leads to Truth. Love is also said to give birth to the good: "The good is the foundation of life. The good is the soil of life and at the same time its nourishment. Only the good can sustain life, only the good can nourish it."

Swedenborg expresses a similar relationship: "It is from the fact that the Divine Essence is Love and Wisdom that all things in the universe have relation to Good and Truth. For everything that proceeds from Love is called good and what proceeds from Wisdom is called Truth."

Swedenborg goes on to say that Divine Love and Wisdom are substance and its form. This corresponds to some extent with Beinsa Douno's formulation that Love is the source of life and that Wisdom creates forms between the alpha of Love and the Omega of Truth. For Swedenborg Love flows into the will (but corresponds with feeling) and Wisdom into the understanding, while in Beinsa Douno the will is associated with Truth, Love with the heart, and Wisdom similarly with understanding and light in the mind. Their formulations come closer, however, in the following explanation by Swedenborg. Rationality is the faculty that enables us to understand truth, "while the other faculty is the ability to do what is true and good. This faculty is called freedom, and is a faculty of the will."

Correspondences

Swedenborg explains that the two colours of red and white are fundamental in the celestial and spiritual kingdoms, corresponding to love and wisdom. Love then corresponds to the heart and wisdom to the lungs. Compare Beinsa Douno's description of the Divine World (as opposed to the spiritual): (Chapter 4 of *The Master Speaks*) "There are no religions in the Divine world, there exists only love. The atmosphere of the divine world is love. Therein everything breathes love."

The Love that is Infinite and Eternal manifests itself at four levels in Beinsa Douno's teaching. Its expressions move from the personal and exclusive to the inclusiveness of the Divine. The first level, corresponding with the roots of a tree, is love as an aspiration in the heart—this is the stirring of emotional love. The second level, corresponding with the branches, is love as a feeling in the soul, reaching up to God and expressed in brotherly or sisterly friendship. The third level, love as a force in the mind, corresponding to the flowers, is a rare and evolved form of love found in those who are prepared to live and even sacrifice their lives for the divine cause like Christ himself. Love as a principle in the spirit, corresponding to the fruit, is a supreme and all-encompassing harmony, the ultimate manifestation of love, which has scarcely made an appearance in the world.

Extrasensory perception

Both Swedenborg and Beinsa Douno embodied Love and Wisdom in their lives, as well as making them the cornerstone principles of their teaching. They also had extensive extrasensory capacities (*siddhis* in the Hindu tradition) that are characteristic of people who have reached a certain advanced stage of development. For instance, the episode involving Swedenborg's sensing of the fire threatening his house is well known—he informed fellow diners while in a different city and the correct timing was subsequently verified. Beinsa Douno was able to sense many events occurring at a distance, one of which involved the assassination of the Bulgarian prime minister, with whom he had had an interview the previous year. More often than not, however, these episodes were triggered by a dangerous situation involving one of his followers. It is said in the Gospels that a sparrow does not fall to the ground without God knowing of this, presumably because the whole of creation lives, moves, and has its being within the Divine consciousness. Those who are themselves aligned with Divine consciousness are perhaps able to sense events within this field that remain unconscious for the rest of us, all the more so because a link of love exists between teacher and pupil. My preliminary researches on "feeling at a distance" point to love or empathy as a crucial enabling factor.

I will end with two formulaic prayers from Beinsa Douno:

> The Love of God brings fullness of life,
> The Wisdom of God brings fullness of light,
> The Truth of God brings perfect freedom!
> Great is God in Love!
> Great is God in Wisdom!
> Great is God in Truth!
> In Love God instructs,
> In Wisdom God enlightens,
> In Truth God liberates.
> Merciful and compassionate is the Lord,
> And His Kindness is above all things,
> His exaltation sustains everything,

Everything lives and moves in the Lord.
He is gladness and joy in everything that lives in the world.

There is no Love like the Love of God,
Only the Love of God is Love.
There is no Wisdom like the Wisdom of God,
Only the Wisdom of God is Wisdom.
There is no Truth like the Truth of God,
Only the Truth of God is Truth.
There is no Justice like the Justice of God,
Only the Justice of God is Justice.
There is no Virtue like the Virtue of God,
Only the Virtue of God is Virtue.
There is no Power like the Power of the Spirit,
Only the Power (sila*) of the Spirit is the Power of God.

*Strength can be read for power here.

Beinsa Douno (Peter Deunov, 1864–1944)—a Prophet for our Times

This is an overview given as a lecture to the Study Society in 2018 and written up as an article in its publication Being.

In the summer of 2014, I was driving across the Forth Road Bridge listening to a CD by Dr Wayne Dyer on Divine Love. I am not sure who sent me a copy, but I was astonished when he started talking about Peter Deunov, explaining that he had experienced a number of visions with a spiritual figure whom he did not know. He recounted how, one evening, after he had given a lecture in St Louis, he was approached by a woman who gave him a copy of my 1991 edited book, *Prophet for Our Times*. Seeing the photo of Peter Deunov on the book's cover, he immediately recognised him as the man from his visions. He was already familiar with the work of Omraam Mikhail Aivanhov, who had been a disciple of Peter Deunov as a young man in Bulgaria. Hearing all this sent a shiver down my spine. I subsequently contacted Wayne Dyer, and it was through our new connection that *Prophet for Our Times* was republished by Hay House. Sadly, he died not long after completing the book's foreword to the new edition.

In his foreword, perhaps not surprisingly, Wayne focuses on Divine Love, the love that never changes and never varies and which great spiritual masters not only speak about, but embody and emanate.

He refers to the new person who is now being created, a person of light who lives in joy, the person who is a harbinger of what Deunov called a Culture of Love. Wayne felt a deep, almost celestial, bond with Deunov and was himself inspired to live and teach Divine Love. It turned out that, after St Louis, Wayne had gone on to a meeting in New York about Einstein, to whom the following quotation has been attributed: "The whole world bows down before me; I bow down before the Master Peter Deunov."

Even though books by and about Peter Deunov have existed in English for more than fifty years, his work is still not well known internationally. Bulgaria is the land of the Bogomils (literally, dear to God), an eleventh-century spiritual and Gnostic movement corresponding to the Cathars in Languedoc. These movements regarded themselves as true to the essential spirit of Christ, and the initiates (*parfaits* and *parfaites* in Languedoc) led a pure and very disciplined life of service. They put a special emphasis on the Gospel of John, which was laid on the head of the initiate during the Consolamentum or ordination ceremony (since writing this I have come to believe that it was the Gospel of the Beloved Companion that was used in this way rather than the Gospel of the Beloved Disciple, but that is a long story). The Gospel of John is the symbolic and mystical gospel speaking of Light, Love and Life.

Peter Deunov was born in 1864, and his father was an Orthodox bishop involved in the Bulgarian liberation movement from the Turks. He was a violinist and qualified as a primary school teacher before emigrating to the US in 1888 to study theology and medicine at the Methodist Drew University. This background is important in understanding his dedication to a renewal of Christianity and the style of the lectures he gave, which began with a biblical verse or chapter. After further studies, in medicine, he returned to Bulgaria in 1895. In 1897 he was told that he had been chosen to be a world teacher, and thereafter prepared himself for this role and began to gather disciples. He later received the spiritual name Beinsa Douno, and in 1914 his spiritual initiation was completed by Christ, who appeared to him on a mountain peak. During his lifetime, Peter Deunov was recognised as the world teacher by Krishnamurti, and his spiritual stature was also acknowledged by Rudolf Steiner and Paramahansa Yogananda. The perennial philosopher Rene Guenon wrote that "He is a real messenger of Heaven, he is the greatest person who has come down to earth, the greatest spiritual magnet yet able to appear on the earth."

An ecospiritual wisdom

The kernel of Deunov's teachings are the spiritual principles of Love, Wisdom, Truth, Justice, and Virtue or Goodness, making up the symbol of the pentagram. He writes that

> The first principle on which the whole of existence is based is Love; it brings the impulse to life; it is the compass, the stimulus within the human soul. The second principle is Wisdom, which brings knowledge and light to the mind. The third principle is Truth that frees the human soul from bondage. There is nothing greater than these principles; there is no straighter or surer path. In these three principles lies the salvation of the world!

The application of these principles is what he calls the Third Testament, bringing into the world Love, Wisdom, and Truth. The important point is that these principles are not articles of belief, but rather the foundation of life and living, which we can understand and embody more deeply in our practice. This Love is capable of eliminating hatred and violence, while Wisdom eliminates ignorance and darkness, and Truth frees us and empowers the will. In this way we can aspire to acquire a more loving heart, a more illuminated mind, and a firmer will.

An important part of the teaching is the supporting of physical health, the physical body being our vehicle on earth. Peter Deunov recommended vegetarianism and wrote extensively about the human body, health, and energy. To access and attune to natural and universal energies, he developed the Paneurhythmy, a sacred dance promoting spiritual development, physical health, and social harmony. The Paneurhythmy is performed daily between March and September outdoors in nature shortly after sunrise. He also gave spiritual exercises to help balance masculine and feminine energies, which he called "electric" and "magnetic", corresponding to the right and left side of the body. Each summer from 1929, he took his followers up to camp in the Seven Lakes region of the Rila Mountains. Here, away from everyday city life, in this pure and sublime environment, the disciples connected with higher beings of light and energised their spiritual bodies—a tradition that continues to this day. This contact with nature amounts to an early manifestation of what we would now call ecological spirituality. Also, the simultaneous emphasis on physical health and spiritual development is something found in yoga traditions but very little in Christianity, which has had a deeply ambivalent attitude towards the physical body. The teaching therefore promotes physical, emotional, mental, and spiritual health.

Since its inception until 1989 the teaching endured difficult conditions. The Orthodox Church, a powerful force in Bulgarian life until the communists came to power in 1944, was threatened by this radical interpretation of Christianity and did everything it could to oppose Beinsa Douno. From 1944 to 1989 his followers experienced the even harsher persecution of communism, a time during which the teaching had to be passed on covertly. My book *Prophet for Our Times* was a collaborative project originating in the late 1980s with Bulgarians Krum Vazharov and Maria Mitovska, and my involvement unknowingly coinciding with the last few months of the communist regime. When I first went up to the Seven Lakes camp, in the summer of 1989, just before the collapse of communism in Eastern Europe, one of my hosts—Joro Petkov—had to spend half a day going down the mountain to register us with the police three times a week. Krum was a psychologist, who had been a close disciple of Beinsa Douno from a young age. It was he who selected the extracts from the thousands of lectures, which we organised into a series of nine chapters, covering God, the spiritual world, the divine school, master and disciple, fundamental principles of life, divine and natural laws, the nature of the human being, methods, rules, and recommendations for life, relations with nature and the New Epoch. The extracts are thematically linked, and I provide an introduction to the whole book and to each section. The book can be opened at any page, where there are nuggets of wisdom and a reminder of how to be more conscious on the spiritual path. The extracts were then translated by another disciple, Vessela Ilieva, and further refined by myself.

Recent work

Since 2006 Maria Mitovska has been translating the lectures of the Teacher, Beinsa Douno (the Bulgarian *Uchitel* means Teacher or Master), working with an Englishman, Harry Carr, to adapt them specifically for contemporary readers of the English language. Their work has now produced its first fruit: in 2016 *The Teacher, Volume One: The Dawning Epoch* was published. This book gives the first twelve years of Peter Deunov's talks and lectures, from 1903 to 1915, in which he begins to lay down the essence of his teaching. Using many footnotes, the book establishes the teaching's foundation in the Bible, especially the teaching of Jesus. An essential point presented is that God's Spirit lives within human beings as spiritual light, a concept that can be understood clearly through a mystical reading of certain parts of the Bible. This is also elaborated in the *Testimony of the Colour Rays of Light*, where biblical verses are set out to correspond with certain colours.

Deunov said that what remains to us of Christ's teaching is enough for our salvation, but it does not give us everything we need to live. There is much missing from his life, as St John told us at the end of his Gospel. The Teacher came to give us what we need to live in the new epoch, but always stemming from Christ. He expands on Jesus's words and certain other parts of the Bible, filling out their meaning and explaining how they apply to contemporary life. While taking opportunities to connect with nature, the idea of a general retreat from ordinary life is not part of the teaching. All disciples who were able were expected to have jobs, and only to devote their free time to the teaching. Those who lived in Izgrev, the spiritual community just outside Sofia, the Bulgarian capital, would set off in the morning after dancing Paneurhythmy for work in the city. While developing spiritual qualities, the disciple needs to learn to apply them in the ordinary material world, with all its challenges. The processes given for self-transformation are simple, but challenging in that they require willpower and perseverance.

The Teacher consists of nearly seventy lectures covering an enormous range of subjects and themes, always with an emphasis on the practical application of the many profound insights. Themes include the development of the heart and mind, constancy, love, patience and benevolence, the law of service, the importance of small things, the value of human life, the law of similarity and the law of contrast, the fundamental types of Pharisee and Publican, the making of the precious pearl through integrating the masculine and feminine, and the importance of new wine skins. The book is best read contemplatively (*lectio divina*), a few pages at a time in order to ponder and absorb the content, as well as the significance of the many biblical footnotes, which show Beinsa Douno's encyclopaedic knowledge of the Bible. He also uses many telling stories and parables to bring his points to life.

Rila

Over the years, I have spent a part of many summers in the Seven Lakes area of the Rila Mountains, and have experienced many sublime moments. In August 2017 I took a walk on my own over the main ridge and down into the Urdini Lakes, where one meets only the occasional horse. Otherwise it is a vast unspoiled and uninhabited expanse, giving a real sense of freedom. The sky was cloudless, and the water crystal clear. The rhythm in the camp involves getting up before sunrise and walking down to the Mount of Prayer, where disciples have been assembling during August for nearly ninety years. One looks over a misty valley, with other peaks silhouetted in the distance and the lake of contemplation down to the right. Sometimes the sun comes up red, but if it is very clear a gleaming yellow. At this point we stand up and salute the rising sun. This is followed by prayers, songs, and a lecture, often given in this place during the 1930s.

We then go back to the camp, often stopping at the kitchen for a cup of hot water as recommended by the Teacher. After breakfast, we climb up to one of the places where we dance the Paneurthymy in a circle with live musicians in the centre. One feels part of a larger human organism moving together. After this, we often go on excursions, taking a picnic lunch to one of the many beautiful spots, and if we are lucky, we may be accompanied by a musician or two who will play when we stop to rest.

Returning to Sofia after a few days in the mountains is quite a culture shock when one senses the thickness of the atmosphere of thoughts and feelings, not to mention electromagnetic waves, largely absent in the mountains. However, returning home I continue with daily practice. This includes a prayer on awakening:

> "I thank thee Lord for giving me life and health. Fill my heart with love and strengthen my will so that I may accomplish Thy Will. May everything I do be done in Thy name and for Thy Glory—Amen."

During my walk, I recite the Good Prayer and the Morning Prayer of the Disciple as well as singing one of the songs. There is a specific song and prayer prescribed for each day of the week, as well as a colour corresponding to biblical verses from *The Testimony of the Colour Rays of Light* already mentioned above. I translated the prayers many years ago, and they are still available to purchase. In particular, I love the Formula of the Disciple:

> *May I have a heart as pure as a crystal,*
> *A mind as bright as the sun,*
> *A soul as vast as the universe,*
> *And a spirit as powerful as God and one with God.*

Most mornings I also perform the twenty-one exercises, which feels like a tuning of the physical organism as well as a harmonisation of thoughts and feelings—the movements vary between vigorous and flowing, balancing masculine and feminine energies. Many are accompanied by breathing patterns, and one feels very energised afterwards.

I hope that this brief introduction will encourage you to dig more deeply into the living source of spiritual wisdom that is Beinsa Douno—you will be richly rewarded if you do so.

Tao and the Path towards Integration

This piece began life as an essay delivered to the Speculative Society in 1982 and was later published in New Humanity. *I inherited the complete works of C. G. Jung from a mentor, Rev Norman Cockburn and was reading his work extensively at the time. I had also been studying different translations of the* Tao te Ching *and reading the novels of Hermann Hesse. At the time I was teaching at Winchester College where a significant part of my timetable involved a daily general studies class for pupils in their final year, called "Div", where the teacher ("div don") chose four books every term ("half") for pupils to read and about which they had to write fortnightly essays. Every year we would study a spiritual text such as the* Bhagavad Gita *and also one of the novels by Hermann Hesse. One not mentioned below is* The Prodigy, *which tells the story of a bright boy crushed by the pressure of parental expectation—which could happen at Winchester—and I hoped that reading Hesse would enable my pupils to forge their own path in accordance with a deeper inner calling than social convention and prestige.*

The pre-Socratic Greek philosopher Herakleitos states in one of his Fragments that a man's character is his destiny; the word which is translated as "character" is *daemon*, which was regarded as some control over the individual life. In modern psychological terms it makes little difference whether the determining power is thought to come from inside or outside; at any rate it lies beyond the conscious ego and may be appre-hended either as an internal drive, or else projected onto some external force, or event, or person—you slip because of the ice, or swear that the other man came round the corner too quickly. The relationship between character and experience (which is necessarily mediated through the psyche) has been commented on by other thinkers, and is implicit in the Eastern concept of karma.

Nietzsche asserted that if a man had character, then he also had his typical experience which recurred again and again, presumably until the short circuit was broken. Eliot, who has two quotations from Herakleitos in the front of his *Four Quartets*, took the relationship of our beginning to our end as one of his main themes. And Jung, who became aware of the importance of polarities partly through reading Heraklei-tos, commented in one of his letters: "The humiliation allotted to each of us is implicit in his character. If he seeks his wholeness seriously, he will step unawares into the hole destined for him, and out of this dark-ness the light will rise." In other words, such an encounter will extend self-knowledge and consciousness.

Individuation

In this article we shall examine the process which Jung calls "individua-tion", by which he means the rounding or realisation of our whole being, a state which is ipso facto unattainable in time, but to which we may hope to approximate. This entails the emergence of the conscious ego, involving a differentiation from the primordial wholeness analogous to creation myths. This is followed by the growth of the conscious ego and the gradual development of a separate identity which, being partial by definition, creates its opposite known as the shadow; this shadow is an unconscious constellation of repressed and undeveloped tenden-cies and acts as a compensation to the conscious ego. If the individual is to approximate to wholeness, the shadow must be recognised and integrated into a wider consciousness. People will also have to come to terms with the complementary aspect of the psyche, known by Jung as the *anima* for men and the *animus* for women; failure to incorporate this will result in a one-sided development. The individual who pursues fulfilment only in worldly achievement will find its value questioned by death, while those who seek it by identifying themselves fanatically with some cause will have completely submerged their individuality in the collective. If the first half of life is concerned with the development of the ego, then the second half looks towards transcendence of the ego, escape from its narrow preoccupations into a wider and more unitive perspective, where the individual life is perceived as integrated in a universal process. The necessity of each stage is succinctly expressed by Frances Wickes in her book *The Inner World of Choice*—"Both separation and reunion are necessary steps in the life process of individuation. For without separation and discrimination unity is only unconsciousness, and without interplay and reunion there is only opposition and warfare ... or the dull content of a half life."

Differentiation

The writer of Genesis relates how God created the earth "without form or void", but immediately shows that he is unable to imagine the true meaning of his words by saying that the Spirit of God moved over the face of the waters, which must have had some content and shape. In any event he was trying to express some kind of undifferentiated formlessness; subsequently light is divided from darkness and the land from the sea, thus creating polarities out of the primordial formlessness. Lao Tsu asserts that the Tao that can be told is not the eternal Tao, in the same way that the name that can be named is not the eternal name: thus the nameless is the beginning of heaven and earth. In another passage he hints that Tao is "something mysteriously formed, born before heaven and earth. In the silence and the void, standing alone and unchanging." Tao is notoriously untranslatable; this arises partly from the nature of the Chinese ideograms, which are more suggestive than precise, and partly from the fact that it is easier for us to say what it is not than to establish what it is. The eternal Tao cannot be truly expressed as a limited and individualised term; it can only be apprehended intuitively, as a whole, beyond the inevitable distinctions of the analytical intellect: it is eternal, the still centre of all phenomena, the unchanging element behind the changing appearances.

The same creative emergence from the all-encompassing One can be seen in relation to humans and the world, the individual and the group, and the conscious ego and the unconscious. Indigenous peoples live in an animistic world, where hopes and fears are projected onto the forces of nature. The individual does not at first exist as an independent entity so much as part of a group. This is what Owen Barfield calls "original participation". And the conscious identity can only emerge when children become aware of themselves as a centre of consciousness; at first this awareness will only be spasmodic, but the development of continuing identity through memory leads to the crystallisation of the ego, or ego-complex as Jung calls it, as the ego acts as an organiser and focus of the contents of consciousness. It is important to bear in mind that consciousness in itself presupposes separation and polarity; in the primordial state there is neither consciousness nor form, they arise mutually as phenomena are differentiated from the One.

Alan Watts expresses the relationship as follows—"As the universe produces our consciousness, our consciousness evokes the universe"; being presupposes non-being and sound silence. The classic Chinese formulation of polarity is that of Yin and Yang, originally symbolising the shady and sunny sides of a mountain but also illustrated by man/woman, creative/receptive, and Light/Dark. What is often forgotten is that these do not express a dualism where the two principles are in perpetual conflict, the one being good and the other evil, but rather what Watts calls "an explicit duality expressing an implicit unity". This unity is the undifferentiated and eternal Tao, more fundamental than either of the complementary manifestations.

The first half of life

Jung sees the first half of life as the ascent of the sun to the zenith. The ego-complex, and with it the shadow, is developed; the energies are turned outwards to the establishment of a position in the world, both in terms of occupation and family. This may or may not reflect the inner urge of the individual, what Jung and Herman Hesse call the "inner law" or "vocation". To the extent that external conditions do not correspond to the internal state, the individual has to adapt to the outside world by means of a *persona* or mask, which conforms to the expectations of his fellows. Sartre calls this bad faith, where the role-playing of, say, a waiter submerges his personality; this automatically creates a split between the individual's own character and behaviour, and may have no drastic effects so long as the waiter is unaware of his role-playing. If he becomes aware that he is acting, then he realises that the persona is not a true reflection but a fake, and here arises a corresponding demand by the real character that there should be less of a gap between inner and outer. Everything now depends on whether the waiter is prepared to continue his role-playing consciously, or whether he feels that he must seek another profession more in tune with his level of awareness.

There is another subtler form of "bad faith" which consists of identifying oneself with a "just cause", of which one becomes an instrument. The attachment is frequently unconditional and absolute. Individuals become means rather than ends, and are dispensable for the sake of the cause. This kind of fanaticism is defined by Jung as overcompensated doubt, and is typical of sects of a quasi-religious or messianic variety. Dogmas must be accepted without question, often on the slimmest empirical grounds, and obedience is at a premium; moreover, if such obedience leads to a martyr's death, this is regarded as the highest form of glorious service on behalf of the cause. Thus the individual, such as Kyo in *La Condition Humaine* by Malraux, is said to become the apotheosis of the cause in his death, which is supposed to be his fulfilment. In actual fact it is the last stage in the annihilation of his personality, a process which began with his surrender to the ideals of the group. Ironically this may have been prompted in part by the wish to transcend his own narrow interests, but the group then operates on the basis of a collective egoism, its members being the willing instruments of its ends. Erich Neumann characterises this trend as a massing together and recollectivisation of modern humanity, whereby individual distinction and development are ignored, and quality sacrificed to quantity and equality.

Authenticity in Hermann Hesse

Political fanatics attempt to overcome their sense of isolation by absolute submergence in a cause, but if they become aware of what they are doing, they may well realise that they have not escaped the isolation which belongs to the very nature of consciousness. In his novel *Demian*, Hermann Hesse charts the implications of the awakening of Emil Sinclair as he detaches himself from the calm and ordered existence of his family, and feels the power of all kinds of strange stirrings within himself. He realises that only he himself can come to terms with these forces; this implies responsibility, self-reliance, and standing alone. He concludes that

> There is only one true vocation for everybody—to find the way to himself. He might end as a poet, lunatic, prophet, or criminal—that was not his affair; ultimately it was of no account. *His* affair was to discover his own destiny, not something of his own choosing, and

live it out wholly and resolutely within himself. Anything else was merely a half life, an attempt at evasion, an escape into the ideals of the masses, complacency and fear of his inner soul.

Jung calls this the vocation to personality, a challenge which he claims is not put to everybody—"To the extent that a man is untrue to the law of his being and does not rise to personality (defined as the complete realisation of our whole being), he has failed to realise his life's meaning. Fortunately, in her kindness and patience, nature never puts the fatal question as to the meaning of their lives into the mouths of most people. And where no one asks, no one need answer." Those who have not been confronted with this question will often consider those who have as peculiar, adding that there is no such thing as a vocation to personality, and that their sense of being isolated and different is a form of spiritual arrogance; they should concern themselves with the really important things in life, viz "getting on", and leading an inconspicuously normal existence.

Unfortunately, this lukewarm advice offers no resolution to inner turmoils and imperatives. The problem of integration and fulfilment runs through many of Hesse's other novels. In *Narziss und Goldmund*, two complementary paths of development are traced; Goldmund arrives at the monastery where Narziss (Narcissus) is already teaching, and attempts to emulate the intellectual and ascetic qualities which he so admires. But in doing so he realises that the law of his being points in a different direction, so he sets off as a vagabond, finally realising his potential as a sculptor, while Narziss remains in the monastery. Goldmund reflects that all being is built on opposites, on division: "Man or woman, vagabond or citizen, lover or thinker—no breath could be both in and out, none could be man and wife, free and yet orderly, knowing the urge of life and the joy of intellect. Always one paid for the other, though each was equally precious and essential." At this stage he experienced an eternal craving, although he does eventually die in peace.

Later on Hesse comments on the relative merits of the two paths, wondering whether people were really created to study Aristotle and Aquinas, to know Greek, to extinguish their senses, to stand apart from the world with well-washed hands in a pretty garden of well-trained thoughts. Narziss, in a moment of self-doubt, asks whether it was not more valiant to breast the currents of reality, and to suffer the bitter consequences of sin. Each of the characters may have been true to themselves, but both are aware that they have developed only one polarity, in accordance with their inherent predispositions.

Steppenwolf is another instance of one-sided development: he trains his mind at the expense of his emotions, and fosters his independence to a degree which makes him practically incapable of relating to others, whose balance and compromise he despises. Harry Haller finds himself a human being on the one hand—"a world of thoughts and feelings, of culture and tamed or sublimated nature", but within he also finds a wolf, "a dark world of instinct, of savagery and cruelty, of unsublimated or raw nature", which Jung would call the "shadow". Neither the unconscious unity of childhood, nor the unmitigated savagery of the "wolf" are possible solutions for Harry, who concludes that his ego is multiple and that man is not a fixed or enduring form but rather "an experiment and a transition. He is nothing else than the narrow and perilous bridge between nature and spirit. His innermost destiny drives him on to the spirit and to God. His innermost longing draws him back to nature, the mother." It is what Baudelaire calls a simultaneous postulation towards good and evil, and what is implied by Faust when he laments that he houses two souls within himself. Harry himself is not destined to reach the distant spiritual goal, but he is initiated into the delights of the senses by a mysterious woman called Maria, who gives him a new understanding, insight and love, thus enabling him to relate to her and break out of his self-imposed isolation. He is ordered to live and to learn to laugh.

In the course of a conversation with a musician called Pablo, Harry is informed that the conquest of time and the escape from reality means simply the wish to be relieved of his so-called personality, which is described as a prison; he has a foretaste of this in the intoxication of dancing and love, but never actually attains a state of inner peace and equilibrium. In the novel *Siddhartha*, the central character experiences the desires for possession and love, and achieves considerable worldly success and status. But in the end he still feels discontented and chained by the riches he has acquired. He wanders off into the forest, profoundly disillusioned and wishing only for death.

A chance encounter with a ferryman leads him to fresh insight; he is told that the river will teach him all he needs to know. He learns from it how to listen—"to listen with a still heart, with a waiting, open soul, without passion, without desire, without judgment, without opinions".

This realisation represents the crucial shift of attitude between the first and second halves of life; in the first half Siddhartha strove to impose his will on others in establishing himself, to overcome resistance with force, to adapt the world to himself, his desires, and his needs. Now he suddenly realises that the will to power is self-defeating, that resistance may be overcome with gentleness, and that his integration consists rather in adapting himself to the flow of events.

As we have seen in the cases of Narziss, Goldmund, and Steppenwolf, one of the dangers of psychological development, particularly in the first half of life, is that it may be one-sided and incomplete; there are unlived possibilities, and opportunities missed owing to imbalances of character. This can be more clearly understood within the framework of Jung's psychological types: in addition to the two basic attitudes of extraversion he distinguishes the four functions of thinking, feeling, sensation, and intuition. It is not necessary for our purposes to go into the details of these functions: it is enough to point out that there is a tendency for one function to become highly developed and differentiated, while another remains dormant, and may even wither. For example, the thinker, such as Steppenwolf, may ignore his feeling side, and attempt to deal analytically with all the problems which he encounters. This is not only inappropriate but dangerous, since his feeling function will remain undeveloped; the less developed it is, the more reluctant he will be to use it, and if he is forced to use it he may find himself behaving in such an inept manner that it becomes impossible for him to express his feelings in a way that will be understood and appreciated by another person. Whatever aspects of the personality are undeveloped remain undifferentiated and repressed in the unconscious, and constitute the "shadow", which must be integrated if the individual is to achieve the desirable wholeness. In addition, the man will have to integrate his feminine side of "anima", and the woman her masculine side of "animus".

These factors are by definition unconscious, complementary to the conscious ego-complex, and are projected onto a member of the opposite sex. If the projection does not coincide with the reality of the person, then there is blind infatuation, but if it relates to reality more than to imagination, then the relationship may turn out to be mutually fruitful. Some of the demands of the shadow and the anima may come to light as a result of dreams, which Jung claims "reflect the vital tendencies of the personality, either those whose meaning embraces our whole life, or those which are momentarily of most importance. The dream presents an objective statement of these tendencies, a statement unconcerned with our conscious wishes and beliefs." Obviously these remarks do not apply to all dreams, but only those with evident symbolic content which constitutes a message to the conscious ego-complex. As such they are an important extension of self-knowledge.

"The greatest and most important problems of life are all in a sense insoluble," claims Jung. "They must be so because they express the necessary polarity inherent in every self-regulating system. They can never be solved, but only outgrown." A solution is something final and static, and therefore inappropriate to describe a process which is inherently organic, where the healing of a wound can only take place through fresh growth. In its turn the new state will throw up new challenges and tensions. Knecht, in Hesse's *Glass Bead Game*, resolves that his life should be a perpetual transcending, a progression from stage to stage, which he likens to music moving "from theme to theme, from tempo to tempo, playing each out to the end, completing each and leaving it behind, never tiring, never sleeping, forever wakeful, forever in the present". Each new growth should extend consciousness and knowledge, tending towards the object of Knecht's Psychological Game, which was "to create unity and harmony, cosmic roundedness and perfection".

Towards integration

We must now return to Siddhartha and the river bank, to the moment where he transcends the limitations of the ego and merges into unity— "From that hour Siddhartha ceased to fight against his destiny. There shone in his face the serenity of knowledge, of one who is no longer confronted with the conflict of desires, who has found salvation, who is in harmony with the stream of events, with the stream of life, full of sympathy and compassion, surrendering himself to the stream, belonging to the unity of all things." In a conversation with his friend Govinda he explains his new insight by saying that he had previously spent his life seeking, equated with having a goal, whereas finding is to be free and receptive, to have no goal, having discovered that what one was seeking was to be found within all the time. Siddhartha's formulation epitomises the main characteristics associated with the man of Tao: the state of being beyond the conflict of desires, being in harmony with the flow of events, acting in accordance with this flow, and the sense of being at one with all phenomena. We shall examine these aspects in turn.

Modern man is typified by Frances Wickes as Mr Restless-busyness: he preaches bigger, better, faster, more, in other words that needs are only ever temporarily gratified, and that the sense of gratification can be increased by a superior product. The man or woman of Tao realises that contentment is to be had by tempering desire and knowing where to stop; their view is that people who are attached to things will suffer much, and so they do not concern themselves with loss or gain. "Without desire there is tranquillity," says Lao Tsu; this is achieved by holding to what is called "the centre in the midst of conditions", or being at what Eliot would call the still point of the turning world. He who is rooted in this centre need not be fundamentally affected by the conditions of the flux.

The movement of Tao is like the flowing of water, but more like the tides than the river, since the flow is reversed when the extreme is reached; the *I Ching* is constructed entirely on this basis. Jung wrote the introduction to the edition by Richard Wilhelm. Thus it is said that he who stands on tiptoe is not steady, he who boasts achieves nothing, and he who brags will not endure; the extremes of attitude are inherently unstable and will certainly be transformed into their opposites, as in the *hubris/nemesis* mechanism of Greek tragedy. In more general terms the highest good is defined in terms of water, "which gives life to ten thousand things and does not strive. It flows in places men reject and so is like Tao." This line is further developed into the paradox that the weak can overcome the strong; Lao Tsu observes that nothing is more soft and yielding than water, and yet for attacking the solid and strong, nothing is better. A recurrent drip can make a considerable hole in the hardest stone.

The principle of action in accordance with the flow is known as *Wu Wei*, sometimes rendered misleadingly as non-action or passivity. The idea is better conveyed by such an expression as not-forcing or not going against the grain. Alan Watts extends the image of the flow when he contends that "The art of life is more like navigation than warfare, for what is important is to understand the winds, the tides, the currents, the seasons, and the principles of growth and decay, so that one's actions may use them and not fight them." This involves a degree of acceptance and yielding, and an understanding that force causes resistance; this

force implies interference with the flow of events and an obstinate perseverance which the man of Tao eschews in favour of flexibility.

The ancient masters are described as subtle, mysterious, profound,
and responsive, with a depth of knowledge which can only be dimly
apprehended by contemporary people; these sages are likened in their
simplicity and wholeness to uncarved blocks of wood. Chuang Tsu
claims that "At the still point in the centre of the circle one can see the
infinite in all things," and that "Only he who has transcended sees this
oneness. He has no use for differences, and dwells in the constant." This
is not quite the extinction of the self in Nirvana, as implied by the image
of the dew drop slipping into the sea, but rather the shedding of the illusion of separate existence as a result of this insight into the oneness of
all things; the imaginary limitations of the self and the other. Ethically
this may lead to indifference towards the self and the other. The Western conscience would feel slightly uneasy about the first alternative,
and would prefer Schweitzer's ethical mysticism, which derives loving devotion to all forms of life in the universe from the insight of the
oneness of life, and further maintains that the individual attains self-
realisation precisely through such loving devotion.

In his old age Jung wrote that it was for him a "major effort to escape
in time from the narrowness of its embrace, and to liberate our mind to
the vision of the immensity of the world, of which we form an infinitesimal part". He was also impressed by the frailty and weakness of
our understanding, with the result that he had recourse at his retreat
in Bollingen to the simplicity and directness of immediate experience,
such as the chopping of wood, the cooking of food over fire, and the
sculpting of shapes out of stone. In one essay he wrote that "To rest
in Tao means fulfilment, wholeness, one's destination reached, one's
mission accomplished; the beginning, end, and perfect realisation of
the meaning of existence innate in all things." This condition would be
symbolised by the mandala or Golden Flower. But this end is far too
neat; elsewhere he writes that the "flow of life again and again demands
a new, more comprehensive adaptation. Adaptation is never achieved
once and for all."

In his *Markings* Dag Hammarskjöld writes that "The longest journey
is the journey inwards of him who has chosen his destiny, who has
started on his quest for the source of his being." For Eliot "The end
of all our exploring will be to arrive where we started and know the

place for the first time." The cycle is completed when the original oneness is consciously intuited, and when the personality reaches an approximation of wholeness, having integrated the opposite tendencies into a wider consciousness and self-knowledge. Finality may be unattainable, perfection one-sided, and wholeness imperfect, but this does not absolve us from striving to balance will and receptivity and from attempting to reach the level of awareness where we may catch a glimpse of the underlying Tao. This in turn may enable us to transcend the pattern of character as destiny, and to navigate freely on the tide of events.

Cultivating a Sense of Beauty

I think this essay, written in 1984, speaks largely for itself. My life is still enriched by a sense of beauty in many of the same respects, including music, poetry, and, above all, a connection with nature. We now live a simple life in the foothills of the Pyrenees where there is a richness in the everyday walking, swimming, and relating to dogs and horses. The light is exceptionally beautiful, and just this morning I was appreciating the first rays of the sun on a series of buildings above our house while walking along the river. One other memory associated with this essay is a visit to the Taize Community in France where I had similar experiences in nature in both spring and autumn. The profound spirituality of Brother Roger was a real inspiration, also in its simplicity and innocence.

The English word "beauty", like the French "beauté", is derived from the Latin "beare" meaning to bless or gladden, and "beatus", blessed or happy. The French adjective "beau" or "belle" comes from the Latin "bellus"—enchanting, lovely, agreeable. This word in turn is rooted in an older word "benlos", which is related to "bonus" and "bene", meaning respectively good and well. This etymology provides us with a few intriguing clues about the origins and associations of the word, evoking two themes which will be mentioned below: the beauty of holiness, and the correspondence between beauty and truth. Meanwhile we can make a few preliminary observations. An object or scene which provides the occasion of an experience of beauty does indeed gladden us, as the word "beare" suggests; it may even extend to a sense of bliss, another word close to "bless". Then the adjective "beatus" clarifies the point that an experience of beauty is an experience of happiness, of integration with one's surroundings.

Active perception

The sense of beauty seems to be a special kind of perception, a faculty which we can either cultivate or neglect. Before proceeding any further we will examine perception in a little more detail. This word (perception) is derived from the Latin "per-capere", to seize through. Our senses are the means whereby we seize the world and forge it into some form of unity and order. To perceive is not just passive reception but rather active interpretation in which we create and construct an image. Given our inevitable participation and involvement in the process of perception, it is easy to see that we are actually responsible for the way in which we perceive, order, and construct our own reality.

The truth of the statement for art can be seen by the various opinions and reactions excited by a picture: some may find it beautiful, others literally repulsive and ugly. In other words, those who find the painting beautiful are attracted to it, while those who feel that it is ugly will be repelled; we advance or recoil according to our sense of beauty on a given occasion. What, then, differentiates an indifferent reaction to a painting from one where the sense of beauty is elicited? The answer is a certain quality of perception arousing a delicious sensation of harmony and happiness, an expansion and glow of the being, even a tingle down the spine. If we were cats, we would surely purr ecstatically.

It is often said that beauty is in the eye of the beholder. But what is in the eye? It is the feeling of the heart, even of the soul, which resonated following perception by the eye. The eye is just the instrument—not the faculty which creates a response to beauty. We need both a perceiver and an external object in order to experience beauty, but the sensation links perceiver and object in a mysterious fashion. There is the discovery of an affinity, of a oneness, of a harmony which is not intrinsic in the object itself, but which in conjunction with this special kind of perception plucks a chord within us. We are flooded with bliss, our separate sense melts and dissolves awhile.

Aspiration

In the preface of *Motivation and Personality*, Abraham Maslow asserts that human life will never be understood unless its highest aspirations are taken into account (it is interesting to note that to aspire means to breathe towards). He laments the fact that many in the intellectual and educational community propound an outlook "characterised by a profound despair and cynicism which sometimes degenerates into corrosive malice and cruelty", illustrating the sorry present-day maxim of "Do in your neighbour before he does you in." This "subculture of despair", this "more corrosive than thou" attitude, is particularly insidious when it reaches young people, who often do not have the confidence to rebut it. They do not want to be laughed at by their peers and are afraid of making themselves vulnerable by adopting a less defensive attitude. Better, then, they think, not to commit myself to anything positive for fear of being criticised, ridiculed, or shot down.

A propos of this problem, there appeared, in 1874, a slim volume by Professor Blackie of Edinburgh University (distantly related through marriage) entitled *Self-culture', a Vade Mecum for Young Men and Students*. The book must have proved extremely popular since my edition dated April 1895 is the twenty-fourth. Besides a great deal of sound and noble advice, the book contains a couple of passages of particular relevance to our theme. Blackie warns the young man that the worst thing he can do if he wants to educate himself aesthetically is to begin criticising "and cultivating the barren graces of the *NIL ADMIRARI* (nothing is to be admired)". This maxim, he comments "may be excusable in a worn-out old cynic, but is intolerable in the mouth of a hopeful young man". He has as yet produced no substantial work of his own, his judgment is not yet formed.

In a later section on moral culture Blackie sees little hope in this attitude, precluding as it does the possibility of experiencing wonder and reverence. He quotes Plato as stating that wonder is a truly philosophic passion. It is defined by the psychologist Rollo May as "an opening attitude—an awareness that there is more to life than one has yet fathomed, an experience of new vistas in life to be explored as well as new profundities to be plumbed". And G. K. Chesterton remarks that "The world will never starve for want of wonders; only for lack of wonder." There is plenty to marvel at if only we can discover it; and if we fail to discover anything, it is rather a judgment on our own superficiality than on the nature of the world. Blackie maintains that to be deficient in wonder "argues either insensibility, or that indifference, selfishness, and conceit, which are sometimes to be found combined with a shallow sort of cleverness that with superficial observers readily passes for true talent". It simply is not clever to be cynical. Moreover, if nothing sublime and wonderful is perceived, owing to the atrophy of the faculty, the sublime and wonderful cannot be imitated and embodied in our lives.

Poetic appreciation

One of the qualities of Maslow's self-actualising people (studies of psychologically healthy individuals) is "continued freshness of appreciation" so that a familiar experience is enjoyed in its pristine intensity with the full recognition of the uniqueness of the occasion. We may have seen any number of beautiful sunsets, but none has been identical to this one, nor is our previous reaction a reliable guide to full appreciation of the present. Maslow comments that such people "derive ecstasy, inspiration and strength from the basic experience of life". In other words, they do not allow their sense of beauty to wither and with it their enhanced sense of appreciation. Not only do they not walk around with their eyes closed, but these eyes are open in a particular way which enables them to exercise and strengthen the sense of beauty through keen and harmonious perception giving rise to joy, exuberance, and gratitude.

Wordsworth, in "Intimations of Immortality", talks of the "primal sympathy" of the child with nature, of "the visionary gleam" of perception:

> *Heaven lies about us in our infancy*
> he remarked, then
> *At length of the Man perceives it die away,*
> *And fade into the light of common day.*

The magic, timelessness, and oneness of childhood perception is lost and wistfully regretted. Elsewhere he speaks of "observation of affinities in objects where no brotherhood exists for passive minds", picking up a point already referred to: that perception is active interpretation, and that the "passive mind" will altogether miss the affinity and hence the beauty. Wordsworth found that "all my thoughts were steeped in feeling", and that he was only contented "when with bliss ineffable I felt the Sentiment of Being spread o'er all that moves and all that seemeth still". This sensation is beyond the reach of all thought, invisible to the eye, "yet liveth in the heart"; a quality and sensation of bliss.

The Indian poet Tagore encapsulates the same thought, taking it even further: "As we become conscious of the harmony in our soul, our apprehension of the blissfulness of the spirit of the world becomes universal, and the expression of beauty in our life moves in goodness and love towards the infinite." Harmony and bliss lie both within and without, the same essence pervades the soul and the object in nature. Three more passages from Wordsworth convey and elaborate the bliss of beauty, hinting at the insight into the infinite in all: the end of "Intimations of Immortality".

> *Thanks to the human heart by which we live,*
> *Thanks to its tenderness, its joys, its fears,*
> *To me the meanest flower that blows can give*
> *Thoughts that do often lie too deep for tears.*

The next two excerpts are from "Tintern Abbey":

> *Until, the breath of this corporeal frame*
> *And even the motion of our human blood*
> *Almost suspended, we are laid asleep*
> *In body, and become a living soul:*
> *While with an eye made quiet by the power*
> *Of harmony, and the deep power of joy,*
> *We see into the life of things.*

There is a sense here in which we see into the life of ourselves by seeing into the life of things. Wordsworth also indicates the peace of mind, the "holy calm" which is a prerequisite to such an experience. "The beautiful", says Simone Weil, "is that which we can contemplate." And for genuine contemplation we need silence and stillness of mind, even solitude; other thoughts and distractions will only shatter the perfection. Wordsworth continues on the following page:

> *And I have felt*
> *A presence which disturbs me with the joy*

> *Of elevated thoughts, a sense sublime*
> *Of something far more deeply interfused,*
> *Whose dwelling is the light of setting suns,*
> *And the round ocean and the living air,*
> *And the blue sky, and in the mind of man;*
> *A motion and a spirit, that impels*
> *All thinking things, all objects of all thought,*
> *And rolls through all things.*

Hence his love of nature, of eye and ear—"both what they half create and what perceive". This phrase highlights the subtlety of the process; the half-creation suggesting the contribution of eye and ear, and the word perceive that there is an element in nature already which man has to discern. The something which Wordsworth senses is interfused deeply in nature, aesthetic experiences and in "the mind of man", which completes the process; in which the experience is born. These exquisite verses of Tagore depict the same unity of mind and nature:

> *I feel that all the stars shine in me.*
> *The world breaks into my life like a flood*
> *Flowers blossom in my body.*
> *All the youthfulness of land and water smokes like*
> *an incense in my heart; and the breath of all things*
> *plays on my thoughts as on a flute.*

Before speaking more personally of beauty in nature, it is worth noting the beauty in the images and rhythms of the poetry itself; beauty reflecting beauty, the evanescent perception evoked in words which may convey in joint degree the sensations of the poet. Joubert expresses it thus: "Lovely verses are breathed forth like sounds and scents … every word used by a true poet holds a kind of phosphorescence for the eyes, a kind of nectar for the taste, an ambrosia for the mind which is in no other words." By rereading the Wordsworth aloud, the reader may catch a glimpse of the sublime.

Experiencing beauty

Last April I sat for a few moments, or was it minutes, in paradise. Bathed in glorious sunshine we were on a wall overlooking a garden in which three cherry trees were in full blossom. The whiteness wafted gently in the wind, radiant and ethereal; it rustled to the soft accompaniment of visiting bees. The slumbering world was awakening to joy and warmth. The vividness and vibrancy was in the flowers and in ourselves; there was an ecstatic evaporation of stillness and movement into joy. On the cliffs of Cornwall one can hear majestic waves crashing onto the rocks below; feel the breeze in one's hair, and watch the glistening sparkles of light dancing out at sea. In pine forests the treetops sing a soft melody, the nostrils swell with the scent from all around. And when these experiences have passed, the memory remains. Tagore again: "My flower of the day dropped its petals. In the evening it ripens into a golden fruit of memory." Even if the sensation of beauty is fleeting, the mind and memory can conjure up the past delight, recreating the green in the course of more grey days.

It goes without saying, however, that no such memories can exist without the initial keen observation and appreciation. Next time you go out into your garden or on a walk, take the trouble of examining a flower really closely—its structure, shape, colour, and texture. You can be sure to take some joy home with you.

In an essay on pleasure in nature, Viscount Grey of Fallodon illustrates the delight which can be derived from the study of birds. First there is their flight: think of the swallow, the swan, the goose, even the flit of the wren or the flash of the kingfisher over the water. Then their plumage: the mallard duck's blue, the peacock, the pheasant, the goldfinch, the wonderful hue of the bullfinch (even if it does eat your fruit). Then their eggs: the dappled blues and greys, the shape, the delicacy, the wonder of seeing half a dozen in one nest. Finally, their song, the expression of pure joy; the lark on a summer's day, the pheasant's call at sunset in winter, the mistle thrush perched on the highest branch of a tall tree. Grey sums up pleasures in nature with a sentence from Jeremy Taylor: "I sleep ... I drink and eat, I read and meditate, I walk in my neighbour's pleasant fields, and see all the varieties of natural beauty, I delight in that in which God delights, that is, in wisdom and virtue, and in the whole creation, and in God himself. And he that hath so many forms of joy, must needs be very much in love with sorrow and peevishness, who loseth all these pleasures, and chooseth to sit upon his little handful of thorns"—a charming image.

Many great cathedrals are symphonies of beauty—the sculptures and stained glass at Chartres—especially the North Rose; the texture and grace of the curved arches. My brother and I were once visiting Amiens Cathedral. There were no seats in the immense nave, so that the beauty of the tiled floor was fully revealed. The eye travelled up to the ceiling, liberated into a sense of angelic space. Then, suddenly, from high up at the west end, came the sound of the first notes of Bach's Toccata and Fugue in D minor; we reeled, literally overwhelmed by wonder and beauty. I have had similar sublime musical experiences in Notre Dame de Paris with Bach's Dorian Toccata and Fugue and in King's College Chapel with the fugue from the Passacaglia.

Appropriately, Albert Schweitzer characterises Bach's music as Gothic: "Just as in Gothic architecture the great develops out of the simple motive, but enfolds itself in the richest detail instead of in rigid line, and only makes its effect when every detail is truly vital, so does the impression Bach work makes on the hearer depend on the player communicating to him the massive outline and the details together, both equally clear and equally full of life." Personally, I find the greatest delight in the fugues of Bach, beginning from a simple line and developing complex layers of interweaving, all discords resolving into a final harmonious chord. And, as Eliot puts it, it is "music heard so deeply that it is not heard at all, but you are the music while the music lasts". There is the same resonance, the same affinity and discovery of the depths of self in and through another medium.

"The most beautiful thing we can experience", claims Einstein, "is the mysterious. It is the source of all true art and science. He to whom this emotion is a stranger, who can no longer stand rapt in awe, is as good as dead; his eyes are closed." It is enough to gaze at the stars for such a sensation to well up. Koestler describes the relationship of beauty to truth in his *Act of Creation*; where something previously chaotic is suddenly seen in another light, order emerges and the phenomenon becomes transparent with the new perspective. He calls it the "Eureka process", the intellectual aspect of which is "spontaneous illumination". "The perception of a familiar object in a new, significant light", while the emotive aspect "is the rapt stillness of oceanic wonder".

In both senses it is the achievement of or insight into overall harmony, peaceful order. In another fine image Tagore says that "Love is life in its fullness like the cup with its wine." Love makes faces beautiful and seem more beautiful. A radiance shines from clear eyes, exudes from the very features. Then there are beautiful smiles, sacred acts of kindness and compassion, a rhythm and grace in movement.

These features create joy and elicit the same harmonious serenity, perhaps even more deeply than nature, but less profoundly than the ineffable mystical experience, the ultimate revelation of peace, unity, meaning, and reality.

In the world we can all be receivers and transmitters of beauty. We must open our senses to the richness of our surroundings (without, of course, losing our awareness of suffering), fill our minds and hearts with joy, cultivate our sense or faculty of beauty. Then in becoming richer in ourselves, we will have more pearls to share with others. The fountain of joy which wells up within will overflow, sprinkling little sparkling petals into a corroded cynical world.

The Encounter of Eastern and Western Cosmologies—Speculations on Radhakrishnan and the "Implicate Order"

*T*his essay dating from 1984 compares the work of the theoretical physicist Professor David Bohm FRS (1917–1992) and Professor (Sir) Sarvepalli Radhakrishnan FBA (1888–1975), who was the first Spalding Professor of Eastern Religions and Ethics at Oxford—I put his knighthood in brackets as it reflects the British Empire of the time. Radhakrishnan was a close friend of both Gandhi and Nehru, who sent him as Indian Ambassador to Moscow—he later became president of India. My first encounter with the work of Radhakrishnan occurred on a visit to Foyles bookshop in London in the late summer of 1974. I headed for the section on comparative religion and bought his books A Hindu View of Life and An Idealist View of Life. I later inherited his scholarly editions of the Upanishads, Bhagavad-Gita, and Dhammapada and subsequently acquired a whole shelf of his books. Radhakrishnan was awarded the Templeton Prize in 1973.*

I first heard David Bohm speak in Winchester at the 1983 Mystics and Scientists Conference, a series I have been organising myself for more than thirty years. He was a shy individual with an extraordinary clarity and penetration of thinking. I don't know if he had himself encountered the work of Radhakrishnan, but he had extensive published dialogues with Krishnamurti and was fascinated by the interface between East and West, also paralleled in the exchanges between Einstein and Tagore. One of the books I bought at the conference was his 1980 Wholeness and the Implicate Order, *which contains an extensive discussion of etymology reflected in the essay below. In his later years, he became very involved in the dialogue process, and we organised a weekend dialogue where he and his wife Saral were both active participants. What he recommended then is more important than ever, namely deep listening and suspension of one's own assumptions and presuppositions.*

Fritjof Capra has coined the phrase "crisis of perception" to characterise the widespread sense of unease concerning the validity of current modes of thought in the sciences, social sciences, and philosophy. The issue at stake is not so much that the old view is wrong while the new approach is correct, but rather that the scope of the old view is inadequate. It tries to explain the whole in terms of one of its aspects, as if one kind of lens were sufficient to ensure that the whole perspective of the picture was focused. One lens will operate most clearly for close-ups, while we require another for a sweeping view; the close-up lens will blur the background, while the long-view lens will not prove sharp enough to catch the foreground detail. "The present crisis in human affairs", claims Radhakrishnan, "is due to a profound crisis in human consciousness, a lapse from the organic wholeness of life. There is a tendency to overlook the spiritual and exalt the intellectual." The job of the intellect is analysis, discrimination, and classification. Etymologically, the word means to read or choose between. The intellect divides (literally "sees as two") and separates the object of its investigation. When applied to the outside world, as has been the case in Western science over the past 300 years, it naturally selects the separate aspect of phenomena which it may then combine in classification.

To classify is then equated with understanding. A moment's reflection suffices to show that this is not the case: the classification is simply a larger part; it remains nonetheless separate from other groups, distinguishable from them. The range of understanding has certainly been extended, but it is still limited by the kinds of classification employed, or, to return to our lens analogy, by what is focused by the particular lens. As human beings, the scope of our comprehension is evidently not infinite; we are by definition finite and limited in our perception and understanding; but this does not excuse us from attempting to extend the width and depth of our views as far as possible, thus enlarging the context and perspective of our knowledge.

World views

The thinker who claims to be "objective" is wearing a contact lens which he has forgotten about. It is so intimately connected with his vision that he no longer realises or admits that his view is conditioned by time and temperament—he is unaware, in other words, that he has an implicit world view which structures and orders his perceptions and judgments. Sir Karl Popper illustrates this point by instructing his students to "observe"; they are naturally nonplussed—observe what? An object must be selected and then considered in a particular way, first through perception itself and then in terms of the questions posed by the observer. If, for instance, you choose a table, exactly what do you want to know? The wood used, the maker, its age, its style, etc.? Each different analysis requires a distinct kind of observation. David Bohm remarks at the beginning of his *Wholeness and the Implicate Order* that it has become a presupposition of most work in modern physics that the principal aim of human knowledge is prediction and control in relation to technical utility. He then continues by asserting that such a presupposition is in accord with the general spirit of our age.

In his view, we cannot simply dispense with an overall world view: "If we try to do so, we will find that we are left with whatever (generally inadequate) world views may happen to be at hand." If we accept, whether explicitly or not, the prevalent view, it will in all probability be for social and/or emotional reasons. Jung states that "The spirit of the age cannot be fitted into the categories of human reason," because it is an emotional tendency carried along by the force of suggestion: it is constituted by our unconscious assumptions and reinforced by social pressure. The popular view, argues Jung is "decent, reasonable, scientific and normal"; whereas "To think otherwise than our contemporaries is somehow illegitimate and disturbing; it is even indecent, morbid or blasphemous, and therefore socially dangerous for the individual." Such censorship will be exerted on the nonconformist in any field. Conservative authority is reinforced by social sanction.

It is unwise, in view of the history of ideas and science, to assume that our current preconceptions correspond with the truth; moreover, as indicated earlier, human understanding is limited by definition. We should be very wary of those who wish to stamp relative truths as absolute or transform hypotheses into definitive statements. Thus Whitehead is right when he contends that the certainties of science are a delusion, hedged around as they are with unexplored limitations and presumptions. He makes a distinction between the Observational and the Conceptual Order. The latter is our general way of conceiving the universe and ourselves (the word "conceive" literally means to grasp with); it supplies the concepts with which we interpret the Observational Order. This order, however, does not follow from an impartial assessment of the facts: "The order prominent in observation is in fact a distortion of the facts." We choose and highlight certain facts. Thus there are two levels of interference in our interpretation. Both thought and observation are canalised within predetermined limits.

As for transformation, Whitehead observes: "Systems, scientific and philosophic, come and go. Each method of limited understanding is at length exhausted. In its prime each system is a triumphant success: in its decay it is an obstructive nuisance." Such systems are like coal seams which can potentially yield a number of valuable insights; but their initial freshness spells eventual obsolescence. They may illuminate certain fields more brightly than hitherto, but they neglect others by the same token. The obstructiveness emerges when the adequacy of the conception is surpassed by a more comprehensive theory—generally regarded with great suspicion by the incumbent experts whose position confers on them a vested interest in preserving the supremacy of the outgoing view.

Process

"The flux of things is the one ultimate generalisation around which we must weave our philosophical systems," claims Whitehead. It is mankind's first general apprehension, and has been expressed in numerous forms in the course of the history of ideas. Transience is lamented by the Psalmist and by Ecclesiastes in the Old Testament; here the tone is one of wistful regret. In Heraclitus the point is made more neutrally: "You cannot step twice into the same rivers; for fresh waters are ever flowing in upon you. It is cold things that become warm, and what is warm that cools; what is wet dries, and the parched is moistened." Anaxagoras develops the ideas to explain the emergence of stable forms in the flux: "The Hellenes are wrong in using the expression coming into being and passing away; for nothing comes into being or passes away, but mingling and separation takes place of things that are. So they would be right in calling coming into being mixture, and passing away separation." Marcus Aurelius expresses the idea in terms of the physical insignificance of man in relation to space and time: "Of human life the time is a point, and the substance is in a flux, and the perception dull, and the composition of the whole body subject to putrefaction, and the soul a whirl and fortune hard to divine, and fame a thing devoid of judgement." From this he eventually evolves a resigned philosophy of life: "... waiting for death with a cheerful mind, as being nothing else than a dissolution of the elements of which every living being is compounded"—the equivalent of "separation" in Anaxagoras.

If the notion of flux is universal, so too is the idea of a stable entity or element behind the flux, a substance out of which the flux of forms arises, the realm of Being rather than Becoming. For centuries philosophers have argued about which of these notions is primary; it is characteristic of the Western mind that it should attempt to reduce one to the other on the basis of Aristotelean logic which claims that T cannot also be not-T. Aristotle had no room for complementary substances or ideas, but instead formulated propositions in terms of contradictions. On the other hand, Chinese philosophy is actually based on the complementary symbols of yin and yang, neither of which can be reduced to the other. They are equally real and equally necessary.

In Indian thought, the bondage of time is expressed in the word *Samsara*. The world is a perpetual procession of events, a succession of states in which nothing abides. The universe is not static; it is "a process whose possibilities are infinite ... transiency is the character not only of human life but of the very structure of reality." We shall come back to this analysis when we consider the relation of the manifest to the unmanifest in a subsequent section.

As a child, Bohm found himself fascinated by the nature of movement, and sees in this the germ of a lifelong quest towards clarification of his understanding in this respect. Forms in the world, including our physical bodies, are processes. Our minds, according to some, are nothing more than the stream of thoughts and consciousness; our understanding of the world is an understanding by one process or another. Further analysis of the mind as a stream of consciousness gives rise to the same structural problem discussed above in relation to stability behind the flux: is there a soul or spirit underlying the process, and if so, which is more "real", the stream or the underlying entity? But this is not the place to pursue this question in detail. Analysing the flux or flow in modern physics, Bohm arrives at the insight of "undivided wholeness in flowing movement", a view which implies that "The flow is, in some sense, prior to the 'things' that can be seen to form and dissolve in this flow." This new formulation reverses the traditional idea that the permanent underlying substance is static. Bohm makes it quite clear that it is dynamic, as are the forms which emerge from and dissolve back into the flow: "Thus … each relatively autonomous and stable structure (e.g. an atomic particle) is to be understood not as something independently and permanently existent but rather as a product that has been formed in the whole flowing movement and that will ultimately dissolve back into this movement." The process is strikingly similar to the extract quoted above from Anaxagoras: for "formed", read "mingling", and for "dissolve", read "separation" (in the sense of disintegration).

Bohm develops these ideas further in a chapter entitled "Reality and Knowledge Considered as Process". He defines process as follows: "Not only is everything changing, but all *is* flux. That is to say, *what is* is the process of becoming itself, while all objects, events, entities, conditions, structures etc. are forms that can be abstracted from this process." The underlying reality is a process, becoming, flux. Limited forms are abstracted (literally "withdrawn") from process and manifest as stable systems and structures, such as the human body, which are temporarily extant and independent sub-processes. As we saw in Marcus Aurelius, physical death destroys the autonomy of the body-process, and the elements are resolved into new forms. By the same token, Bohm argues that knowledge is a process, an abstraction from the all-encompassing flux (or holomovement as he terms it). This thought is a reformulation of some of our earlier points about the inherent limitations of any world view. It can only be a partial abstraction from the whole.

Time exemplifies a further application of this notion of process. In the *Timaeus* Plato explains that the Living Being, whose nature was eternal, set out to make the universe resemble it as far as possible, but could not bestow the attribute of eternity fully on the created universe; instead, the best he could come up with was "an eternal moving image of eternity", which we call time. In a sense, then, Plato envisaged time as a material abstraction from eternity. Since, for Bohm, the holomovement is the reality, moments in time and events are necessarily abstractions from it. The etymology of event indicates as much—it is something which "comes out of" (compare the words emerge and merge). As for the derivation of moment, it comes from the Latin "momentum", meaning movement: to use the word statically is tantamount to a contradiction in terms.

Underlying reality

Underlying reality has traditionally been associated with masculine symbolism, while the visible world is conceived in terms of the feminine. As spirit it is the breath of force which moves (Atman in Hinduism derives its root from the word "to breathe"); sky gods represent the all-pervading supreme paternal deity. Other formulations of the underlying reality include the nameless, the formless, the *esse* (as opposed to the *existere*, literally, "that which stands out"), the Tao, and the holomovement of Bohm. In this section we shall examine these last two conceptions, leaving Whitehead and Hinduism until the next one.

The *Tao Te Ching* opens with the verse:

> *The Tao that can be told is not the eternal Tao.*
> *The name that can be named is not the eternal name.*
> *The nameless is the beginning of heaven and earth.*
> *The named is the mother of ten thousand things.*

The formless, the nameless, the infinite, the eternal cannot by its very nature be encapsulated in words which are limited, however suggestive they may be. This leads both Chinese and Hindu thinkers to the use of negative terms to characterise the Supreme Reality. If one cannot define it in words, at least words can be employed to suggest what it is not. The *Tao Te Ching* supposes that the nameless is the source of the named (or limited forms), while some primal form derived from the formless (as equivalent of the demiurge) is responsible for the material manifestation of phenomena.

Later in the book, an attempt to pin down the Tao disintegrates:

> *Something mysteriously formed,*
> *Born before heaven and earth.*
> *In the silence and the void,*
> *Standing alone and unchanging,*
> *Ever present and in motion.*
> *Perhaps it is the mother of ten thousand things.*
> *I do not know its name.*

Call it Tao.
For lack of a better word, I call it great.

Being great, it flows.
It flows far away.
Having gone far, it returns.

A number of further images appear here: silence, void, and unchanging (yet flowing). Noise arises from silence, form from void, and the changing from the unchanging flow. Once again it is nameless, and the word "great" is used with considerable reluctance. The theme is once more taken up in chapter 32—"The Tao is for ever undefined ... Once the whole is divided, the parts need names." So long as the whole remains undifferentiated, there are no separate forms, therefore no need for names. Form is manifestation and limitation—individuality which requires naming and classification.

For Bohm the underlying reality is the holomovement, which is "undefinable and immeasurable", in other words nameless and formless in terms of the Tao. Moreover, regarded in its totality, Bohm claims that it includes the principle of life, the "named" in terms of the Tao— the mother of ten thousand things. The all-embracing nature of the holomovement means that life and inanimate matter are not fragmented, nor is life reduced to a by-product of matter. They share a common source. Matter is one form or degree of abstraction, life another. There is, however, an intermediary "stage" between the primary, self-existent, and universal holomovement and physical forms. This is called the "implicate order", in which "everything is enfolded into everything". The idea derives from the hologram, a three-dimensional laser image where the whole picture is reflected and contained, albeit imperfectly, in any part. In Bohm's formulation "The form and structure of the entire object may be said to be *enfolded* within each region of the photographic record. When one shines light on any region, this form and structure are then *unfolded* to give a recognisable image of the whole object once again." From this unfolding Bohm arrives at the notion of an "explicate (physically visible) order" in contrast with the implicate order explained above. It is important to bear in mind that this implicate order is not to be equated with the underlying holomovement, even though it exhibits a unity absent from the explicate order. A partial analogy illustrating the relationship between the two orders can be drawn in the unfolding of the plant from the seed.

God

Transcendence and immanence are two conceptions widely used to characterise the Divine. To transcend means "to climb across", while immanence indicates "dwelling in". The transcendence of the Christian God is expressed in fear, awe, and worship, in the notion of the infinite, and in the idea of God as "wholly other", the impartial judge of mankind; His immanence on the other hand is suggested by the phrase "the kingdom of heaven within", and to some extent by the image of a loving personal father and the all-pervasive Holy Spirit. Bohm quite rightly points out that the conceptions of immanence and transcendence are abstractions, although as ideas they are "relatively independent sub-totalities" encompassing a wide range of thoughts about the Divine. We must continually remind ourselves that ideas, however sweeping, are not reality. The Isa Upanishad confirms the limitations of ideas: "Into deep darkness fall those who follow the immanent. Into deeper darkness fall those who follow the transcendent." The liberated man is he who knows both—"with the immanent overcomes death, and with the transcendent reaches immortality". The knowledge referred to here is not so much abstract as lived and experienced—hence its effect.

The Upanishads use the word *Brahman* to indicate the supreme reality "which remains identical and persists through change", the root of the word hidden from the senses but discernible to reason. It is derived from *brh*, meaning to grow, to burst forth—creative vitality. It is characterised in the Upanishads as "That which is sufficient to itself, aspiring to no other, without any need, is the source of all other beings, the intellectual principle, the perceiving mind, life and body." As such, it shares many of the qualities of the Tao and the holomovement. Radhakrishnan goes on to point out that Brahman can be considered under the three aspects, which are not to be confused with human qualities: 1) the Absolute, 2) God as Creative Power, 3) God immanent in this world. The succession is logical, not temporal. The Absolute contains only possibilities, which must exist before Divine Creativity can choose one; then the world-spirit must exist before there can be a world. The world is seen as unfolding from these three integrated aspects of the Divine.

Like the Tao, the Absolute is nameless, beyond the sphere of forms and qualities. Being all-inclusive, nothing exists outside it, and it is misleading to attempt to describe it; the description imposes a form, a limitation, which contradicts its very nature. Like the holomovement, the Absolute is immeasurable: to measure also implies form.

God as Creative Power is seen as the source of all forms: "All things are forms of one immutable being, variable expressions of the invariable reality." Another way of expressing the same relationship is to state that "The finite is the self-limitation of the infinite." In turn, this implies that "The manifestation of Primordial Being is also a concealment of His nature." We shall return to this point in more detail when talking of *maya* below. In the meantime, these statements serve to highlight the paradoxical nature of Brahman's relationship to the world: "He lives in all things and yet transcends them"; he is more than the sum of all existing forms; he fills all of these forms, while remaining beyond them. He is transcendent with respect to the manifest world, yet beyond all manifestation he is transcendent in the Absolute, where there are no forms, just potentialities. Words, as the reader will readily appreciate, can only reach out clumsily to express these ideas.

Before looking at the complementary Hindu idea of Atman, we shall divert back to the West to examine Whitehead's scheme of the relationship between God as manifest and unmanifest. He distinguishes what he calls the primordial and consequent natures of God. The primordial corresponds to Hindu Absolute; it is conceptual, unchanging, and finally complete; as such it has no need to become manifest. God's consequent nature is explained as derivative and dependent on the creative advance of the world. Broadly speaking these two classifications—or abstractions—reflect the complementarity of being and becoming as analysed in the section on Process above. If, following Plato, the flux is regarded as unreal while the real is the underlying substance, then the idea of God is robbed of the dynamic element and tends towards the static and remote; the pendulum swings from immanence to transcendence. In its most extreme form, the transcendence of God becomes his total absence from or abandonment of the world, as suggested by Bonhoeffer, the German theologian who died at the hands of the Nazi regime.

Whitehead is anxious to keep in balance the immanent and the transcendent, the primordial and the consequent, the conceptual and the derivative. He sees God and the World as opposed elements connected by mutual requirement; the Chinese would say "mutual arising", rather than requirement, in so far as God was treated as a concept: "For God the conceptual is prior to the physical, for the World the physical poles are prior to the conceptual poles." That is to say, the World exists for God first as an unmanifested idea, but for the World the conceptual emerges in the course of evolution from the physical. Whitehead describes the purposive interaction of God and the World in his customary dense style: "God and the World are the contrasted opposites in terms of which Creativity achieves its supreme task of transforming disjoined multiplicity, with its diversities in opposition, into concrescent unity, with its diversities in contrast." The forms in the World, being "relatively autonomous sub-totalities", are "disjoined"; all the more so if they are self-consciously aware of their separation from life. They are therefore said to be in opposition. The aim is unity, or rather the unification of opposites (*Mysterium Coniunctionis* in the language of Jung's individuation); the word is in the present participle, the unity referred to is dynamic, flowing. At this stage the initial oppositions (literally "placed over against") are resolved into contrasts (literally "to stand with"): while there is still differentiation, there is no longer any conflict. Whitehead characterises this thrusting of the many (forms) towards the one as "the basis of religions …. The story of the dynamic effort of the World passing into everlasting unity." The consequent and derivative nature of God is reabsorbed into the primordial and conceptual nature.

We can now return to Hinduism, with its further conception of ultimate reality as *Atman*, a word derived from *an* "to breathe". In this respect it can be compared with, among others, the Latin *spiritus* and the Greek *pneuma*: inspiration is breathing in, expiration (expiry, expire) to breathe out. *Atman* is "the principle of man's life … the soul that pervades his being, his breath, his intellect and transcends them". It is the true self, awareness unfettered by intellectual conceptions. Through it comes understanding of the Brahman, and thus a beautiful unification of these two abstractions from the Divine: "God is not merely the transcendent numinous other, but is also the universal spirit which is the basis of human personality and its ever-renewing vitalising power." Thus the transcendent limits itself by dwelling immanently in the finite forms of human beings, but for us it is this indwelling immanence which enables us to catch a glimpse of the transcendent. The universal limits and expresses itself through forms, but these forms reach some autonomous understanding of the universal. Nature evolves individual forms of consciousness, but these consciousnesses strive to understand nature. Consciousness transmitted through the brain sets about understanding the workings of the brain. The completed circle renews itself.

Manifest reality

We have already said a good deal about manifest reality in the context of other sections. Here we shall examine a few points in greater detail. It will be remembered that Bohm considered describable entities and objects to be abstractions from an unknown and undefinable totality of flowing movement, which, like the Absolute, is pure potentiality. These entities or objects are relatively autonomous sub-totalities, or stable self-organising structures, as Prigogine would say. The bodily form presents an appearance of stability, but in reality it is in a state of flux, and only able to maintain itself by constant breathing in and out, ingestion and excretion, and circulation of the blood through the heart. Prigogine calls such open systems (as opposed to closed systems like a stone) dissipative structures—they constantly interact with and fit into conditions in the physical world, maintaining a delicate balance between stability and change. If the change is not too drastic, it can be adapted to, but if it is overwhelming, as in physical death, there then occurs a radical restructuring of the parts. Matter disintegrates irrevocably from the context of its present shape and re-forms in another. So far as the individual subatomic particle is concerned, it manifests successively in a number of aspects. When one form disintegrates, it is reintegrated into another, in a different form of abstraction from totality.

Maya

In the earliest Hindu scriptures, the *Rig Veda*, *maya* was "the divine art or power by which the divinity makes a likeness of the eternal prototypes or ideas inherent in his nature": not so much the veil as the dress of God, as Radhakrishnan remarks. Plato's analysis of time is expressed in similar terms (see Process above). The root of *maya* is *ma*, meaning "to measure". This is remarkably significant in the light of Bohm's observation that "measure" originally meant "limit" or "boundary". Thus *maya* denotes measure, form, the finite, the limited in the absence of which there could be no vehicle for individual consciousness. Given the world as the self-limitation of the unlimited, the partial abstraction from the underlying totality, individual forms *participate* in the real, in the total-ity, in accordance with the very nature of such a form. The clearest anal-ogy for this is a container which shapes its contents.

Radhakrishnan explains the relationship of Brahman and the world as follows: "The world is not a deceptive façade of something under-lying it. It is real though imperfect. Since the Supreme is the basis of the world, the world cannot be unreal." In so far as the world is based on and understood in terms of Brahman, it is real. It is unreal only if the relatively autonomous sub-totalities are assumed to be completely autonomous and self-sufficient. The illusion is not manifest reality itself, but the assumption that manifest reality is the ultimate and only reality. By this definition the materialist who thinks that matter is the basis of everything which exists (including consciousness) is deluded by an inadequate conception.

Avidya

Avidya is ignorance; to the Hindu the materialist viewpoint is an act of ignorance. The materialist has succumbed to a subtle temptation: "The world has a tendency to delude us into thinking that it is all, that it is self-dependent, and this delusive character of the world is also desig-nated *maya* in the sense of *avidya*." Here *maya* is used to indicate misap-prehension; it relates not to the existence of the world but to its status and meaning, to our view of its context.

When applied to individual egos *avidya* is the belief that each ego is separate and different from all other egos; the apparent isolation of the self is taken as absolute. This view has emotional, ethical, and intellectual consequences. Emotionally, the self feels alienated, uncon-nected, perhaps even insignificant and meaningless; this alienation is expressed in atheism and suggests the preoccupation of much twenti-eth century Western literature, of which *Waiting for Godot* is one of the most devastating examples. The listlessness of the two tramps is echoed in their featureless view of life. The ethical and spiritual result of this ego-isolation is fragmentation, violence, destructiveness: "a failure to enter into harmony with the universe". Man gives way to helpless-ness and despair, lashing out from time to time to express his frus-tration, thus compounding and reinforcing the very bondage against which he vigorously rebels. Violence can only aggravate already acute fragmentation.

The intellectual consequences of *avidya* require more extensive consideration. Bohm contends that "wholeness is what is real, and that fragmentation is the response of this whole to man's action, guided by illusory perception, which is shaped by fragmentary thought". If the lens or the theory is fragmented, then perception and reasoning will reflect this. It is important to realise the degree of abstraction involved in our understanding. This starts with perception, and reasoning will reflect this. It is also important to realise the degree of abstraction involved in our understanding. This starts with perception itself. Once again, etymology gives us a clue. The word perception is derived from *per-capere*, "to seize through", while both comprehension and concept mean "to seize with". The seizing instrument, the human brain, inevitably filters and interprets the information which it receives and processes. In other words, per-ception is organised and classified by con-ception. In the act of understanding a physical object—for example in recognition of a distant landmark—percept and concept are inseparable. I recall a particular instance of this in France when I saw a ruined tower in the distance and only saw its real shape—with a squared off rather than round wall—as I got closer.

We are now in a position to consider the nature of our understanding of "reality". This word comes from the Latin *"rere"* meaning "to think", which is in turn related to *"res"*, a thing; so that reality is what can be thought about—in this way the inconceivable is unreal because it cannot be grasped by the mind. This is a serious admission of the limitations of our understanding, since logically there is no reason to suppose that what lies beyond our comprehension is unreal. For instance, if underlying reality is immeasurable and undefinable it cannot be fully understood by human reason; as the source of sensory or explicate reality it cannot be any less real than what is perceptible through the senses. The job of the intellect is differentiation, distinction, and analysis—literally to carry apart, to stand as two, and to loosen. For the scientist this process has been helped by the lens which "greatly strengthened man's awareness of the various part of an object"—think of microscopes and telescopes—and of the relationship between these parts. In this way, it furthered the tendency to think in terms of analysis and synthesis. Bohm pursues this line of thought by indicating that the great error—*avidya*—was to assume that anything not measurable by their instruments (which considerably extend the range of sense-perception) did not exist. As Radhakrishnan puts it: "Those who have no contact with reality, no insight into truth, accept the relative symbol for the absolute truth"; and "Intellectual activities are a derivation, a selection, and, so long as they are cut off from the truth which is their secret nature, a deformation of true knowledge."

Where there is separate consciousness, there is duality (conscious means "know with"), division (seeing as two), and objective knowledge (in its true sense of "being thrown in front of"). In Hindu philosophy this objective knowledge is equated with estrangement; Bohm would express it as fragmentation and alienation. What needs to be grasped is what he calls the "formative cause" of such fragmentation—and this applies as much to the process as the content of thought, since these two terms are aspects of the whole. A fragmentary approach will be reflected in a corresponding (answering with) fragmented idea of conception. We have to begin by realising that we cannot fully grasp the immeasurable and indefinable whole; if we thought we could do so, it would amount to a grand self-deception. What we grasp is an abstraction from the whole, one of its aspects, and we do this by means of our concept expressed in static language—a further limitation. We use categories (from *ageiro*, "to collect") to organise and classify our ideas.

We reason within the framework of our theories (from the Greek *theoria*, a spectacle—compare also speculation), in other words through the way in which we see or view things. When explaining an idea, we ask the other person whether they "see" what we mean. Theories are supposed to correspond to facts, but facts are literally what are made—therefore what we call a fact depends on our theoretical approach. The grave risk lies in misunderstanding a strange or new phenomenon because we rely on the validity of a traditional approach or on our previous experience of something similar—what William James calls apperception, the process of incorporating the new into the already known. The reflexes of both theory and thought may channel the mind into a misleading or inadequate explanation. Such is the case with many "nothing-but" interpretations of paranormal occurrences. We need to appreciate both the range and the limitations of any particular theory in order to use it appropriately.

Vidya

As opposed to divisive, discursive, mediated *avidya*, *vidya* is unitive and immediate knowledge, intuitive apprehension or *gnosis*, which cannot always be adequately expressed in words. While *avidya* stresses the "separateness, mutual independence and strife", *vidya* emphasises "the harmony and interconnections which make up the world". To stop at *avidya* is to take fragmentation (*maya*) as ultimately real, without discerning underlying connections and unity in the world. The flash of insight—into unity, for instance—is essentially a reordering of perception and/or conception. The problem is approached from a new angle, the parts are reorganised into a new whole. Bohm argues that such insight is not personal, but supreme intelligence's ability "to rearrange the very structural matter of the brain which underlies thought so as to remove the message which is causing confusion [literally melting together], leaving the necessary information and the brain open to perceive reality in a different way". At present, he explains, the brain is blocked by conditioning which creates a pressure to maintain the familiar and the old, thus excluding the possibility of a fresh approach.

We can now return to our starting point of Capra's "crisis of perception". "The task of philosophy", asserts Whitehead, "is to recover the totality obscured by the selection of consciousness." We have seen how consciousness and intellect necessarily select in terms of perception and theory; how this selection tends to highlight the separate and fragmented aspects of reality; and consequently how reality is interpreted as what is manifest and explicate. We need not discard the spectacular successes of the scientific analytical mind; but nor should we assume that this faculty conveys a complete picture—it is a partial form of insight, an abstraction from the whole. Furthermore, our ideas of the whole are themselves abstractions, although they are able by analogy to help us appreciate the unfolding of the manifest from the unmanifest, or the relatively autonomous sub-totalities from the undefinable and immeasurable holomovement. If we can look beyond the apparent fragmentation of forms in the physical world as ultimately real and self-subsistent, we can see ourselves, our thoughts, and our theories in a true perspective. Such mental proportion is vital accompaniment to spiritual development in its multifaceted quest for unity and integration.

Consciousness and Spirituality:
Widening the Scientific Perspective

*T*his essay from 2001 draws on the work of various special interests of the
Scientific and Medical Network, with which I have been associated since
1983 (www.scimednet.org). Different groups discuss the relationship
between science and spirituality, science and consciousness, and science and
esoteric knowledge, while our flagship conference Mystics and Scientists discusses the interface between science and mysticism. More recently, our major
Galileo Commission Report addresses these issues relating to science and philosophy in considerable depth and detail—see www.galileocommission.org.
Our basic proposition is that science needs to expand and move beyond a purely
materialistic world view, which can only be maintained by studiously avoiding
looking "through the telescope" at conflicting evidence. It needs to re-exam-
ine its basic philosophical assumptions, as also proposed by many of the great
twentieth-century physicists, including Max Planck and Erwin Schrödinger.

Fritjof Capra once asked Krishnamurti how he could best reconcile
his humanity with his profession as a scientist. The response was immediate and conclusive: you are a human being first and a scientist second.
Much the same message became a slogan for Einstein's and Russell's
anti-nuclear protest of the 1950s: remember your humanity and forget the rest. How does this all relate to science, consciousness, and

spirituality? By insisting on the centrality of consciousness as a basis for understanding in both science and spirituality.

The word "science" comes from the Latin "scientia", the root of which is "scire", meaning to know. Consciousness contains the same root, namely "con-scire", meaning to know with. So consciousness is the means by which we know. More precisely, we organise our knowledge through our perceptions and concepts, words which are both derived from the Latin "capere", meaning to grasp. So perception is "grasping through" (per-capere), while concepts imply "grasping with" (con-capere—the word "comprehend" has a similar root since "prehendere" also means to grasp). An alternative set of metaphors proposes that truth is seen rather than grasped: the origin of the word "theory" goes back to the Greek word for contemplation "theoria", from which the word theatre is also derived. Hence consciousness and knowledge are intimately related, whether through grasping or seeing.

What about spirituality? This is a difficult word to define, and one where the *Concise Oxford English Dictionary* is of little help: "spiritual quality", it says, before mentioning the now outdated usage of spirituality as a tithe due to the Church. The word "spiritual" is often used in contrast to "religious", a distinction that many churchgoers would be reluctant to accept. The word can also be contrasted with "secular" or "worldly", implying a sense of priorities and values committed to the sacred dimension of life. Spirituality entails commitment to a practice of some kind and the living out of spiritual principles such as love, compassion, and freedom in everyday life. It also embraces a broader and deeper world view than currently envisaged by modern science.

Origins of the modern scientific world view

Before we address the question of how to widen the scientific perspective on consciousness and spirituality, we need to explore how science arrived at its current understanding. While mediaeval theologians such as St Thomas Aquinas developed a highly sophisticated use of reason, they applied it primarily to the proof of doctrine. Ironically, Kant used the very same tool to overturn the classical theological arguments for the existence of God. Indeed, the keynote of the Enlightenment was the application of *Reason* to human affairs, including the emergent modern science. However, modern science brought with it another key principle, namely the *experimental method*, whereby hypotheses could be formulated and tested independently by different scientists (the word "scientist" was invented by William Whewell in the nineteenth century).

Another key distinction was elaborated by Galileo (and Descartes), between so-called *"primary"* and *"secondary"* qualities. Underlying this distinction is an argument about the nature of reality and knowledge. Primary qualities were defined as concrete and visible: they could be touched, weighed, and measured. The real world was a world of physical bodies moving in space and time. Secondary qualities relating to consciousness, by contrast, were regarded as nebulous, relative, and subjective. Primary qualities are in the realm of knowledge, while secondary qualities lie in the realm of mere opinion. The implication to grasp here is that if reality is defined primarily in terms of the material and the bodily, then spirit, mind, and consciousness are *derived from and therefore secondary to matter, body, and indeed the brain*. This is illustrated in the chart below where it is supposed that the elements in column 2 can be explained by those in column 1:

Causality and explanation

Primary	Secondary
External	Internal
Visible	Invisible
Objective	Subjective
Quantity	Quality
3rd person (it)	1st person (I)
Matter-energy	Spirit-mind
Body/brain	Consciousness

If reality is defined exclusively in terms of the elements composing the first column, then we have a *physicalist* or *materialist* world view. Furthermore, if the right-hand column is explained in terms of the left, we have a form of *reductionism* whereby matter gives rise to mind and brain to consciousness, so that the inner, spiritual dimension is stripped of intrinsic reality. Our conscious experiences become *nothing but* a fluctuation in the brain, as people like Nobel prize-winner Francis Crick assert. Even more fundamentally, there can be no question of any form of conscious existence that is not tied to a physical body, that is, of survival of consciousness beyond bodily death. If brain gives rise to consciousness, then death is logically the extinction of consciousness.

In summary, the materialist understanding is mind = brain, therefore death = extinction.

These categories might be continued by adding three more lines:

Knowledge	Opinion
Experiment	Experience
Science	Spirituality

Science is based on repeatable experiment, while an understanding of spirituality emerges from subjective experience (although, interestingly, both words derive from the Latin root "experiens", meaning to try thoroughly. However, experience is direct while experimenting on something is indirect). Science has focused on the objective or impersonal, while spirituality engages with the subjective and personal. A key question, to be pursued below, is whether valid knowledge is restricted only to the realm of science and experiment. In addition, the dominant metaphor of scientific thinking since the seventeenth century has been *mechanism*, and this mechanistic picture tends to reduce human beings to the same status as the function of machines. This view can be stated more formally in terms of current assumptions about the nature of being or existence (*ontology*) and the nature of knowledge (*epistemology*):

Materialist /physicalist ontology (nature of reality, as related to consciousness)

- The universe is a unified closed physical system
- Matter gives rise to mind in the course of biological evolution
- Nervous systems and brains give rise to consciousness, therefore:
- The death of the brain is the death of the person.

Materialist epistemology (way of knowing)

- Empirical knowledge can only be acquired through physical senses and instruments
- The observer can study the world impersonally and separately from himself
- Causes and explanations can only be physical
- We understand things only through analysis of their component parts
- Purpose and meaning are to be excluded from scientific discourse

Moreover,

- This procedure has proved so successful in theory and practice that any evidence contravening these assumptions is unthinkable and can be summarily dismissed
- It is only a matter of time before everything (including consciousness and spirituality) is adequately explained along these lines.

Scientism

The last two propositions underpin what has come to be known as *scientism*, which can be logically distinguished from science. Huston Smith suggests in his book *Why Religion Matters* that science is "a body of facts about the natural world that controlled experiments require us to believe, together with logical extrapolations from those facts, and the added things that scientific instruments enable us to see with our own eyes". Scientism, he says, adds a further two propositions: "first, that the scientific method is, if not the *only* reliable method of getting at the truth, then at least the *most* reliable method; and second, that the things science deals with—material entities—are the most fundamental things that exist". The first is a claim about *epistemology*, or the way in which we can know things; and the second a claim about *ontology* or the nature of existence or reality, as explained above. The combined effect of these claims is, as Smith puts it, to "erase transcendence from our reality map". Furthermore, if, like Peter Atkins and Richard Dawkins, one believes this scientific world view to be true, then these episte-mological and ontological claims are not regarded simply as opinions but rather as self-evident facts backed by the immense authority and achievements of science. In other words, *scientism* or *scientific material-ism* is not the same as science or the scientific method, it is an *ideology* or a self-consistent world view whereby consciousness is regarded as a secondary by-product of physical processes and spirituality a com-forting illusion. There is no room for widening this particular scientific perspective on consciousness and spirituality.

Science within consciousness

We therefore need a new view of consciousness and spirituality if we are going to widen the scientific perspective. This will be based on different assumptions about the nature of reality and knowledge. If the view outlined above can be characterised as "consciousness within science", then the new view will explain a "science within consciousness", insisting that spirit, mind, and consciousness are in fact more fundamental categories than our current science assumes.

In the introduction to his book *The Perennial Philosophy*, Aldous Huxley makes the following important observation: "Knowledge is a function of being. When there is a change in the being of the knower, there is a corresponding change in the nature and amount of knowing." This is true of growth and education in general, but applies especially to the relationship between modes of consciousness and modes of spirituality. Philosophers and scientists concentrate on the exercise of reason to phenomena revealed by the senses. In the words of the mediaeval theologian St Bonaventure, they are using the eye of sense along with the eye of reason. However, they are not exercising what he calls "the eye of contemplation", and even tend to deny its existence. These could be called the outer, logical, and inner eyes respectively, corresponding to the physical senses, the reasoning faculty, and the intuition. As Bonaventure elaborates:

- The *eye of the flesh* enables us to perceive the external world of space, time, and objects—(*lumen exterius et inferius*)
- The *eye of reason* enables us to attain knowledge of philosophy, logic, mathematics, and the mind itself—(*lumen interius*)
- The *eye of contemplation* enables us to rise to a knowledge of transcendent realities—(*lumen superius*).

Although scientific creativity makes use of intuition, scientists are not trained in its use and extension in the development of the inner senses. Our current science restricts its scope to the eyes of sense and reason. If a mystic is being tested in the laboratory, the instruments can only record changes in EEG patterns not changes in consciousness. The experiment cannot validate the inner nature of the subjective experience. In this spirit, the Indian philosopher-president Radhakrishnan wrote that "A physicist who rejects the testimony of saints and mystics is no better than a tone-deaf man deriding the power of music."

Science and spiritual experience

The pioneering work of William James and Richard Maurice Bucke at the beginning of the twentieth century has led to the scientific study of spiritual experience and altered states of consciousness. Transpersonal psychology began to emerge with C. G. Jung and Abraham Maslow, and now has a flourishing section within the British Psychological Society. In 1969, the zoologist Sir Alister Hardy founded the Religious Experience Research Unit. His work and that of his colleagues has now resulted in the classification of some 6,000 spiritual experiences. We now know that such experiences are much more common than previously thought, occurring in around two-thirds of the population. Since the early 1980s, near-death experiences have been studied in detail, and have provided a rich seam for those interested in the interface between consciousness and spirituality.

Experiencers report that their consciousness and sense of self is not identified with the body, and some of them enter into deep mystical states that are not necessarily experienced only close to death. Here the NDE and Hardy's work cross-refer in throwing up examples of mystical experience where the sense of a separate self disappears and the subject is immersed in a sea of light, love, peace, and bliss. Such experiences have a profound and lasting effect on experiencers. The sense of the oneness of creation is known directly and first-hand in a way that leaves absolutely no room for doubting its reality. In Indian philosophy this is expressed as the union of *Sat-Chit-Ananda*, or being, consciousness, bliss. The experience transcends both reason and the senses: the inner eye of contemplation is opened and apprehends directly through an experience of *gnosis* (higher intuitive knowledge) the inseparability of love from light or wisdom.

The poet Tennyson expresses it like this: "All at once, as it were out of the intensity of the consciousness of individuality, individuality itself seemed to dissolve and fade away into boundless being, and this was not a confused state but the clearest, the surest of the sure, utterly beyond words." Near-death experiencers speak in similar terms:

- "I went forward toward the light and as I did so I had such a feeling of freedom and joy, it's beyond words to explain. I had a boundless sense of expansion."
- "I came into the arc of pure golden love and light. This radiation of love entered me and instantly I was part of it and it was part of me."
- "It's something that becomes you and you become it. I could say, 'I was peace, I was love.' I was the brightness, it was part of me."
- "'In the middle of one circle was a most beautiful being … an immense, radiant love poured from it. An incredible light shone

through every single pore of its face ... I was consumed with an absolutely inexpressible amount of love ... I was filled with an intense
feeling of joy and awe."

You can imagine that such experiencers will not be overly impressed
to learn from their scientifically trained doctors that these experiences
are mere hallucinations generated by a disorderly brain function. Such
interpretations reflect the preconceptions of scientific materialism outlined above. However, a different response is possible, as researchers
like the neuropsychiatrist Dr Peter Fenwick have shown. They have
already widened their scientific perspectives through personal experience of meditative practices and states, so that the language of the
mystic is no longer foreign to them. They recognise the underlying oneness of consciousness and the limitations of the mechanistic metaphor.
Renée Weber observed a decade ago that "A parallel principle drives
both science and mysticism—the assumption that unity lies at the heart
of our world and that it can be discovered and experienced by man."
The universe is one, it is our perception that fragments it and alienates
us from our intrinsic sense of belonging.

A science of interconnectedness

If mystical and near-death experiences demonstrate the underlying unity
of consciousness, science itself offers new principles of the interconnectedness of life forms. Ecology and biology have built on the systems
view of the world introduced in the 1940s by Ludwig von Bertalanffy.
His key insight is the distinction between open (organic) and closed
(mechanistic) systems where the former interact and exchange with the
environment in a dynamic way. Life forms and habitats (ecosystems)
are both complex open systems. As Fritjof Capra observes, the very
principles of ecology are applied in holistic biology: "interdependence,
recycling, partnership, flexibility, diversity, and, as a consequence, sustainability". The metaphor of the "web of life" says it all, beautifully
expressing both unity and interconnectedness. Other concepts from
biology include *symbiosis*—cooperation between organisms for mutual
benefit—and *synergy*, where individual elements within a system work
together for the good of the whole. Then Jim Lovelock's Gaia hypothesis questions the sharp distinction between organism and environment,

arguing that organisms regulate the composition of the atmosphere for their own benefit—this is mutuality in action.

Atomistic conceptions of isolated particles, genes, or individuals which put an emphasis on separation rather than unity contribute to a sense of isolation in an indifferent cosmos that has led to widespread alienation and loss of meaning. On the other hand, more holistic concepts in science stress participation and belonging as ways of overcoming this sense of alienation. And Arthur Koestler has provided the useful idea of a "holon", which is at once a whole and a part: cells are individual but form elements of organs; organs are in turn individual but forms part of the body, just as the body is part of the earth and the individual a part of society. And the earth is part of the solar system, which is in turn part of the Milky Way galaxy and so on.

Physicist John Archibald Wheeler has asserted that "the universe does not exist 'out there', independently of us. We are inescapably involved in bringing about that which appears to be happening. We are not only observers. We are participators. In some strange sense this is a participatory universe." The inseparability of observer from the observed has been a standard element in quantum theory since the 1930s even if many physicists do not share the view that consciousness actually "collapses the wave function". The physicist and philosopher David Bohm elaborated a new view whereby unity is prior to separation with his ideas of the "implicate" and "explicate" orders (literally enfolded and unfolded orders). For him, reality is "undivided wholeness in flowing movement" (his best-known book is *Wholeness and the Implicate Order*), so wholeness is primary and part-ness or separation is secondary and derived from this. These ideas all stress wholeness, participation, and connectedness (see essay on Bohm and Radhakrishnan above).

The last ten years have also witnessed an explosion of interest in the scientific study of consciousness. Much of this, however, still takes place within the narrow confines of scientific materialism and is based on the premise that consciousness is a product of brain function, even if the so-called "God Spot" has been identified by neuroscientists. Because it seems to contradict its presuppositions, parapsychology is still marginalised by mainstream science, which is still managing to focus the debate on the absurd question of whether psychic experiences ever actually occur at all. Quantum non-locality is acceptable but non-locality of mind is not.

Postulates for a new science of consciousness

If science is to widen its perspective on consciousness and spirituality, then it will need a new set of postulates that transcend and include its current approach. Science will need to recognise its own inherent pre-suppositions and move beyond them. This means a new ontology and a new epistemology along the following lines:

- The universe is an organic multi-levelled interconnected unity with manifest and unmanifest aspects pervaded by life and consciousness
- The evolving and self-organising universe reflects creative intelligence, order, meaning, and purpose
- Knowledge can be acquired not only by means of sense perception but also intuitively—there are different ways and degrees of knowing
- Explanations need not be restricted to the physical realm
- Consciousness in a cosmic sense is both fundamental and formative—it drives evolution from within
- Life is experienced as energy and consciousness
- Consciousness is not invariably tied to physical bodies; hence human consciousness may be non-local and may in some form survive the death of the brain
- The universe is participatory (beyond the duality of subject and object) and the human mind is one of the ways in which it knows itself.

This last point is elaborated by Richard Tarnas in his seminal book *The Passion of the Western Mind*. Scientists are familiar with biological evolution, but less so with the idea of the evolution of consciousness towards more all-embracing, universal, and compassionate expressions. Indeed, most scientific focus is on biological—that is genetic—manipulation or engineering, to use the mechanistic metaphor. Tarnas discusses the relationship between the human mind and the world, commenting that the mind is "ultimately the organ of the world's own process of self-revelation". Our understanding is progressively widened and deepened through our own active engagement. If "the human mind is ... an expression of nature's essential being" then "a developed inner life is indispensable for cognition". In other words, the more consciously we develop our inner life, the deeper we see and the more we know: the eyes of reason and sense cannot take us as far as the eye of contemplation.

Several thinkers have addressed the question of the evolution of both individual and collective consciousness (used here in the sense of identity). These can be summed up in five broad stages:

- Undifferentiated or embedded consciousness (identity merged)
- Individualised consciousness (identity individualised)
- Collective consciousness (identity collectivised)
- Global or planetary consciousness (identity planetised)
- Cosmic consciousness (identity felt as part of cosmic consciousness).

The eighteenth-century Enlightenment saw the rise in the West of individual rights corresponding to the growing sense of individual selfhood. The nineteenth and twentieth centuries developed both the positive and negative aspects of collective consciousness, with socialism, communism, and nationalism. The twentieth century also laid the groundwork for global consciousness with its planetary institutions and communications network, while the task of the twenty-first century is to consolidate a positive sense of planetary consciousness and the emergence of a growing sense of the oneness of both nature and the universal mind or consciousness of which we are all a part. This will then lead to what I call an ethic of interconnectedness based on a knowledge of the underlying unity of consciousness and a felt sense of being a part of the web of life.

Conclusion

The historical development of modern science has relegated consciousness to a secondary role and has tended to erase spirituality from our maps of reality. The dominance of the mechanistic metaphor favours impersonal and functional models of mind and consciousness that alienate people from a sense of belonging to the universe. Science has deliberately restricted its scope to the eyes of sense and reason. However, the intuitive eye of contemplation is beginning to open, revealing larger vistas of reality and showing a way in which the scientific perspective on consciousness and reality can be widened. The core of mystical and near-death experiences enables people to have an immediate sense of certain fundamental principles of spirituality such as love, wisdom, peace, and bliss. Scientists who study these experiences, or better still who have a contemplative spiritual practice of their own, can

come to a wider and deeper understanding of the nature of consciousness and spirituality. Instead of perpetuating a dichotomy between the
objectivity of science and the subjectivity of conscious experience, the
world opens up as a process of creative participation and unfolding
expression.

Acknowledgements

I have benefited from the insights of many authors in formulating these
thoughts, as well as from conversations within the Scientific and Medical Network's special interest group on Science and Esoteric Traditions.

CONSCIOUSNESS, DEATH
AND TRANSFORMATION

The Challenge of Death

Most of us have experienced the numbing shock at the announcement of the unexpected death of a friend or relative. What is its meaning and significance for us? Do we regret the way we treated the person in question? Death comes as an intrusion into the routine of our daily lives, sometimes forcing us to adapt radically; in any event encouraging us to ask some of the deepest questions about life and its purpose. A subject which is normally dismissed as "morbid" pushes to the front of the stage and demands consideration. Written for a discussion group in 1985.

We live in a society where there is a widespread, if largely unacknowledged, fear of death. Science and technology have made gigantic strides towards control of many hitherto fatal infectious diseases, although we are beginning to realise that its prowess in the face of degenerative diseases is not so spectacular. Technology, however, cannot eliminate death, only postpone it and affect its timing, thus rendering more acute the dilemmas of doctors about whether or not to prolong life under artificial conditions. These dilemmas have been further reinforced by a materialist theory of life which tends to cling to physical existence without admitting the possibility of a spiritual dimension beyond it. The patient passively submits to the sophisticated techniques and instruments of modern medicine, isolated from friends and family. For the doctor, death can be an uncomfortable admission of failure, as well as a tacit reminder of his or her own mortality.

The problem of death will not disappear if we ignore it. Sooner or later we must come to terms with our own nature and destiny. What is the nature of man, of death, and what are the implications of the nature of death for the way in which we live our lives? The first two questions amount to asking about the nature of consciousness.

We know that consciousness is intimately associated with the brain, but exactly what is the nature of this association? Broadly speaking there are two possibilities: either consciousness is produced by the brain, therefore perishing with it at physical death, or else it is transmitted through the brain into the material world; in which case it need not be extinguished at bodily death. Materialists who insist that the brain produces consciousness usually cite the effect of brain damage, alcohol, and drugs on our awareness and state of mind. This, they contend, indicates such a close correlation between consciousness and brain that it is inconceivable that physical death should not mark the extinction of the conscious self.

The strongest apparent evidence of this is the dead physical body. But is the self extinguished or just absent? The transmissive theory would not deny any of the materialist's observations but would dispute this interpretation and conclusions. If the instrument is damaged, manifestation of consciousness will be distorted or incomplete. It might appear that the programme was being produced by the radio, an impression arguably strengthened by dropping it on the floor or into water—the sound is blurred, crackly, or perhaps even fades out altogether.

The programme is still there, but the damaged receiver/transmitter can no longer reproduce if faithfully; and the destruction of the instrument does not annihilate the radio waves, it just makes their manifestation in the physical world impossible. On the basis of normal experience, therefore, it would seem impossible to decide which of these two stories is correct—both fit the evidence. It is here that some aspects of psychic experience may throw some light on the problem.

Although in my book *Survival* (new edition 2017) I have dealt with apparitions and out-of-the-body experience separately, I shall confine myself here to a brief consideration of the near-death experience in so far as it relates to the nature of perception in this world. At a point of great physical distress, the patient might feel their conscious self rising out of the physical body and be able to perceive it and the surrounding area as if from a point near the ceiling. They will be able to observe the attempts of the medical staff to resuscitate the physical body, will feel no pain, but rather a sense of calm and detachment from the resuscitation work. They may even hear themselves pronounced dead.

At length people find themselves once more back in the physical body with its cramping pain. They are then able to describe accurately to the nurses and doctors the procedures involved in the resuscitation as well as conversations and actions which took place while they were ostensibly unconscious, even dead. The doctors and nurses frequently confirm the accuracy of such observations and are astounded—to them it looked as if the patient was absolutely unconscious, and yet they are able to recount the exact sequence of events which took place during resuscitation (see *The Self Does Not Die* by Rivas, Dirvan, and Smit). It is impossible here to convey the details of such experiences or the plausibility of various alternative explanations advanced.

My own conclusion is that the patient really did perceive the events described and that therefore the bodily senses are not essential for perception—while the conscious self is. Just because we normally perceive by means of the physical body does not mean that we cannot perceive independently of it. Moreover, those who have had out-of-the-body or near-death experiences testify that they felt a greater sense of reality than in the physical body, and were free from the constraints of space-time. This line of reasoning is also suggested by post-mortem communications describing physical death; the parallels with the near-death experience are striking, to say the least. In the light of such evidence, the theory that consciousness is produced by the brain can no longer be sustained—it must give way to the transmissive hypothesis.

Those who undergo a near-death experience no longer fear death (the attitude among those resuscitated without any memory of conscious experience remains unchanged). They also realise the absurdity and futility of exclusive preoccupation with the temporal values of money, status, fame, and power; they become less concerned with past and future, more focused on appreciation of and attention to the present; and they become interested in spiritual knowledge and relating lovingly to those whom they encounter: the pursuit of wisdom and the practice of love, values which can help us live in the light of the eternal recognised in the present moment. Such is the challenge of death.

Religious and Scientific Implications of the Near-death and Related Experiences

*T*his article appeared in an edition of the Scientific and Medical Network
    newsletter in 1985, partly as a response to an article by Prof John
    Milsum, as can be gathered from the content. I had become involved
with setting up the UK branch of the International Association for Near
Death Studies with psychologist Margot Grey as chair and neuropsychiatrist
Dr Peter Fenwick as president. Margot's book Return from Death *came out*
in 1985 and we began to collect our own case histories by doing radio inter-
views and the occasional TV feature. After an interview with Selina Scott, we
received 200 letters—not emails in those days—which began to build our own
database and enable us to contact experiencers, many of whom became mem-
bers of IANDS (UK). In 1988, we invited cardiologist Dr Pim van Lommel to
give our annual lecture at the Oxfordshire home of John and Janet Tomlinson.
His seminal Lancet *article was not published until 2001, and his bestselling*
book a number of years later. The NDE has opened up conversations about the
meaning of death, and hence implicitly about the meaning of life. My 1990 book
Whole in One *explores the ethical implications of the NDE.*

> *I knew the mass of men conceal'd*
> *Their thoughts, for fear that if reveal'd*
> *They would by other men be met*

With blank indifference, or with blame reprov'd;
I knew they liv'd and mov'd
Trick'd in disguises, alien to the rest
Of men, and alien to themselves—and yet
There beats one heart in every human breast.

(Matthew Arnold, from The Buried Life)

At the outset of his article Professor Milsum comments that our beliefs about our role in the "overall cosmic space-time unfolding" must necessarily affect the way in which we choose to behave on this earth. In other words, there must be a close relationship between a person's metaphysics and their ethics, between their philosophy of life and their conduct and attitudes. My first reaction to this was to wonder in how many people this was *explicitly* the case: in other words, how many actually sit down and consider the questions of life, its meaning and destination in any detail? Here the extract from Matthew Arnold was a timely reminder not to be over-presumptious about what "most people" think, especially if judging by superficial social criteria; we do not share our deepest thoughts lightly. Indeed, those thoughts may only surface in the wake of testing and critical experiences in life. At such times our conventional defences crumble, our philosophy of life is shown up in sharp relief, its adequacy undergoes a stringent test. Elisabeth Kübler-Ross's patients are often faced with the prospect of a sudden and drastic curtailment of their life-expectancy: a cancer is diagnosed and the patient has six weeks to live. What genuine inner resources has the person in question accumulated over their lifetime? Will they enable a positive response to the challenge of impending physical demise? Or does the crisis provoke the shattering realisation that the individual has no philosophy of life adequate either to their present imminent physical death, or, on reflection, to the context of life as a whole? Consideration of such possibilities applied to oneself makes it clear that an adequate philosophy of life is, despite everyday preoccupations of an apparently more pressing nature, an urgent priority which one can ill afford to neglect.

Facing impermanence

In this connection one can glean some useful signposts from the implications of the near-death experience review, to which Professor

Milsum refers in his article: the impulse to love more, sometimes resulting from a mystical insight into the oneness of being and humanity;
and the urge to increase one's knowledge of the natural and spiritual
world—the pursuit of wisdom. It is interesting to note that these two
themes are regarded by Swedenborg as the complementary attributes
of the Divine—Love and Wisdom, relating to the will or heart of man
on the one hand, and to the reason and understanding on the other.
The seminal point emerging from this particular experience is that the
individual almost invariably reorients his values away from exclusive
focus on material concerns towards a spiritual perspective. Perhaps the
most succinct account of this reorientation can be found in *The Human
Encounter with Death* by Stanislav Grof and Joan Halifax, who have done
a great deal of psychedelic therapy with terminal patients:

> Psychological acceptance of impermanence and death results in a
> realization of the absurdity and futility of exaggerated ambitions,
> attachment to money, status, fame, and power, or pursuit of other
> temporal values. This makes it easier to face the termination of
> one's professional career and the impending loss of all worldly
> possessions. Time orientation is typically transformed; the past
> and future become less important as compared with the present
> moment. Psychological emphasis tends to shift from trajectories
> of large time periods to living "one day at a time". This is associ-
> ated with an increased ability to enjoy life and to derive pleasure
> from simple things. There is usually a distinct increase of interest in
> religious matters, involving spirituality of a universal nature rather
> than beliefs related to any specific church affiliation. On the other
> hand, there were many instances where [a] dying individual's tra-
> ditional beliefs were deepened and illumined with new dimension
> of meaning.

Psychologically and in terms of values there is a process of death and
rebirth. Planning for the material future is put into perspective and
may even now be felt to be under providential guidance; it need not
be a source of crippling anxiety. The individual realises that it is mis-
guided to cling to a transient earthly identity and its equally ephemeral environment and possessions. Such factors now assume a relative
rather than an absolute significance. One can no longer afford to invest
one's entire sense of identity in professional status or function; there is

a deeper layer to be uncovered. The shift in time orientation brings the individual into line with what Maslow terms self-actualising people, models of psychological health. One of their characteristics is "continued freshness of appreciation", which reflects the "increased ability to enjoy life and to derive pleasure from simple things", an ability which, by definition, involves living fully in the present. The last point in the extract, referring to spirituality also deserves comment. The experience leads to a deepening of spiritual awareness, whether from inside or outside a church affiliation. If from inside the person will probably be drawn towards the mystical and contemplative stream of their tradition with its emphasis on shift of being and consciousness on the intuitive/ intellectual side and on the compassion and tolerance associated with unitive insight.

What assumes importance is not the exclusive and divisive exoteric dogma, but rather the experiential core of the religion which points to underlying affinities with other belief systems. For humanists, the challenge is of a different order: they have now gained a personal insight into one of the universal human experiences. This may lead them to seek parallels in the experience of other people and to strive to reach an understanding of any patterns which they may discern. In both cases, it seems, the quest is for an underlying unity, for depth, for universality.

The psychic and the spiritual

The Christian contention that the paranormal is irrelevant to bringing about the Kingdom of God ignores the overlap between the psychic and the spiritual. It is certainly a more constructive position than dismissing the entire field as an invention of the devil, a stance which can only disintegrate in the wake of a close study of the material available through automatic writing. The real spiritual danger of psychic powers or "*siddhis*" is not only that they divert the individual from the essential goal of the spiritual quest, but also that they actually work against it: instead of the ego being transcended, it is inflated: humility is engulfed by pride.

The important positive contribution of the paranormal towards religion, however, is that it weakens the position of reductionist materialism, the thesis that we are nothing but physical organisms whose consciousness will be extinguished at death. Many of those with psychic ability have also had mystical experiences, so that they go beyond even the dualist model of body and spirit to the insight that the goal of human endeavour is union with the Divine, with Ultimate Reality; here they confirm and reiterate the teachings of the great mystics of the Christian and other traditions. Far from being a historical curiosity, these experiences are catalysing spiritual transformation in the present. Because they were autonomous and claimed authority for their own insights, there has historically been some tension between mystics and the Church; Eckhart came under the eagle eye of the Inquisition, although it is recognised today that he is one of the most profound and penetrating Christian thinkers.

As Professor Milsum indicates, it would be a pity for the churches not to take a lead in this field. Contemporary experiences have plentiful historical parallels which can be used as a context and framework of understanding, as well as an indication of the continuing and consistent activity of the Holy Spirit across the ages. Religion can then move away from rigid adherence to articles on faith, which have to be accepted unquestioningly on an intellectual level, towards a spiritual philosophy of life and conduct based on the insights of those with direct experience of the Divine—which is the case with all founders of the great religions. Tradition will assume a new role in discerning the value of new formulations in relation to the old. Such a revised mystical basis would be less susceptible to the possessions of dogmatic fanaticism, which elevates principles above humanity: the starting point would not be unswerving assent to an unprovable proposition, but rather that the Ultimate Reality as Love is best expressed in mutual compassion and understanding.

Evidence and proof

The question of proof and the paranormal is a vexed one. The near-death experience is clearly not amenable to repetitions in the laboratory. I have discussed the issue in detail in my book *Survival?*, but a few observations are in order here. Since it is impossible to adopt a strictly scientific experimental approach to the NDE, one must instead tackle the problem on a legal-historical basis. Evidence is marshalled, and explanatory hypotheses are advanced to account for it. The hypothesis which one provisionally accepts should be that which is most adequate to the data in question. The matter is further complicated by attitudes towards evidence of the paranormal. There are those who regard such occurrences as *a priori* impossible, so that ostensible evidence of the paranormal, or, in this case, any paranormal explanation of the NDE is inadmissible. They argue that no individual case is perfect and conclusive, so an aggregation of these cases is best represented by the image of a leaky bucket.

By contrast, I take the view that the convergence of features gleaned from diverse and independent sources strengthens the case for these being interpreted on the basis of a transcendent model of consciousness and the brain. Instead of the leaky bucket, the image proposed by the logician Archbishop Whately is a bunch of faggots where each case represents a stick which when added to the next makes a cumulatively stronger case as a faggot.

We do, however, have a further pointer in the interpretation of NDEs as realistic prototypes of part of the experience of physical death. In my book I have analysed the features of post-mortem descriptions of bodily death received through mediums and found that these seem to be a logical extension of what is described by NDE experiencers. Once again, this does not constitute scientific proof, but, in my view, the hypothesis of the survival of consciousness is certainly the most adequate in the light of the data.

Karma and reincarnation

The doctrine of reincarnation has a long if controversial ancestry in Western thought. In the last hundred years the Theosophical Society has done a great deal to revive interest in the possibility. Dissatisfaction with the traditional linear view of one life leading to heaven or hell, in the light of inexplicable inequalities of station and opportunity, has further enhanced our curiosity. Some distinguished but underrated or forgotten philosophers such as John McTaggart and F. C. S. Schiller professed belief in reincarnation. A study of Orphic, Pythagorean, Platonic, and neo-Platonic philosophy is a rich source of inspiration. There is also a fascinating anthology by Joseph Head and S. L. Cranston.

Some of the most illuminating remarks on karma, freedom, and rebirth were made by the Indian philosopher Sir Sarvepalli Radhakrishnan, who was the first professor of Eastern religions and ethics at Oxford; he subsequently became vice-president then president of India. Radhakrishnan begins by pointing out that the word karma means action, deed: "All acts produce their effects which are recorded both in the organism and the environment. Their physical effects may be short-lived but their moral effects are worked into the character of the self. Every single thought, word and deed enters into the living chain of causes which make us what we are." He explains that karma is less of a principle of retribution than of continuity: "Man is continually shaping his own self."

Since all things in the world are both causes and effects, it follows that karma is better characterised as a limiting condition of existence rather than destiny as such; it is like a hand of cards which can be played well or badly; it has both a retrospective and a prospective aspect. It naturally entails a moral responsibility which cannot be glibly passed on to the determining impositions of environment, a factor less important than the exercise of the human will. Life as constant self-creation signifies constant and vigilant moral sensitivity.

For the individual, karma is a kind of psychological or spiritual heredity, underlying both social and physical heredity. It operates in rebirth by a kind of adaptive affinity whereby the soul chooses earthly circumstances which, from a spiritual perspective, offer opportunities for evolution and development. A similar process is depicted in Plato's "Myth of Er". I have omitted here any discussion of Radhakrishnan's replies to various objections to reincarnation. For him the aim of individual human consciousness is union with the Absolute, in which the soul realises its true nature in a state of liberation from the limiting conditions of individual human existence. Such liberation, relating as it does to the frame of mind, does not depend on embodiment or non-embodiment. The liberated soul is free from "the egoistic self and its tyrannous desires" and also convinced of the unity with all, so that it has love for others. This means that it works for universal liberation, for "that cosmic harmony which is the destiny of the historical process; they are in cooperative union with God, their task remaining uncompleted while the goal is unattained". On present reckoning, this must be an extremely distant prospect.

In closing, I would like to echo Professor Milsum's Wordsworth with some Browning. In it the reader will discern the title of an important book on physics, psychical research, and mysticism by Raynor Johnson:

> *Truth is within ourselves; it takes no rise*
> *From outward things, whate'er you may believe.*
> *There is an inmost centre in us all,*

Where truth abides in fullness; and around,
Wall upon wall, the gross flesh hems it in,
This perfect, clear perception—which is truth.
A baffling and perverting carnal mesh
Binds it, and makes all error: and, to KNOW,
Rather consists in opening out a way
Whence the imprisoned splendour may escape,
Than in effecting entry for a light
Supposed to be without.

Aspects of the Near-death Experience in the Light of the Tibetan Book of the Dead and the Experiences of Swedenborg

*T*he material for this 1985 article also constituted part of my research for
my first book Survival, published in 1984. I was struck by the parallels
between the processes described in The Tibetan Book of the Dead and
the personal experiences around death recorded by Swedenborg expressed in
a very different language. In both cases, there is a process of seeking a level of
consciousness corresponding to essence or what Swedenborg would call the
ruling love—I don't use the word soul as the self in our sense is not recognised in Buddhist thought. Later, in the 1990s, Sogyal Rinpoche and Andrew
Harvey published their magisterial The Tibetan Book of Living and Dying,
and I remember attending the launch in Kensington where Sogyal stood up on
a table and semi-mockingly thanked us for taking time out of our busy lives
to be there. The reality of death brings a radical reordering of values and priorities on which it is advisable to reflect before being overtaken by events. As
I read recently in a Japanese garden on Maine Island in British Columbia,
"I intended never to grow old, but the temple bell sounded."

Background

The *Bardo Thodol* (Tibetan Book of the Dead) literally means "liberation
by hearing on the after-death plane", and was read to the dying person

as a guide to the states which he or she was undergoing. It was written down in the eighth century AD, although the oral tradition reaches back well beyond that era. Lamas were thought to have had the ability to pass through the various stages of the experience and then transcribe their impressions. The book describes the death of the physical body and the stages intervening prior to subsequent rebirth or, ideally, liberation from the cycle; reincarnation was axiomatic. The relevant terms employed are "consciousness-principle" for the ego (in which the Buddhists do not believe); the psychic nervous system, corresponding to the physical counterpart; the Bardo body which is etheric and resembles the physical body, also known as the propensity or desire body. Just as birth is the incarnating of the consciousness-principle, so death is regarded as its discarnating.

Swedenborg (1688–1772) was one of the universal geniuses of his day—scientist, mathematician, engineer, politician, and, after 1743, seer and mystical philosopher. A number of striking instances of his ESP powers are extant; he also predicted the date of his own death and paid his London landlady until the end of the appropriate month. The empiricism exhibited in Swedenborg's scientific works is carried over into his theological books. He claimed to have conversed with discarnate spirits ("proved to me by the daily experience of many years"), and to have died himself in order to be able to give an account of the experience to others. Swedenborg was a dualist: on the one hand he was the internal man, soul or spirit—the source of rational life and sense experience; acting, on the other hand, through a physical body which cannot *of itself* sense or think. The philosophical climate of Swedenborg's day was one of growing scepticism. Under the pervasive influence of Descartes the soul, an immaterial and unextended substance, was conceived as an aerial, fiery, thinking entity and general vital force. Some sceptics thought that such a notion was unintelligible. Swedenborg comments on the contemporary "complete ignorance of the nature of the soul, especially in the learned world"; they did not realise that the soul was "the man himself". According to Swedenborg "separation or death occurs when, from some sickness or accident, the body comes into such a condition that it is unable to act in unison with its spirit … yet the man does not die; he is merely separated from the corporeal part of that which was of use to him in the world."

The near-death experience has been characterised as a report of conscious experience continuing when the physical body is ostensibly unconscious or even clinically dead. The terms of the modern debate about the nature of humans are the physical body or brain on the one hand, and the mind or conscious self on the other. Broadly speaking there are two possible explanations of the nature of consciousness: either it is produced by the brain, in which case it perishes at physical death, or else it is transmitted through the brain, thus leaving open the option of its survival of bodily death. The philosophical climate of our own day has been influenced by a number of complex and interrelated factors, which it is impossible to analyse in detail here. The impact of Marx, Darwin, and Freud has been immense and has contributed to the decay of formal religious belief and the rise of a materialist view of life and society. Science has edged out traditional religious formulations, and many scientists find themselves espousing a view where only physical cause and effect are valid. Although among philosophers the most popular position is the identity theory (that mental processes are brain processes which cannot conceivably continue after the death of the body), there are signs that various disciplines are moving beyond this: the holistic revolution in medicine, David Bohm's unifying implicate order in physics, and Rupert Sheldrake's morphic resonance in biology. Death may look less like extinction and more like the release of the conscious self from the confines of space-time.

The near-death experience

We have already characterised the experience as consciousness continuing while the physical body is apparently unconscious or even dead. This hints at what may be a fundamental distinction between what death looks like from the outside and how it is viewed from the inside. Michael Sabom analyses the experience in two stages: the autoscopic kind, where the immediate environment (and perhaps the physical body) is viewed from a vantage point outside the physical body; and the deeper transcendental experience, in which the subject is conscious in non-physical surroundings. These are generally, but not invariably, of a heavenly nature. In any event the experience belies the apparent unconsciousness of the physical body. Although records go back to the end of the nineteenth century, widespread public interest has only been generated since the publication in 1975 of Raymond Moody's *Life after Life*.

More recent scientific studies were carried out by Kenneth Ring (*Life at Death*, 1980), and Michael Sabom (*Recollections of Death*, 1982).

The first British study will be published next year [*Return from Death*, 1985] by Margot Grey. In the USA there is an International Association of Near-Death Studies (IANDS), which publishes a newsletter and journal entitled *Anabiosis* (now *The Journal of Near-Death Studies*). As is the case with Swedenborg and *Bardo Thodol*, the basis of these reports is human testimony and experience, which must naturally be carefully sifted. In the transcendental cases, as in dreams, we have nothing to go beyond the word and trustworthiness of the experiencer. In some autoscopic cases, however, it is possible to verify at a later stage details of what the subject claimed to have seen or heard while unconscious. Sabom has six very impressive cases which he correlates with the appropriate medical records.

As for the incidence of the experience among those who come close to death, the latest figures suggest that it is about 40% (later studies suggest a lower figure, nearer 15–20%). What happens, then to the other 60%? My own conjecture follows analysis of our known sleep patterns: the distinction between REM or dream sleep and deep dreamless sleep. It may well be that subjects pass into a state corresponding with deep sleep, thus there is nothing to report; or else they may have an experience which is followed by deep sleep. We do not remember dreams which we had at 2am unless we wake up at the time. All this is not to assert that the experience itself is dreamlike; the subjects insist that it is much more vivid, and, moreover, that it can be distinguished from hallucinations.

Autoscopic NDEs

These seem to me to be special cases of the out-of-the-body experience, if one interprets the term literally. It is hard to envisage a materialist explanation for the type of veridical case outlined by Sabom (see Rivas, Dirvan, and Smit in the bibliography). The subject experiences feelings of detachment, peace, calm, and bliss—there is no longer any pain, but a sense of release in every sense. As we have just mentioned, the experience is characterised by a sense of reality which transcends the dream state. Mental processes are said to be very clear, the senses distinct, and the mind extremely alert. Space-time collapses; it is "no longer a meaningful construct". Jung asserted that for him this world (during a near-death period of 1944, recounted in *Memories, Dreams, Reflections*) was "utterly real, absolutely objective" and spoke of "the ecstasy of a non-temporal state in which past, present and future were one".

Swedenborg talks of the exquisite nature of the senses—especially those of sight and hearing—in the non-physical state. Our present senses, he maintains, are gross and obtuse, adapted to this natural world. Then, according to his scheme, it is the spirit which possesses the power of sensation: this manifests itself in the physical body by means of what he calls influx. As for space-time, he asserts that our thoughts are normally confined by this category and by causality. Thought is clearer and more perfect in the spiritual state. The origin of space and time is explained as stemming from the idea of motion in an internal sense, which corresponds to a change in the state of mind. In an entirely mental world, then, a change in the state of mind would be represented as a change of location. Eternity is regarded as an infinite and change-less state. Any change of place/state is caused by desire, so that to think of someone or something is immediately to find oneself in their or its presence. Similarly, by the law of affinity in which like attracts like, a similar state will correspond with a similar place. Swedenborg comments, on the basis of his experience, that "These things seem incredible, but yet they are true."

In a passage in the *Bardo Thodol*, the consciousness-principle finds itself out of the body and is bewildered by the experience: "Am I dead or not?" It cannot determine. "It seeth its relatives and connexions as it had been used to seeing them before. It even heareth the wailings." And yet it is unable to communicate. Swedenborg also refers to the confusion of recently deceased people, especially if they had no conception of a continued existence. The paradox of being dead and yet feeling alive is resolved by some only be by assuming that they have not died physically at all.

Trancendental NDEs

One of the most significant aspects of the experience is the so-called review or judgment. Subjects see an unfolding panorama of their life experiences, and pass judgment on themselves. It seems as if a "higher" self is judging the empirical personality. There are some illuminating cases of this in Kenneth Ring's book *Heading toward Omega—in Search of the Meaning of the Near-Death Experience*. One subject experienced every emotion which he had felt in his life, the basis of how the emotion had affected his life—"what my life had done so far to affect other people's lives using the feeling of pure love that was surrounding me as the point of comparison". The subject was devastated by such an assessment when unconditional love becomes the central criterion for assessing the quality of our life and contribution to the happiness of others. Another way of expressing the same point is found in Crookall's post-mortem analyses: "All the pain he had given to people he experienced himself, and all the pleasure he had given he received back again ... He becomes aware of all the emotions aroused by his acts ... and is purified through his identification with the sufferings." It is a self-revelation of all the motives behind our actions. An awesome prospect for most of us. The profound implication is that we are one another, that love is in an expression of the unity towards which we are all striving, and that we should be continually refining our sense of compassionate understanding.

The review experience calls into question the nature of memory and seems to support the contention that memories are not exclusively stored in the brain; that the brain is a filter which actually prevents us from remembering everything all the time, as Bergson suggests. That memories are not lost is suggested by the mechanism of hypnosis, where conscious interference is removed and certain memories are able to be retrieved. Swedenborg explains that all states can be recalled after death, that we take everything with us except the physical body. Details are drawn forth from the memory and reviewed—in the light of heaven they appear as an image as if read in a book: "Every least thing that a man has willed, thought, spoken, done or even heard or seen is inscribed on his internal or spiritual memory." It is never erased, and moreover "The spirit is formed in accordance with the thoughts and acts of its will." The persona or mask is no longer sustainable, the man stands nakedly revealed in his innermost will and thoughts. As Jung put it: "I was what I had been and lived." In the *Bardo Thodol* there is a symbolic counting and weighing of black and white pebbles. If the person attempts to lie, the Lord of Death consults "the mirror of karma" (the memory); lies are of no avail, the judgment is undertaken by the conscience which assesses the images projected by memories of the existence which has just terminated.

A good many subjects experience a bright light, a thousand times the luminosity of the sun, but which yet does not hurt the eyes. It corresponds to impressions of surpassing peace and beauty and tends to dissolve the subject/object distinction, thus making it almost impossible for the experiencers to describe adequately. Swedenborg states that the light of heaven "exceeds by many degrees the noonday light of the world … the brightness and splendour are such as cannot be described … the things that I have seen in the heavens have been seen in that light, thus more clearly and distinctly than things in the world." Ineffability is characteristic of such experiences or states of consciousness.

Such light is also referred to in connection with the experience of death. According to Swedenborg, he found himself in a state of insensibility in which his thoughts and mental life remained unimpaired. He then became aware of the presence of celestial angels corresponding in a sense with warmth of heart. If the spirit is unable to associate with such beings, through lack of affinity, they withdraw and are replaced by spiritual angels of light. These withdraw in turn if there is no harmonious correlation, and are replaced by good spirits: "The experience is repeated until he comes into association with such as are in entire harmony with his life in the world," in accordance with the general or ruling affection which a man had (or rather was) in the world. The hierarchy of being descends from ineffable light towards impenetrable darkness.

In the *Bardo Thodol* it is thought that supreme union and enlightenment may take place at death, but only if the aspirant is able, by means of his spiritual qualities, to recognise and merge into Fundamental Clear Light of Reality. This is usually prevented by various forms of ignorance, fear, and desire; liberation is not attained. Various other lights are encountered, which the consciousness-principle is enjoined not to fear, but from which the aspirant usually shrinks—back into the confines of what Westerners would term the ego. Fear and terror may arise from within and be projected out as images. The consciousness-principle is encouraged not to follow the earthly lights, but to abandon its egoism and surrender to the spiritual light. If this proves impossible, the consciousness-principle gravitates back to embodiment and chooses an incarnation in accordance with "the habits of the former life". In Plato, this is expressed by saying that those seeking rebirth "assume a character appropriate to their choice". The past conditions the future, and the cycle is perpetuated.

In his book *Easy Death*, Da Free John (later Adi Da) elaborates the scheme of the *Bardo Thodol*. He explains that the core of lights is "The Brilliant White Clear Light", and that there are other lights that correspond to different worlds and to those reported by many experiencers. The key to enlightenment is recognition of the Light, which can only occur beyond self-limiting identification with the body-mind. Failure to participate in a larger field of consciousness, to surrender our limitations, results in the limited self returning into incarnation. If one accepts Da Free John's analysis, then we are all to some extent imprisoned within self-imposed limitations; this is precisely what the mystics urge us to transcend.

The near-death experiencers arrive now at some boundary beyond which they know they cannot go if they wish to return to earth. They find themselves deciding to return, principally because of the pull of loved ones or unfinished business—they want to return in order to live their lives differently. The immediate reaction on finding themselves once more in the physical body ranges from disappointment to anger and resentment. The freedom and bliss are abandoned for a box-like and relatively unreal world. The after-effects of the experience are treated in detail in Kenneth Ring's *Heading toward Omega*; we only have space for the barest outline here. There is a universal decline in the fear of death, accompanied by the conviction that a life after death is a reality. There is an increased desire to live in the present, to appreciate beauty and nature; a concern for and an acceptance of others as they are, together with an emphasis on the values of love, compassion, and giving; a search for wisdom and spiritual understanding; and finally a decreased concern for material wealth and status. One of Ring's interviewees summed up his new set of values: "The most important thing we have is our relationships with other people … It all comes down to caring and compassion and love for your fellow man … *Love is the answer*. It's the answer to everything."

In concluding, we need to stretch our sense of identity beyond conventional boundaries. As Ramana Maharshi says: "The body dies but the Spirit that transcends it cannot be touched by death." He defines the Self as "that out of which the sense of the personal arises and into which it will have to disappear". Absorption in this Self (higher self/oversoul/Overself) banishes the fear of death, which represents the ego contracting away from Transcendent Reality. Paradoxically, it is only with the breakdown of the phenomenal ego that there arises the possibility of enlightenment—in the ego's dissolution and surrender lies its ultimate fulfilment, representing perfect love, perfect sacrifice, and perfect freedom. If we regard the transcendental near-death experience as a kind of initiation and spiritual pointer, it can open up a vision of the meaning of life and the task of the individual: an essentially spiritual process in which our sense of identity is expanded and expressed in growing sensitivity and empathic understanding.

Swedenborg and Survival

Presidential address, Swedenborg Society, May 2001

The relationship between Immanuel Kant (1720–1804) and Emanuel Swedenborg (1688–1772) can still be regarded as an archetype of how philosophy and reason relate to mysticism and experience. Kant is celebrated as a pivotal figure in the Enlightenment, while Swedenborg's philosophy is marginal in its influence. Kant was one of the very few people to order a copy of Swedenborg's Arcana Celestia *explaining the spiritual significance of biblical passages, and sent his own investigator to verify the stories circulating about Swedenborg's extrasensory capacities. He was in fact satisfied with the veracity of the reports, but as my initial quote spells out, he was unable to accept the implications for fear of ridicule and instead chose to publish a scurrilous and indeed libellous book entitled* Dreams of a Spirit Seer *in 1766. Very few modern philosophers—with some notable exceptions like C. D. Broad and H. H. Price who held chairs of philosophy at Cambridge and Oxford respectively—seriously consider the implications of psychic and spiritual experiences, preferring instead to remain safely within materialist orthodoxy for fear of being considered unsound. This brings to mind the quotation from Bernard Shaw, where he said that "Reasonable men adapt themselves to the world, while unreasonable men try to adapt*

the world to themselves. Therefore all progress depends on unreasonable men."
Unreasonable maybe, but irrational certainly not.

> *Philosophy, which on account of its self-conceit exposes itself to all sorts of*
> *empty questions, finds itself often in an awkward embarrassment in view*
> *of certain stories, parts of which it cannot* doubt *without suffering for it,*
> *nor believe without being laughed at.*
>
> —Kant

> *No choice is uninfluenced by the way in which the personality regards its*
> *destiny, and the body its death. In the last analysis, it is our conception of*
> *death which decides our answers to all the questions that life puts to us.*
> *That is why it requires its proper place and time—if need be with right of*
> *precedence. Hence, too, the necessity of preparing for it.*
>
> —Hammarskjöld

These two quotations are an apposite starting point for Swedenborg's views on survival and their relevance to our time. Some of you will know of Kant's parody of Swedenborg, *Dreams of a Spirit Seer*, but his quotation here indicates that he was in a quandary when confronted with well attested accounts of Swedenborg's telepathic capacities. Kant thought that the interaction of the soul and body was beyond our (sensory) knowing but argued for the existence of immortality on moral grounds. He elaborates that the philosopher (i.e., himself) is caught between the "affirmations of a reasonable and firmly convinced eyewitness and the inner resistance of insurmountable doubt"—which is partly fear of being credulously duped and ridiculed. Kant relates three well-known stories, including the Marteville receipt and the Stockholm fire (see below) as examples of what he is talking about.

Resistance

The so-called "inner resistance of insurmountable doubt" is nothing other than the investment in a philosophical view that denies the possibility of phenomena that are not amenable to a materialistic explanation, as was becoming the fashion even in Swedenborg's day, as exemplified in Hume's *Essay on Miracles*.

What Swedenborg calls the hypothesis of "physical influx" or physicalism "arises from the appearance of the senses, and the fallacies thence derived". The problem with this hypothesis for Swedenborg is that it is based on a threefold ignorance: "ignorance as to what the soul is, ignorance as to what is spiritual, and ignorance respecting the nature of influx—these three things must first be explained before the rational faculty can see the truth itself". And he adds, knowingly: "For hypothetical truth is not truth itself but a conjecture of the truth."

He sees a danger that ignorance of the existence of a spiritual world could make a person "so far infatuated as to become an atheistic materialist", remarking that his mission was precisely to enlighten people about the nature of spiritual worlds in a manner acceptable to the critical intellect. Those who know nothing of these worlds, he says, are liable to fall into blindness, "because the mind, depending solely on the sight of the eye, becomes in its reasonings like a bat, which flies by night in a wandering course"; into darkness because the sight of the eye is deprived of all spiritual light; and into stupidity, "because the man still thinks, but from natural things concerning spiritual, and not contrariwise".

Here one is reminded of the three eyes of St Bonaventure (1217–1274): the eye of sense, the eye of reason, and the eye of contemplation. Contemporary science and philosophy are generally restricted to the first two eyes, denying the validity of the third or inner intuitive eye which in Swedenborg was so remarkably developed. Kant also confines himself to reason and sense. Yet a complete account of reality, and more especially consciousness, cannot afford to ignore the testimony of mystics and sages. In the early Church, Clement of Alexandria wrote of the roles of faith (*pistis*) and contemplative knowledge (*gnosis*) that "Faith is a compendious knowledge of the essentials, but *gnosis* is a sure and firm demonstration of the things received through faith ... carrying us on to unshaken conviction and scientific certainty." He goes on to explain that the second kind of saving change, after that from heathenism to faith, is from faith to gnosis: "And this latter, as it passes on into love, begins at once to establish a mutual friendship between that which knows and that which is known." Here he refers to consciousness knowing its own nature, source and goal, which is not ultimately separate from itself. Or, as the Hindus would put it, the self becomes aware of its identity with and within the larger Self.

Swedenborg's psychic perception

A number of incidents are recorded which indicate that Swedenborg possessed what would now be regarded as psychic capacities: some involve clairvoyance, one is a case of precognition, and three others were explained by Swedenborg himself by his ability to converse with spirits; modern researchers, depending on their presuppositions, might advance alternative explanations. The first clairvoyant incident took place in July 1759, when Swedenborg was one of fifteen guests at the house of Gothenburg merchant, William Castel. At six in the evening Swedenborg suddenly became alarmed and explained that there was a fire burning in Stockholm, 300 miles away. He described where it was burning, where and when it had started, but was relieved when he informed the company that its progress had been halted not far from his own house. Swedenborg related the details to the governor on the following day, and only two days after the fire did messengers arrive with reports that corresponded in every detail with Swedenborg's description. The fame of this incident spread far enough to arouse the curiosity of Kant, who sent his own investigator to check up on the facts; this is one of the incidents referred to above.

There was a similar occurrence in Gothenburg around 1770 at a dinner held in Swedenborg's honour. A manufacturer called Bollander was also present; he owned extensive cloth mills, and suddenly found himself being abruptly addressed by Swedenborg who told him, apparently without any explanation, that he had better go to his mills. The manufacturer left immediately, and on arriving at his mills he discovered that a large piece of cloth had fallen down near the furnace and had started to burn. Any delay would have resulted in the complete razing of his property. On returning to the dinner he thanked Swedenborg and explained what had happened.

Swedenborg replied that he had seen the danger and that there was no time to be lost—hence the abrupt tone. On another occasion he was attending a dinner (another public function) in Amsterdam just after the Russian Emperor Peter III had fallen from power and had been replaced by his wife Catherine. Swedenborg suddenly became unaware of his surroundings, and his expression changed radically; on recovering he was asked what had happened and at first refused to say anything; but he was then prevailed upon and described the gruesome death of Peter III, urging his fellow guests to note the date and his account. A few days later the newspapers featured the story, which corresponded to Swedenborg's description. Modern equivalents to this kind of story can be found in accounts from Kyriakos Markides's books on the Magus of Strovolos—the late Stylianos Atteshlis—as well as in the life of the Bulgarian sage Peter Deunov. They suggest that highly developed people have a more sensitive and universal consciousness field that is more aligned to the Divine and can therefore pick up incidents that are removed from the present in space and time.

The next incident could either be classified as a case of precognition or, as Swedenborg himself would probably have said, an example of correct information conveyed to him by the world of spirits. One evening in company he was put to the test: he was asked to state which of the assembled company would die first. After a few moments of silence, he said that the first to die would be Olof Olofsohn—at 4.45 the next morning. One of Olofsohn's friends resolved to go to his house the next morning to see if the prediction was fulfilled. On the way he met one of Olofsohn's servants who informed him that his master had just died, and that the clock in the apartment had apparently stopped at the moment of death, at 4.45.

In 1770 an Elberfeld merchant wanted to test Swedenborg himself: he related that he had had an important discussion with a friend shortly before he had died, and asked Swedenborg to find out what the topic of conversation had been. Some days later he returned and informed the merchant that the subject was the restitution of all things. The merchant is said to have turned pale on hearing the correct reply and must have been even more surprised to learn that his friend was not yet in a state of bliss as he was still tormenting himself about this subject. Swedenborg explained that a man takes his favourite inclinations and opinions with him, and he advised the merchant that they were better laid aside before death. This story might equally be explained by Swedenborg reading the mind of the merchant, although the details about his friend's condition, if true, could not have been obtained in this way. A comparable contemporary account comes from a Bulgarian friend who dreamt of a friend of her father's after his death and was instructed to pass on to him the message, "There is a transcendental world." The father was deeply moved as he had had discussions fifty years previously with this same friend and they had agreed that whoever died first would try to find some way of sending a message to the other—and, in this case, they always used the term "transcendental world".

Queen Louisa Ulrica of Sweden had heard reports of Swedenborg's powers, and had serious doubts about his sanity. But she was reassured by Count Scheffer, who arranged for Swedenborg to come to court. The queen questioned him about his abilities and asked him to take a commission to her dead brother. Some time later Swedenborg was once again brought to court and had a private audience with the queen; no one ever found out what Swedenborg told her, but she was so shocked that she had to retire—later she explained that she had been told something which no person living knew. An intrepid reporter made further attempts to find out what had been said, but he was dismissed with sovereign contempt—"Je ne suis pas facilement dupée" (I am not easily fooled).

If the last two incidents can be explained by thought-reading, the same is not true of the following account, also referred to by Kant. In 1761 the Countess de Marteville came to Swedenborg to explain that her husband, who had been ambassador to the Netherlands, had given her a valuable silver service before his death. The silversmith was now demanding an exorbitant payment, even though she was sure that her husband had paid for it already; but the receipt was nowhere to be found. The countess asked Swedenborg to contact her husband to ask about the receipt. Three days later he told her that he had spoken to her husband, who had informed him that the vital document was in a bureau upstairs. The woman replied that the bureau had already been searched, but Swedenborg insisted that she should remove a certain drawer and pull off its false back. The papers were duly found in the secret place, whose existence was only known to the dead count. The story is related by eleven different sources and vouched for by Swedenborg himself when he was later questioned about it.

The only alternative hypothesis to a "conversation" with the dead man in this instance is some form of so-called post-cognition, whereby Swedenborg had picked up the information from a sort of "event bank", but this theory is extremely unspecific and is little more than a sophisticated and desperate question-begging device—as Sir Cyril Burt pointed out. The modern term for this theory is the "super-ESP" hypothesis, which is a last-ditch attempt to discredit the survival hypothesis. In his defence, Swedenborg observes: "Many will say that no one can possibly speak with spirits and angels so long as he lives in the body; and many will say that it is all a phantasy, others that I relate such things in order to gain credence, and others will make other objections; but by all this I am not deterred, for I have seen, I have heard, I have felt."

Interaction of soul and body

Elsewhere, he refers to things which "have been proved to me by the daily experience of many years"; and when talking of the fact that a man is essentially unchanged after death he asserts that this "has been proved to me by manifold experience". In other words, Swedenborg retains the empirical approach—indeed the radical empiricism of William James—and analyses these uncommon experiences in the same way as he would go about the examination of a crystal or a part of the anatomy. He never dramatises his writings, but relates the facts about the nature of the soul, its relation to the body, and its persistence after the death of the body in a straightforward and down-to-earth manner.

Swedenborg gives a succinct definition of the soul and its relation to the body: "As regards the soul of which it is said that it will live after death, it is nothing but the man himself who lives within the body, that is, the interior man who in this world acts through the body, and gives life to the body. This man, when freed from the body, is called a spirit."

The terms spirit, soul, and internal man are used synonymously most of the time, although above spirit is used to denote the man freed from the body; occasionally soul is used to mean the spirit of a man while still in the body, a distinction which Swedenborg seems to have derived from Augustine (the use of the preposition *in* when referring to the relation of the soul to the body is significant and illustrates Swedenborg's idea of instrumentality). The other term, "internal man", is peculiar to Swedenborg, who uses it in contrast with the external man who is manifest through his physical body. The use of these terms will become clearer in reference to the after-death state. One further synonym emerges, that of mind: "The mind of man is his spirit and the spirit is the man because by mind are understood all the things of man's will and understanding." These two faculties of will and understanding are said to act in harness: the understanding contains all that a man thinks of, while the will is all the things that affect a man (emotionally), thus the will operates through "affections" and the understanding through thoughts.

Swedenborg considers the explanation of the understanding self-evident, but admits that the function of the will is harder to grasp. He compares the understanding to the sound of the voice, and the will to its tone: the meaning of the sentence is given in its structure, while the subtler emotional message can be grasped in its tone. In practice these two operations are separated; only in a reproduced synthesiser would the tone carry no significance. As the affection is related to the will, so it is related to love; not in the ordinary sense, but rather in terms of preoccupations and habits, which Swedenborg terms the ruling loves— the lines along which a man's thoughts usually run in opinions, tastes, and inclinations. The qualities of the essential inner man are manifest in his thoughts and emotional tendencies.

Swedenborg expands on the nature of soul and body, and their respective functions in a very similar way to Plotinus:

> Whoever duly considers the subject can know that the body does not think, because it is material, but that the soul, which is spiritual, does. The soul of man, upon the immortality of which many have written, is his spirit … this is also what thinks in the body, for it is spiritual … all rational life that appears in the body belongs to the soul, and nothing of it to the body; for the body, as said above, is material, and the material, which is the property of the body added to and, as it were, almost adjoined to the spirit, in order that the spirit of man may be able to live in the natural world, all things of which are material and in themselves devoid of life; and because the material does not live but only the spiritual, it can be established that whatever lives in man is his spirit, and that the body merely serves it, just as what is instrumental serves a moving living force. An instrument is said indeed to act, to move, or to strike; but to believe that these are acts of the instrument, and not of him who acts, or strikes by means of an instrument, is a fallacy.

This formulation turns on its head most of the twentieth-century ways of thinking, and may require some mental acrobatics to appreciate: it is not the body which feels, but the *spirit which feels through the body*, a view which follows the line of Plato and which anticipates those of F. C. S. Schiller, William James, and Henri Bergson, as elaborated in my book *Survival*; the matter of the dead body has no sensation unless the spirit is operating within it, in the same way as a severed limb automatically loses sensation. More will be said below about the senses after death.

Explanation of death

From the above conception that the soul is the man within the body, it follows that death is the separation of the soul from the body:

> Separation or death occurs when, from some sickness or accident, the body comes into such a condition that it is unable to act in

unison with its spirit … then man is said to die. This takes place
when the respiration of the lungs and the beatings of the heart
cease. But yet the man does not die; he is merely separated from
the corporeal part that was of use to him in the world, for the man
himself lives. It is said that the man himself lives, since man is not a
man because of his body but because of his spirit, for it is the spirit
in man that thinks, and thought with affection makes man.

This is a very clear exposition. In brief, for some reason or other the
spirit and body are no longer able to act in conjunction, so that a separation takes place; because it is the spirit which lives in man, it continues
to exist while the body decays.

Swedenborg explains that as soon as the heartbeat ceases the man
is "resuscitated", which means that the spirit is drawn out of the body.
In order better to report the details, Swedenborg himself claims to have
undergone the experience. He was brought into a state of bodily insensibility with his interior life, though unimpaired so that he could retain
the memory of the experience. He describes that he first perceived celestial angels (he explains elsewhere that all angels have been men, and
that heaven is divided into three broad categories, the highest of which
is celestial, then spiritual, then natural—the highest angels come first);
these celestial angels represent the highest and most spiritual forms of
thought, corresponding to the Fundamental Clear Light of the *Bardo
Thodol*—those who can accept the light attain liberation. If the spirit is
not of celestial quality, he will feel uncomfortable in the presence of
celestial angels and will long to escape from them. Next come angels
from the spiritual kingdom, corresponding to the secondary clear
light; they will likewise withdraw if the spirit feels uneasy, and are
then replaced by angels from the natural kingdom—"But if he lived
such a life in the world as would prevent him enjoying the company
of the good, he longs to get away from them, and this experience will
be repeated until he comes into association with such as are in entire
harmony with his life in the world; and with such he finds his own
life, and what is surprising, he leads a life like that which he led in the
world." Thus a spiritual gravitation takes place, whereby the novitiate
spirit finds the milieu which corresponds to his inner disposition. In a
reincarnation framework, this would correspond to the choice of a new
life, as in Plato's *Republic*, but reincarnation is specifically rejected by
Swedenborg.

Swedenborg describes sensations of bewilderment in the novitiate in similar terms to the *Bardo Thodol*:

> I may state that much experience has shown me that when a man comes into the other life he is not aware that he is in that life, but supposes that he is still in the world, and even that he is still in the body. So much is this the case that when he is told that he is a spirit, wonder and amazement possess him, both because he finds himself exactly like a man, in his senses, desires and thoughts, and because during life in this world he had not believed in the existence of the spirit, or, as is the case with some, that the spirit could be what he now finds itself to be.

Similar descriptions might be given from contemporary accounts of near-death experiences. Swedenborg points out that no sight or hearing is possible in the absence of the appropriate organ, hence that the spirit as well as the body has to be in a form, a human form, which enjoys senses when separated from the body. The fact that the body is a duplicate of the physical body accounts for the confusion of many of the recently deceased, who can only associate body with matter; thus when they see that they are in a body they conclude that they must still be in a material body.

The senses, then, are manifest through another body which is substantial in the sense that it has form, but not in the sense that the form is material. This body cannot be seen with the eyes of the body but only with the eyes of the spirit, to which it seems like a man in the world. His senses are supposed to be far more exquisite "for the things of the body, being comparatively gross, had rendered the sensations obtuse, and this all the more because the man had immersed them in earthly and worldly things". The thoughts are much clearer and more distinct— "There are more things contained in a single idea of their thought than in a thousand of the ideas that they had possessed in this world."

Again, this compares interestingly with descriptions of very clear mental processes in contemporary NDEs. The speech is said to be interior, thus communication is wordless—that is, telepathic—and thoughts pass from one to the other without the medium of spoken language; nor can the thoughts be concealed, as their expression is immediate and spontaneous—an embarrassing prospect of those who, like Voltaire, reckon that our tongues are for concealing our thoughts. In conclusion,

Swedenborg points out that "Life consists in the exercise of sensation, for without it there is no life, and such as the faculty of sensation is, such is the life"—a conception of life in terms of continued experience similar to the assumptions made by H. H. Price in his essay on *Survival and the Idea of Another World*. After death we find ourselves in a spiritual body which has more refined senses than its physical counterpart.

Christopher Polhem

Reactions to the burial of the physical body are mixed. Swedenborg explains that the scene can only be perceived by the spirit through his eyes (material) not through the dead person's own, and even then only because the spirit is in the unique position of being in both the natural and spiritual worlds at once. Yet one does read elsewhere of people witnessing their own funeral not apparently through the eyes of a witness. One of Swedenborg's friends told him at his funeral that they should throw his body away, because he himself was alive. The distinguished engineer Christopher Polhem, however, is reported by Swedenborg to have experienced a good deal of confusion or cognitive dissonance owing to his previous views:

> Polhem died on Monday. He spoke with me on Thursday; and when I was invited to his funeral he saw his coffin, and those who were there, and the whole procession, and also when his body was laid in the grave; and in the meantime he spoke with me, asking why he was buried when he was still alive: and he heard, also, when the priest said that he would be resuscitated at the last judgment, and yet he had been resuscitated for some time; and he marvelled that such a belief should exist, as that men should be resuscitated at the last judgment, when he was still alive; and that the body should rise again, when yet he himself was sensible of being in a body.

Polhem's witnessing of his own funeral should have enabled him to appreciate his true state. Swedenborg tells of acquaintances with whom he had conversed after their death, and who have

> wondered exceedingly that during the bodily life no one knows or believes that he is to live when the bodily life is over … they have desired me to tell their friends that they are alive, and to write and

tell them what their condition is, even as I have related to themselves many things about that of their friends here. But I replied
that were I to tell their friends such things, or to write to them
about them, they would not believe, but would call them delu-
sions, would scoff at them, and would ask for signs and miracles
before they would believe; and I should merely expose myself to
their derision.

Scepticism about life after death

Sadly, this is probably true, even today. If one is to believe a message
purporting to come from Bertrand Russell through Rosemary Brown,
he would not have believed his own message while still in the body (see
my account in *Survival*). Swedenborg is extremely pessimistic about the
possibility of convincing those still in the body of the continued existence of their friends. He gives three main arguments for scepticism
about the immediate resuscitation of consciousness: that the spirit can
have no existence apart from the body; that men will sleep until the
day of judgment; and that the nature of the soul is to be unextended in
space. The first two arguments are forms of materialism, in that neither
can conceive of an existence apart from the physical body—the first a
rationalist and the second a religious version. The third derives from the
Cartesian assumption that while the body is substantial and extended
in space, the soul or mind is unextended, and can therefore have no
form. We shall look at each of these in turn.

Swedenborg comments that "When the sensuous and corporeal man
thinks about the separation of the spirit from the body, it strikes him as
an impossible thing, because he places life in the body, and confirms
himself in this idea from the fact that brute animals also live, but do not
live after death."

But, Swedenborg argues, he has forgotten his rational faculty, which
distinguishes him from animals and which Swedenborg calls the
"in-most"; as we have seen, Aristotle and others made the same distinction. The corporeal man also contended that the spirit cannot exist
because it is invisible, to which Swedenborg replied that it was invisible
only to the corporeal eyes, not to those of the spirit. Men who can only
think in bodily categories, he concludes, find the existence of a separate
spirit impossible to conceive.

We have already indicated the problems inherent in resuscitation at the last judgment with respect of Polhem's funeral. Swedenborg describes this theory of bodily resurrection as "so universal that almost everyone holds it as a matter of doctrine". But this opinion has prevailed "because the natural man supposes that it is the body alone which lives; and that therefore unless he believed that the body would receive life again, he would deny the resurrection altogether". In some cases, Swedenborg asserts, the last judgment has been awaited so long that it is believed that the soul will never rise again. He goes on to give his own view, which we have outlined above, of immediate resuscitation. And on one occasion he records having asked some spirits whether "they wished to be clothed again in their earthly body, as they had thought before. On hearing this they fled far away at the very idea of such a conjunction, being filled with amazement that they had so thought from blind faith without understanding."

The learned, it is remarked, have the idea that the spirit is abstract thought, and are unwilling to grant that it may have any extension. The thinking subject has extension in space (form), but the thought has none; and if the spirit has no extension, it can have no substance, and cannot be in any place. Swedenborg comments on this state of affairs (or rather confusion):

> But an abuse arises from the fact that philosophers abide in terms, and dispute concerning them without coming to an agreement, from which all idea of the thing itself perishes, and the comprehension of the man is rendered so limited that he ceases at length to know anything but terms. Accordingly, when such persons would master a subject by their terms they do nothing but heap them up, obscuring the whole matter, so that they can understand nothing of it.

A practical example of this is recorded: Swedenborg is conversing with one who in the world believed that the spirit has no extension, and asked him how he now thought of himself, seeing that he was a soul with all his senses and supposed himself to be exactly as if in the body. He replied that spirit was thought, whereupon Swedenborg pointed out that no senses could exist without the appropriate organs, and that the brain is required for the transmission of thought in the body; therefore the body in which he now found himself must be of some organic substance, even though not material, for without it there would be no sensation, and without sensation, no life (i.e., consciousness), "whereupon he confessed his error, and wondered that he had been so foolish".

The common thread running through the above three varieties of scepticism is the paradoxical situation which arises when people still find themselves conscious and in a body after death. Much of this phenomenon has been recorded by William Baldwin and others in their work on spirit attachment. According to the materialists, they should have ceased to exist; but they are still conscious and alive in a sense, hence their first reaction, as we have seen, is to believe that they are not dead at all, but still alive in the physical body; only gradually, by conversing with other spirits, do they rid themselves of this illusion. The philosophers are less surprised to find themselves alive than to find themselves in a body, as they had equated the substantial with the material, thus concluding that anything which was not material would not be substantial or have extension. Their experience slowly convinces them of the real nature of their survival, so that in the end all their *a priori* categories are abandoned, and they experience themselves as they now are. The empirical approach should also be applied to an unfamiliar set of circumstances.

Spiritual evolution

We shall now look briefly at Swedenborg's account of human development in the spiritual world; readers who wish to examine this in detail are referred to the original texts. People arrive in the spiritual world with everything except their earthly body: their disposition and memory are not changed in any respect. Swedenborg distinguishes two kinds of memory, the internal and the external: on the internal memory is inscribed everything that a person has thought, willed, spoken, done, or even heard. Hence nothing whatsoever is lost and the person can be judged by the re-creation of all their acts, thoughts, and intentions concerning any hidden crime or misdemeanour—this constitutes the life review (see my book *Resonant Mind* for a detailed treatment): "Deceits and thefts ... were also enumerated in detail, many of which had been known to scarcely any in the world except themselves. These deeds they confessed, because they were plainly set forth, with every thought, intention, pleasure and fear which occupied their minds at the time."

The record is read as if in a book; and this book has been compiled by ourselves, so that our character has been built up by the thoughts of our mind and by the acts of our will.

The person, then, corresponds essentially to the "ruling love" or primary disposition, in terms of which they think and act, and which is responsible for their initial gravitation to a certain milieu or society. At first there may be some discrepancy between the "internal" and the "external", between what is thought and willed on the one hand, and what is spoken and done on the other. As the former internal person is the more essential, it gradually comes to predominate, thus eliminating the initial division; there is no longer any external restraint to be taken into account, so that people are able to act in accordance with their own nature. Corresponding to this, the face is transformed into an image of the ruling love, of which it is the outer form: "All in the other life are brought into such a state as to speak as they think, and to manifest in their looks and gestures the inclinations of their will. And because of this the faces of all become forms and images of their affections."

When this is complete the person gravitates to their "natural" abode in heaven or hell, a process which rounds off the gravitation expressed in the experience of dying described above.

Swedenborg makes two further important points: first, that no one comes to heaven as a result of immediate mercy. In other words, there is no justification by faith alone or last-minute repentance; mere knowledge without action is not manifested through the will, and is therefore not part of the essential person. In addition, because the person's ruling love is their life, destruction of an evil ruling love would involve annihilation of the person. The one whose bodily life has been the opposite of heaven cannot miraculously be transformed into the opposite of their nature. For a person to gain access (or rather gravitate) to heaven, their thoughts and affections must correspond to the heavenly.

Second, Swedenborg reassuringly maintains that it is not so difficult to lead a heavenly life as is believed. He warns against the hermit whose sorrowful life will continue to be sorrowful after death "since life continues the same after death". On the contrary, people are exhorted to live in the world and engage in duties and employments there. They must live an internal and an external life at the same time, but must not content themselves with practising virtues because of the restraints of the law, but rather because it accords with divine laws; thus they act not out of fear but from love, with the result that there is no division between their internal and external.

In terms of subject matter, we have come a long way from the practicalities of the Board of Mines, but for Swedenborg this transcendent exploration was an extension of the empirical approach and of reason into the realms of the spiritual. He writes of experiences which few have had, some of which are only now becoming more familiar in the light of parallel experiences in our own time. Fittingly, he predicted the day and time of his own death in March 1772, and paid his landlady exactly up to the end of the month.

Conclusion

It is clear from the foregoing analysis that Swedenborg gives priority to the first-person perspective and to his own experience, treating an exclusively third-person view based on the evidence of the senses as a superficial fallacy. He asserts the existence of the soul and the continuity of the self and consciousness through death. He also seems to envisage the long-term persistence of the personality—as witnessed in his accounts of conversations with Luther—which other schools of thought contest as the self becomes more identified with the Universal Self and therefore loses some of its limiting boundaries. And yet identity does imply a degree of separation or distinction from any Ground of Being. My personal conviction is that we cannot become less than we are at death as growth always implies that we can become more, and can manifest potentials hidden from us in the body and obscured by the time-bound personality. Indeed, Swedenborg himself says as much when he insists that all angels were once human beings.

Swedenborg, the Soul and Modern Consciousness Studies

Swedenborg Society presidential address, May 2002

It is not well known that Swedenborg wrote a 700-page book on the brain, in which he was the first to suggest complementary roles for the two hemispheres. My neuroscientist friend Peter Fenwick was taken aback by its sophistication and himself gave a lecture on this book to the Swedenborg Society. The difference between Swedenborg and mainstream philosophers writing about mind, brain, body, and consciousness is that he had personal experience of how the soul interacted reciprocally with the physical body and also of undergoing the death process and communicating with many deceased people, as noted in a previous lecture. The evolution of concepts about consciousness since Swedenborg has been largely driven by an outside-in third-person perspective, while Swedenborg's formulations stem directly from analysing his own experience— first-person inside-out, but no less rigorous on that account.

I recently reviewed a volume entitled *From Soul to Self* in which most contributors consigned the Platonic idea of the soul to history. I should explain that there are two popular concepts of the soul: the Platonic idea defines the soul as the divine, imperishable element of the human being that is separable from the body at death. This was historically transmuted into the rational soul—*res cogitans*—of Descartes, which is also

separate and distinct from the *res extensa* of matter. In Aristotelian philosophy, though, the soul is understood as the "form" of the body. The
trend since Descartes has been against dualism of any kind, so that most
scientists now consider consciousness or the self to be entirely dependent on material brain processes. In a wider sense the self is understood as a social construct. As such, it can be socially deconstructed
and indeed much modern psychology goes further in psychologically
deconstructing the self into a bundle of properties. Such a model was
advanced by David Hume in the eighteenth century but is currently
espoused by a number of psychologists including Guy Claxton and
Susan Blackmore, both of whom draw inspiration from Buddhism.

Definitions

The terminology itself has evolved. Traditionally, in Christian theology,
the spirit (*pneuma, spiritus*) was distinguished from the soul (*psyche,
anima*) as an intermediary principle between the spirit and the body
(*soma, corpus*). Many people now use soul and spirit interchangeably,
and also use them in a different sense without the definite article.
Etymologically, spirit is associated with breath (*ruach* in Hebrew) while
the soul (Latin *anima*) is the animating principle. Interestingly, the San-
skrit word for soul, *atman*, is also derived from a word "an", meaning
to breathe. For the Indian scholar Radhakrishnan the *atman* is the "life,
soul, self or essential being of the individual", the unborn and immortal
element (a concept which he argues influenced Plato). So, "Our true self
is a pure existence, self-aware, unconditioned by the forms of mind and
intellect." The individual soul is sometimes referred to as the *jivatman*,
where "*jiv*" also means to breathe. The soul as defined here survives the
death of the physical body. As mentioned above, it is the rational soul
of Plato that reappears as the *res cogitans* (mind) in Descartes, located
in the pineal gland. It is worth mentioning that Plato recognised the
animal and vegetable souls, which we shared respectively with animals
and plants. The concept of the soul has thus shrunk through the ages
until it is scarcely recognised.

For Swedenborg the soul is defined in a number of ways as:

• The internal/interior man who lives after death, the man who lives
  in the body Every soul of man is in a spiritual body after death
• Equated with spirit and even mind

- As the very life, that which lives (animates)
- The good which lives from celestial love
- A spiritual substance, purer, prior, more interior

There is a reciprocity between the soul and the physical body such that they are reciprocally united. The soul "acts in the body but not through the body ... everything of the soul is of the body, mutually and reciprocally."

Swedenborg characterises the view that the soul depends for its existence on the body as "physical influx", which he claims "arises from the appearances of the sense and the fallacies thence derived", that is, from an exclusively third person or outside-in view. In India this view would be regarded as an illusion (*maya*) manifesting spiritual ignorance (*avidya*—literally "not seeing"). As Radhakrishnan comments: "The world has a tendency to delude us into thinking that it is all, that it is self-dependent, and this delusive character of the world is also designated *maya* in the sense of *avidya*." Swedenborg echoes this sentiment when he says that there can be such a degree of ignorance about the spiritual world that a man can become "so far infatuated as to become an atheistic materialist".

The decline of the soul

Swedenborg's views are based on his own inner perceptions or "spiritual influx"—where causation moves from inner to outer. He claims that there are two worlds: spiritual and natural, with two suns, two lights. The spiritual world is one of being while the natural world is one of manifestation. If we examine why the concept of the soul has gone out of fashion—a "damaged concept" according to Templeton Prize Winner Sir John Polkinghorne, then a number of factors can be identified. The modern self is not a substance in the way the soul was previously defined.

1) Cartesian interaction of incommensurable substances is regarded as impossible—how can an immaterial mind interact with a material body? Dualism is not an intellectually attractive option and is espoused by only a handful of philosophers and theologians like Oxford's Richard Swinburne. Most opt for a monistic (one principle) materialism whereby matter gives rise to mind, which is entirely dependent upon it.

2) The soul as an "immaterial substance" seems an oxymoron to modern thinkers.

3) The inconceivability of disembodied existence: this arises because Western philosophers have no concept of subtle bodies or subtle energy. Psychical research and mysticism both point in the direction of subtle bodies that can serve as vehicles for consciousness.

4) Descartes thought of animals as machines. Since his time, Darwinism has come to stress the continuity of humans and animals in evolution so the logic has proceeded to imply that since humans are animals, humans are also machines. This trend has been encouraged by the determinism of classical physics, which still predominates in molecular biology in spite of twentieth-century advances in quantum physics; and by computer metaphors prevalent in AI research.

5) All causation is thought to be physical, bottom up. Consciousness is an epiphenomenon, like the steam rising from a kettle. This view causes considerable problems since it goes against our immediate intuitions and undermines our sense of free will.

6) Most neuroscientists support a version of the mind-brain identity theory—brain produces consciousness rather than transmits it—the view put forward by William James, Henri Bergson and F. C. S. Schiller.

7) Science is underpinned by philosophical materialism, methodological reductionism and positivism.

8) The concept of the unconscious and its influence has gained currency within psychology, so that the role of the conscious mind becomes secondary.

9) Finally, there has been a general erosion of the belief in God, even though many contemporaries now report powerful spiritual experiences. The main reasons for this decline have been the problem of theodicy or the reconciliation of the existence of evil with the idea of a loving and omnipotent God. I regard this view as understandable but superficial.

The focus of almost all conventional thinking is on the normal and the abnormal, while no attention is paid to the supernormal or paranormal. Indeed, such studies are avoided since they seem to call into question the metaphysical premises on which modern science is based. Over 100 years ago, the Harvard philosopher and psychologist William James had a complete psychology including psychical research. His father,

Henry James Sr., was an ardent Swedenborgian, and evidently some of this interest rubbed off on the son.

James discusses the soul in his great *Principles of Psychology,* defining it as "immaterial, substantial and simple" and describing it initially as "the line of least logical resistance—better than mind-stuff or material monad". However, he continues, "the immediate phenomenon is a state of consciousness rather than the soul itself"—that is, the soul is an inference from experiencing its states. James is aiming at a positivist and non-metaphysical psychology so he thinks it superfluous so far as accounting for the actually verified facts of conscious experience goes. The stream of thought that we experience with putative immortality may come to an end. The soul is also "the guarantee of the closed individuality of personal consciousness". He concludes that, although it is scientifically superfluous, this does not imply its non-existence. Some of James's successors have been less logical when they deny the existence of the soul on scientific grounds.

James takes a different tack in his 1898 Ingersoll Lecture on immortality. Here he asks if the formula "Thought is a function of the brain" logically compels us to disbelieve in immortality? While acknowledging the close relationship between mind and brain, he questions T. H. Huxley's view that consciousness can be compared with "Steam is a function of the tea-kettle". James's logic is subtler. It is plausible that consciousness may in a sense be transmitted by the brain (as in a TV) or permitted by it—in both these cases consciousness is not actually produced by the brain. James argued, rightly in my view, that only a transmissive theory made sense of psychic experiences. While normal and abnormal evidence might point to the productive view, this is inadequate when one takes the supernormal into account.

James was influenced in this position by a book by the Oxford philosopher F. C. S. Schiller, *Riddles of the Sphinx,* published anonymously in 1891, probably on account of the scepticism of fellow Oxford philosophers, which would still be the case today. Schiller maintains that "Matter is not that which produces consciousness but that which limits it and confines its intensity within certain limits." This view, he argues, fits the alleged facts as cogently as materialism while also enabling us to understand facts which materialism rejects as "supernatural". For instance, from the outside (third person perspective) death may look like the cessation of consciousness while for the first person consciousness continues in a more intense form.

Another contemporary of James and Schiller was F. W. H. Myers, a classicist fellow of Trinity College, Cambridge, who was one of the founders of the Society for Psychical Research. Myers's magnum opus *Human Personality and Its Survival of Bodily Death* was published post-humously, and there is good evidence in the cross-correspondences for some cogent communications from him from the other side. His use of terminology—human personality rather than the soul—is interesting, since it represents the components of memory and iden-tity. The word "soul" is not actually in the index, which I think fairly astonishing. Myers's earlier work was on apparitions or phantasms, about which he published a monumental two-volume work, *Phan-tasms of the Living* (with Gurney and Podmore) in 1886. His alleged posthumous work through Geraldine Cummins (*Beyond Human Per-sonality*) defines the soul as "a finite focus or centre for imagination", a definition that comes close to those of Douglas Fawcett and Raynor Johnson.

Soul as formative, particle, and wave

You will recall that I mentioned earlier Aristotle's idea of the soul as the "form" of the body. This is an idea that has re-emerged in the biol-ogy of morphogenesis where a "morphogenetic field" is postulated as an organising principle underlying the genesis of physical form and indeed its recovery in healing. The idea of soul has metamorphosed here into that of a field. Ian Stevenson, in his researches on children who remember previous lives, has found that some memories correspond to birthmarks, which in turn correspond to the place of a fatal injury in the remembered life. So, for instance, one child had a memory of being shot through the head. The name given corresponded to a man whose hos-pital records showed that he had been shot in the very place where the birthmark was found. On the basis of such cases, Stevenson speculates that there must be a form-carrying principle to establish a certain conti-nuity between the bodies—and one that also carries the corresponding memory. He calls this template the "psychophore". So here we have a continuity not only of memory and identity, but also of the body via birthmarks. This suggests that an adequate model of the soul might require it to be the carrier of memory and identity as well as being the formative principle of spiritual bodily continuity. I should mention here that Swedenborg's interpretation of such cases would involve telepathy from a deceased person, but this would not account for the indications of bodily continuity.

It seems to me that we exist within a sea of consciousness and that we as individuals are particular expressions or manifestations of this universal consciousness. Mystical experience suggests that our sense of self is continuous with the universal consciousness, and that an expansion of consciousness equates with an expansion of freedom. So one of the basic dynamics of consciousness is expansion and contraction.

Let us suppose that consciousness, as in quantum mechanics, has both a wave and a particle aspect. The wave aspect corresponds to what Rupert Sheldrake calls the extended mind, or Larry Dossey non-locality of consciousness. The particle aspect might then be represented by the soul-hypothesis—the seat of inner continuity and individuality. It seems to me that both wave and particle aspects are required to explain the full range of paranormal phenomena.

The wave aspect is required for telepathy, clairvoyance, precognition, and telesomatic phenomena (feeling other people's bodily sensations at a distance). In so far as this wave aspect is adequately rendered by the notion of a "sea of consciousness", we are immersed in it and can pick things up from it with the requisite ability and training—as indeed Swedenborg himself was capable of doing.

The particle aspect of consciousness—the soul—seems to me required to make sense of OBEs, NDEs, conscious apparitions, memories of previous lives with somatic transmission of birthmarks, trance mediumship, and survival. In the OBE and NDE, people describe themselves as conscious apart from the body (in a Platonic sense) and are convinced on this basis (certainly with an NDE) that their essential self survives the death of the body. The findings of trance mediumship, where another personality seems to communicate through the medium's body, require the existence of a soul if one is to suppose that more than simple memory residues are being picked up. Finally, the notion of individual survival after death makes no sense without the soul. Naturally, most scientists regard this case as far from proven, but their attitude stems from a combination of ignorance of the data and downright resistance to investigating phenomena that would upset the interlocking and comprehensive materialism that underpins modern science.

My conclusion is that the concept of the soul is not at all fashionable in modern psychology—it is dismissed as a relic of folk psychology or superstition, especially by scientific materialists. They are still challenged by the "binding problem" (the unity of conscious experience) and many opt for a "bundle" understanding of the self. However, Swedenborg would continue to uphold the existence of the soul in a modern context, on the basis of his own experience. My contention is that the explanatory value of the soul concept lies in the areas referred to above and which are largely ignored by science. It seems to me that the way forward does not lie in dualism as such (although I believe that it is required to explain survival) but rather in the kind of dual-aspect theory advanced by Mark Woodhouse, allied to a view that postulates consciousness as fundamental rather than incidental in our universe. Woodhouse observes that consciousness (inner) and energy (form, outer) are required in any world where there might be persons interacting. Without body or form there can be no individuality, and without consciousness no personality. The soul remains an essential concept that corresponds to a deeper understanding of life.

The Near-death Experience and the Perennial Wisdom

*T*his essay written in 2005 and updated for Being *in 2016 brings together two strands of my quest in understanding the implications of NDEs with their transformative outcome moving towards becoming an embodiment of love and wisdom, which is also the very essence of esoteric perennial philosophy, itself based on profound spiritual experiences. I have gradually come to regard the principles of love and wisdom as quintessential for life, expressed as they have been by sages down the generations, and which form the kernel of the teaching of Swedenborg and Beinsa Douno, as explained in a previous essay. At a certain point it becomes critical to enter in depth into a single tradition rather than keep flitting around at the bottom of the mountain—and all the great living traditions focus on the development of love/compassion and wisdom/understanding, integrating heart and mind while put into practice through the cultivation of a disciplined will. This essay was first published in* Being.

> *The eye with which I see God is the same eye with which God sees in me: my eye and God's eye, that is one eye and one vision, one knowledge and one love.*
>
> —Meister Eckhart

It is not we who know God, it is God who knows himself in us.
—Frithjof Schuon

The human intellect can reach "theosis"—knowledge of God—through the rediscovery of its own essence … to know God is to recall what we are.
—Seyyed Hossein Nasr

It is now some forty years since the appearance of the first books explicitly devoted to the near-death experience (NDE). Public interest in the phenomenon has been sustained over that period by a spate of new books ranging from the academic to the popular, most recently those by Anita Moorjani and Eben Alexander. Journalists and broadcasters still regularly make contact, wanting to produce programmes and speak to experiencers. The field has branched out in a number of directions and disciplines: neurobiology, medicine, psychiatry, various psychologies— ranging from cognitive to transpersonal—anthropology, sociology, philosophy (including the nature of perception), metaphysics, and religion. The NDE lends itself to an interdisciplinary approach, and indeed cannot be fully understood without considering a variety of aspects and levels. This essay will focus on the relationship between the NDE and what I call the perennial wisdom, arguing that the deeper aspects of the experience are a kind of *gnosis* that give an insight into the nature of a reality which transcends the physical.

The term perennial philosophy was popularised by Aldous Huxley's 1945 book of the same name, but the ancestry of the term goes back a good deal further. I am using it here in the sense advanced by Frithjof Schuon and others that there exists an underlying thread which unites all expressions of religious traditions. Two of the cardinal principles of this are love and wisdom, principles which can be used as a benchmark or criterion of religion and spirituality: if love and wisdom are not central within a tradition, then, in my view, such a tradition is not a genuine spiritual expression.

Two views of consciousness

By no means all researchers would agree that reality can transcend the physical dimension. The dominant philosophy in modern neuroscience, medicine, and psychology is still mechanistic, materialistic, and reductionist, whether this is formulated as physicalism, functionalism, or even "biological naturalism". It amounts to stating that conscious experience is produced by brain activity and that perception is only possible by means of the five senses. It follows from this that the NDE must be a purely physical phenomenon and that brain death spells the extinction of personal identity and memory. Without an active physical brain, no consciousness is possible. This was neurosurgeon Eben Alexander's view prior to his own NDE, which completely changed his attitude, failing to explain "the rich, robust, intricate interactivity" of what he calls the Gateway and Core Experiences.

An alternative view postulates that consciousness is not so much produced by as transmitted through the brain. Thus conscious states would be correlated with rather than caused by brain activity. The distinction is a crucial one, since it allows the possibility that the mind or soul might operate independently of the physical brain and have access to non-physical aspects or dimensions of reality. Furthermore, the death of the brain need not necessarily spell the extinction of the individual, but possibly a transformation or transition to a different state of consciousness. In this view, the brain could be regarded as the space-time limitation or localisation of consciousness, while consciousness itself is neither intrinsically limited nor localised.

This theory is capable of accounting for the kind of out-of-the-body perception reported in NDEs, while the brain-based approaches are obliged to ignore or dismiss such evidence. The fundamental issue here is this: is the physical world a closed self-sufficient system so that everything can be causally explained in physical terms? Or does it open into inner dimensions that transcend the physical realm? The modern scientific world view assumes the former position, while all types of spiritual world view insist that there is something more.

Witnesses

The quotations at the top of this essay make very little sense to those who do not believe that there is a God to discover or know. Yet throughout history there have been reports of "otherworld journeys" from those who have come back from the borderland of death. One of the earliest analogies to the traveller's tale is Plato's simile of the cave in the *Republic*. The prisoners in the cave take the shadows thrown by the fire on the wall opposite as reality, and are reluctant to believe in the existence of anything else. Yet, as Plato argues, there are many other degrees of reality that are more real than what can be perceived inside the cave. There is a gradual ascent from illusion through belief, reason (*dianoia*) and intelligence (*nous*) to a "vision of the form of the good" represented by looking at the sun.

It is here that Plato's symbolism begins to meet the phenomenology of the NDE. The stages described seem to indicate a gradual withdrawal from the physical realm and entry into another, spiritual realm that is always sensed as more real than the physical on the traveller's return. An interesting reflection on this point is provided by "Bertrand Russell", ostensibly communicating through medium Rosemary Brown while commenting that he himself would not have believed this while he was alive …

> Now here I was, still the same I, with capacities to think and observe sharpened to an incredible degree. I felt earth-life suddenly seemed very unreal almost as if it had never happened. It took me quite a long time to understand this feeling until I realised at last that matter is certainly illusory although it does exist in actuality; the material world seemed now nothing more than a seething, changing, restless sea of indeterminable density and volume. How could I have thought that that was reality, the last word of Creation to Mankind? Yet it is completely understandable that the state in which a man exists, however temporary, constitutes the passing reality which is no longer reality when it has passed.

"Russell"'s remark that his capacities to think and observe were sharpened to an incredible degree is typical of the NDE and flies in the face of the materialistic assumption that a dying brain could only result in confused perceptual processes. The evidence for this comes from reports of veridical OBEs during the NDE, where subjects are able to give an accurate report of events going on around them when they were apparently completely unconscious. This is all the more remarkable in cases of cardiac arrest investigated by the Dutch cardiologist Pim van Lommel. We know the exact physiology involved in cardiac arrest and subsequent recovery of consciousness. In one of his cases, a man was brought into hospital following a heart failure and subsequently transferred to intensive care without recovering consciousness. A few days later he was brought back to the ward. Not only did he recognise the nurse (whom he had never seen before) as having been present at his resuscitation, which he described in detail, but he even asked her where she had put his false teeth! The subject had seen him (the nurse was male) place them on a gurney. The nurse was flabbergasted, as there was no normal way in which the subject could have known this.

Sceptics argue that such reports could have been reconstructed from residual hearing, but such an interpretation does scant justice to the detailed visual nature of the experience and the fact that many actions or phenomena reported were not actually verbalised by the medical staff. This stage of the NDE is the first point of contact with the perennial wisdom, which speaks of subtle bodies or vehicles of consciousness beyond the physical form or envelope. The subjects realise that they are more than their physical body, and sometimes even hear themselves pronounced dead in spite of the fact that they are still conscious and often looking down on the scene from above.

The next stage of "going through the tunnel" almost sounds like emerging from the Platonic cave into the light. The "light" is described as very bright, but harmless to the eyes. It is clearly not physical light, but rather spiritual light, a distinction which has its counterpart in Latin (*lumen/lux*) and Bulgarian (*videlina/svetlina*). Light has from time immemorial been the symbol of the Divine, but, as Eckhart indicates in the quotation above, this light is also knowledge and love. Experiencers write (quoted from my book *Resonant Mind*):

> I found myself travelling towards this tremendous light, so bright that it would have blinded me if I'd looked at it here, but there it was different. I reached the light which was all around me … and I felt this wonderful love enfolding me and understanding me. No matter what my faults, what I'd done or hadn't done, the light loved me unconditionally.

Again:

> A light was glowing invitingly—I was encouraged by a strong feeling to enter the light. I approached without haste as I felt that the light was part of the jigsaw to which I rightfully belonged. As I entered, I felt the light glow. I was peaceful, totally content and I understood why I was born on earth and knew the answer to every mystery.

These two accounts show that the light has both cognitive or intellectual and affective or emotional aspects. In terms of the perennial philosophy this can be translated into wisdom and love respectively. It is significant that the root of the Latin word for wisdom—*sapientia*—comes from *sapere*, which means to taste. Wisdom, therefore, is derived from experience, and the NDE, in this sense, could be regarded as a taste of love and wisdom. This experience in turn influences the documented after-effects of the experience. Melvin Morse even goes on to argue that the transformative effects of the NDE are due to the light, a hypothesis consistent with other research in religious experience by Sir Alister Hardy and colleagues, indicating profound transformation following spiritual encounters.

A central feature of the experience of the light is that it is unitive: there is a sense of complete oneness—at-onement—in which the sense of self is nevertheless retained and expanded at the same time. Eben Alexander remarks that he became part of anything he experienced and that thoughts entered him directly. Plotinus writes that the infinite can only be grasped "by entering into a state in which you are your finite self no longer … when you cease to be finite and become one with the infinite". The poet Tennyson similarly records: "All at once, out of the intensity of the consciousness of individuality, individuality itself seems to fade away into boundless being." The Zen scholar Suzuki suggests that *satori* is an expansion of the individual into the infinite. It is as if the normal boundaries of the limited and contracted and seemingly separate self are suddenly dissolved. It is perhaps this transcendence of the ego which produces a loss of the fear of death.

Knowing and being

Modern NDE accounts are typical of what is known in the West as absorptive mysticism, where the self is absorbed into a higher or deeper order of reality in which light, life, intensity, and certainty all meet. Consider this classic account from Jan van Ruysbroeck:

> And all those men who are raised up above their created being into a God-seeing life are one with this Divine brightness. And they are that brightness itself, and they see, feel and find, even by means of this Divine Light, that, as regards their uncreated essence, they are that same onefold ground from which the brightness without limits

shines forth in the Divine way, and which, according to the simplicity of the Essence, abides eternally onefold and wayless within.
And this is why inward and God-seeing men will go out in the way
of contemplation, above reason and above distinction and above
their created being, through an eternal, intuitive gazing. By means
of this inborn light they are transfigured, and made one with that
same light through which they see and which they see.

This last sentence recalls the circular paradox in the Eckhart quotation,
only here Ruysbroeck refers to light rather than the eye. This change of
perspective and perception is a form of gnosis whereby, as Schuon puts
it, we "participate in the perspective of the Divine Subject". And, in the
words of Parmenides, "To be and to know are one and the same thing."
This kind of knowledge itself represents a change of being which overcomes the division between subject and object.

In the Indian tradition this state is the union of being, consciousness,
bliss (*Sat, Chit, Ananda*). There is no separation between knower and
known, only the knowing; none between the lover and the beloved,
just the love. Such a union between love and knowledge is beautifully
expressed by St Maximus: "If the life of the spirit is the illumination of
knowledge and if it is love of God which produces this illumination,
then it is right to say: there is nothing higher than the love of God."
Seyyed Hossein Nasr (1989) makes the same point: "This illumination
in turn enables man to realise that the very essence of things is God's
knowledge of them and that there is a reciprocity and, finally, an identity between being and knowing. The intellect becomes transformed
into what it knows, the highest object of that knowledge being God."
Such gnosis, according to both Nasr and Schuon, is through the eye of
the heart, which is the eye of the intellect (nous) not reason (the two are
often wrongly conflated—the intellect is what enables us to grasp unity,
while reason is dialectical and dualistic). The essence of the intellect,
according to Schuon, is "light as well as vision, nor is it reason which is
a reflection of intellect on the human plane, but it is the root and centre
of consciousness and what has traditionally been called the soul".

There is one further crucial feature of this gnosis: it is the truth which
makes you free, the *moksha* or deliverance of Hinduism which is beyond
form, beyond limitation, and beyond ego. It is not just a concept, but
a profound experience and, as Schuon says, "If we want truth to live
in us, we must live in it." The return from the light can be painful and

disappointing as the subject wakes up again in the limitations of the physical body. The NDE, though, leaves an indelible impression in most of the experiencers. It is as if they try to live out the values of love, wisdom, truth, joy, beauty, and peace that have transfused their beings. Such a shift of attitude and perspective can create difficulties for close relationships where the partner remains unchanged. There tends to be a change from "having" to "being", that is away from purely material concerns and priorities. Subjects embark on a pursuit of wisdom and make love the central value of their lives.

Transformation

It is illuminating to compare the NDE and its accompanying transformation of values with the effects of conversion and initiation. William James characterises conversion as a change in what he calls "the habitual centre of personal energy", which precipitates "a mental rearrangement" or reordering of priorities and values. The parallels with initiation are even more apparent, since one of its essential features is a ritual death and rebirth, a separation from the old and an embracing of the new. Michael Grosso quotes an early Greek writer, Themistios, as stating that the soul has the same experience at the point of death as those who are being initiated: "First one is struck by a marvellous light, one is received into pure regions and meadows." In this sense, experiencers of NDEs are unwitting initiates who have usually had no preparation whatsoever, in contrast with the careful instruction which preceded ancient initiation rituals.

The poet Rumi writes:

> *O man go die before thou diest*
> *So that thou shalt not have to suffer death when thou shalt die*
> *Such a death that thou wilst enter into light*
> *Not a death through which thou wilst enter into the grave*

In other words, a death leading to a new or second, spiritual birth. In speaking of patterns of initiation, Mircea Eliade remarks on the initiatory character of the ordeals and spiritual crises of life: "It remains true nonetheless that man becomes *himself* only after having solved a series of desperately difficult and even dangerous situations; that is after having undergone 'tortures' and 'death', followed by an awakening to another life, qualitatively different because regenerated. If we look closely, we see that every human life is made up of a series of 'deaths' and 'resurrections'." Eliade observes that such initiations are usually effective only at a psychological rather than ontological level, which I think is by and large true for NDEs although transformations can be so profound as to be clearly ontological—there is literally a change (or revelation) of being.

Some people refer to the NDE as a "telephone call from God", which acts as a reminder of their true nature. Plato's myth of Lethe illustrates human forgetfulness of the nature of being and the purpose of human life. It is a spiritual awakening which makes people conscious of their journey and responsibilities. Typically, the spirituality of experiencers is deepened and they experience a spiritual feeling of closeness to the Divine. The emphasis is therefore on the inner life more than on outer ritual and church attendance. Churchgoers find themselves taking a more mystical approach and become more concerned with an underlying universal core of religions—what Schuon calls "the transcendent unity of religions". They also enjoy spending more time alone and in nature.

Esoteric and exoteric

In their search for the meaning of life and death, a significant number of NDE experiencers become interested, as I said, in more esoteric aspects of religion and spirituality. The life's work of Frithjof Schuon has been to formulate the transcendent unity of religions, showing that esoterism is the true form of ecumenism, not a watered down and compromised liberalism. The problems arise from the fact the Revelation is intrinsically absolute and extrinsically relative, in other words the essence is absolute and the form relative: "Religious revelation is both a veil of light and a light veiled." Restrictive dogma arises when the form is taken to be equivalent to the essence. The esoteric aspects of a religion are its hidden inner essence only accessible through gnosis to those who have developed the appropriate organs of perception; while the exoteric aspects are the doctrines, dogmas, and rituals in which the churchgoer is expected to believe implicitly and often unquestioningly.

Schuon characterises the relationship between esoterism and exoterism as follows:

> Esoterism on the one hand prolongs exoterism—by harmoniously plumbing its depth—because the form expresses the essence and because in this respect the two enjoy solidarity, while on the other

> hand esoterism opposes exoterism—by transcending it abruptly—
> because essence by virtue of its unlimitedness is of necessity not
> reducible to form, or in other words, because form, inasmuch as
> it constitutes a limit, is opposed to whatever is totality and liberty.

He continues further on:

> We could say, simplifying a little, that exoterism puts the form—the
> *credo*—above the essence—Universal Truth—and accepts the latter
> only as a function of the former; the form, through its divine origin,
> is here the criterion of the essence. Esoterism, on the contrary, puts
> the essence above the form … the essence is the criterion of the
> form; the one and universal Truth is the criterion of the various
> religious forms of the Truth … the particular or the limited is recog-
> nised as the manifestation of the principial [sic] and the transcen-
> dent, and this in its turn reveals itself as immanent.

In contemporary terms, we have here the tension and conflict between
the esoteric, universal and mystical approach and the exoteric, literalist,
fundamentalist view. The fundamentalist pronounces his own revelation as absolute, exclusive, and unique, so that anyone not accepting
it on those terms is cast into outer darkness and forfeits salvation. The
near-death experiencer will tend to express a more inclusive philosophy corresponding to the ineffability of the experience. Indeed, one fundamentalist who had an NDE came back with the (to them) surprising
thought that "God isn't interested in theology"! Another experiencer
tells of a presence which asked "What is in your heart?" and added that
what mattered most was the love expressed in one's life; also that there
is no such thing as sin, as humans commonly understand the term. The
emphasis throughout is on being rather than belief, and actions infused
with spiritual qualities.

The core of love

A modern initiate and spiritual master who was also an exponent of
the perennial wisdom is the Bulgarian Beinsa Douno (Peter Deunov,
1864–1944). He taught in Bulgaria from 1900, and began giving systematic lectures in 1914. Between that time and his passing, he gave sev-
eral thousand lectures and talks on every aspect of human existence.

The cardinal principles of his teaching, though, are simple: Love, Wisdom, and Truth:

> The first principle on which the whole of existence is based is Love; it brings the impulse to life; it is the compass, the stimulus within the human soul.
>
> The second principle is Wisdom, which brings knowledge and light to the mind, thus enabling human beings to use the forces of nature in a noetic way.
>
> The third principle is Truth; it frees the human soul from bondage and encourages her to learn, work well and make efforts towards self-sacrifice.
>
> There is nothing greater than these three principles; there is no straighter or surer path. In these three principles lies the salvation of the world.

These are the principles which we have already encountered in connection with the perennial philosophy and the NDE. They are expressed in practical form through the sacred dance movements of paneurythmy. Douno echoes Schuon's remarks about essence and form, but with a distinct emphasis:

> Love does not recognise any religion. It is Love itself which creates religions. In the Divine World there are no religions.
>
> There, only Love exists. Love is the very atmosphere of the Divine World. And everything in it breathes Love.
>
> Since Love cannot manifest on earth, there arose the need for religions. However, if you wish to fulfil the will of God, it is essential to substitute Love for religion.

Religions are therefore the various forms and expressions of the Divine, and all have love or compassion at their core. The statement that Love is the very atmosphere of the Divine World expresses the experience in the NDE of being immersed in love and light (wisdom); and the centrality of the principle of Love in the NDE and its after-effects unites it with the mystical and wisdom traditions in world religions. The success of books on the NDE suggests to me that the spiritual content articulates a message that resonates with many contemporary seekers. It comes directly out of an individual's experience and yet contains universal elements that speak to our condition and but point beyond it to the more profound and systematic teachings expressed in the perennial wisdom and outlined above.

Both Eben Alexander and Anita Moorjani report intense experiences of love. For Alexander, the core of his message is that "You are loved and cherished. You have nothing to fear. There is nothing you can do wrong." His shorter version is "You are loved" and the one-word summary is "love". The unconditional love and acceptance that he experienced on his journey was the single most important discovery of his life, as well as a vital bridge between science and spirituality. After crossing over into another dimension, Moorjani was totally engulfed with love and had a clear insight about why she had contracted cancer as revealed in her title *Dying to Live* (2012). She had not lived her own authentic calling. She writes in her online account that "The amount of love I felt was overwhelming, and from this perspective, I knew how powerful I am, and saw the amazing possibilities we as humans are capable of achieving during a physical life. I found out that my purpose now would be to live 'heaven on earth' using this new understanding, and also to share this knowledge with other people." Her message echoes exactly that of Alexander: "Life is supposed to be great, and we are very, very loved."

Some aspects of the NDE, then, can be seen as an opening into transcendent realms beyond and within the apparently self-sufficient and closed physical system. It reveals to the experiencer hitherto unknown and little explored dimensions of the self, indicating that human beings are more than a physical body-mind, in many cases completely transforming their understanding of life. The experience can be regarded as a seed for spiritual growth in the perennial principles of Love, Wisdom, and Truth. Although these principles are universal, they are lived and experienced by individuals. Future forms of spirituality will, I believe, draw both on individual experience and timeless tradition, which remains a yardstick of its authenticity and sets it in a broader and deeper context.

TAKING RESPONSIBILITY—
ETHICS AND SOCIETY

A Life as an Argument: The Plight of the Individual in Modern Society

*D*r Albert Schweitzer has been a huge presence and inspiration in my *life for over fifty years. I first got to know his work as an organist as my mother had a collection of his recordings, some of which were made in the parish church at Gunsbach (in 1950, when he was seventy-five) where he lived when he was in Europe, and others in Strasbourg and London. In the 1960s, I had an old reel to reel tape recorder on which I played the Toccata and Fugues in D minor and A minor, and the great Fantasia and Fugue in G minor. Since that time I have accumulated an extensive collection of Bach's organ works played by many different organists, and among my favourites are Piet Kee and Marie-Claire Alain. Schweitzer is best-known for his work as a medical missionary, and I describe some of his life path below. He raised money for his hospital in Lambarene by giving organ recitals and lectures in Europe, including the famous Gifford Lectures in Edinburgh—he also received honorary doctorates from many universities, including Oxford and Cambridge. Uniquely, he himself had four doctorates: in philosophy, theology, music, and medicine.*

In 2016, I arranged a conference on the fiftieth anniversary of his death. At that time, he was one of the most famous people in the world, but few people have heard of him these days, still fewer of his writings in philosophy, ethics, and theology. The award of the Nobel Peace Prize in 1954 catapulted Schweitzer to worldwide fame, and he appeared in extensive features in Time Magazine *and* Paris Match, *among others. Erica Anderson made a film about his life, which you can still access on YouTube. He was once asked how best to change the world. He said there were three ways: the first was by example, the second was by example, and the third was by example—recalling Gandhi's famous remark that we have to be the change we want to see in the world. I hope the following two essays, first published in 1981, will provide you with some inspiration.*

The visitor to Kaysersberg, Albert Schweitzer's birthplace, will find a commemorative statue of him in the main square. The inscription is disarmingly simple: Albert Schweitzer 1875–1965, PRIX NOBEL DE LA PAIX. No doubt the local committee soon realised the impossibility of listing his achievements beneath the rugged carved head, hewn from a local stone. Even an enumeration of his various roles of physician, musician, philosopher, theologian, etc. would have appeared cumbersome and long-winded. Hence the laconic epitaph. On the hill overlooking the church and village of Gunsbach, where Schweitzer's father had been pastor, and where he himself built a house and recorded Bach's organ works, there is another statue. It is hewn from the same red stone, but is full-size, and portrays Schweitzer, pencil in hand, concentrating intensely on a book. This statue conveys an impression of massiveness and a rare degree of inner power. These memorials, however, only achieve their full impact in the light of knowledge of the man, his work, and his thought. This article focuses on Schweitzer's diagnosis of the plight of the individual in modern society, the way in which he himself responded to this, and the role which he felt the individual capable of assuming in fostering a more humane climate in human affairs.

Elemental philosophy

In the epilogue of *My Life and Thought*, Schweitzer makes a distinction of crucial importance to those who approach philosophy according to the true meaning of the term, as lovers of wisdom not merely of words: he distinguishes between elemental and unelemental thinking. The former, he asserts, is "that which starts from the fundamental questions about the relations of man to the universe, about the meaning of life, and about the nature of goodness. It stands in the most immediate connection with the thinking which impulse starts in everyone. It enters that thinking, widening and deepening it."

By contrast, unelemental philosophy no longer has as its focal point humanity's relation to the world. Man (I use this term advisedly) becomes an analysing spectator of his existence, as opposed to a participant in it. He indulges in logical and epistemological speculations that are only of peripheral relevance to the central and elemental questions. The logical positivist abolishes metaphysics altogether as unverifiable: philosophising in this sense consists of mastering a virtuosity of technique, while discussions about definitions replace those about problems on fact.

In short, such a philosophy can only further uproot an already rootless modern humanity, and has totally forgotten its original purpose of formulating a meaningful world view. In the preface to *The Decay and Restoration of Civilisation* Schweitzer asserts that "The future of civilisation hangs on our overcoming the meaninglessness and hopelessness that characterise the thoughts and convictions of men today, and reaching a state of fresh hope and fresh determination." He sees humanity bogged down in a swamp of scepticism, whose origins lie in the reaction of disappointment to the optimistic idea of progress engendered by the Enlightenment. As a result of this people have lost confidence in their ability to think for themselves, have laid themselves open to the impinging of external authority, and have stunted their potential for spiritual growth.

The danger of dehumanisation

Schweitzer saw the number of self-employed artisans declining with the rural exodus, and the absorption of craftsmen into larger organisations. These new employees were separated from the soil, their homes, and from nature. Moreover, they were caught up in long hours of monotonous occupations, which made mental collectedness and self-control in leisure hours more difficult. Rather than opportunities for self-improvement, the workers sought entertainment, complete idleness, and diversion from their usual activities. Aided by habit, the mentality of the mass of individuals became spiritually relaxed, thus leading to increased superficiality in culture and reading: not to mention conversation, where a real exchange of ideas was generally avoided, and restricted to banalities.

Furthermore, the immense increase in technical knowledge forced specialisation, hence only partial use of human faculties, and brought with it a concomitant narrowing of horizons and sympathy. Schweitzer found even more worrying the danger of man losing his humanity. We all live in a hurry and work with many other people, often in crowded surroundings. We therefore tend to encounter each other as strangers and do not always feel able to make the extra effort required to treat those we meet as individuals.

In addition, chessboard-like war strategies have encouraged men to think of others as mere objects in the material world. Schweitzer argued that as soon as we forget our relationship towards our fellow human beings, we are on a path to inhumanity, and concluded that "Wherever there is loss of consciousness that every man is an object of concern for us just because he is a man, civilisation and morals are shaken, and the advance towards fully developed inhumanity is only a question of time."

Finally comes the effect of over-organisation of our public life. While not denying that this is to an extent inevitable, Schweitzer contends that, when developed beyond a certain point, organisations operate at the expense of spiritual life—personality and ideas are subordinated to the institution. Public opinion and propaganda threaten our freedom of thought. We are likened to a rubber ball that has lost its elasticity, and preserves indefinitely every impression made on it. Without independence of thought, we will renounce our faith in truth thought out by the individual. Moreover, we also surrender our personal moral judgment if we fail to uphold our personal opinion. In such circumstances, we may bow to public pressure, no longer judging by the standards of morality but by those of expediency, thus accelerating the de-moralisation of the individual by the mass.

C. G. Jung shared Schweitzer's concern for the fate of the individual. In his essay *The Undiscovered Self* he stresses that individuals render themselves obsolete as soon as they combine with the mass and level themselves down to an anonymous unit. And in a letter of January 1955 he emphasises the role of scientific rationalism in reducing the significance of the individual, as well as our own lack of insight into the nature of the group:

> Natural laws are in the main mere abstractions (being statistical averages) instead of reality, and they abolish individual existence as being merely exceptional. But the individual as the only carrier of life is of paramount importance. He cannot be substituted by a

group formed by a mass, yet we are rapidly approaching the state in which nobody will accept individual responsibility any more. We prefer to leave it as an odious business to groups and organisations, blissfully unconscious of the fact that the group or mass psyche is that of an animal and wholly inhuman.

Schweitzer's stand

Early in his school days, Schweitzer became aware of the fact that the other village children resented him being better clothed than they were. He was mortified, and his native stubbornness made him determined not to be better off. He refused to wear a new overcoat and was repeatedly beaten, "but I stood firm", he relates. Then there was a fiasco in Strasbourg over the choice of a new cap; in the end, Schweitzer prevailed in his insistence on a brown one from the unsaleable stock!

By his own account, the most important experience of his childhood concerns a friend's proposal, near the end of Lent, to accompany him on a bird shoot with a catapult. The unsuspecting birds were singing merrily as the hunters approached and took aim. Suddenly the distant church bells rang out, prompting Schweitzer to frighten the birds away and flee home. The bells had driven into his heart the commandment "Thou shalt not kill". This experience foreshadowed his later discovery of the ethic of reverence for life, and also had an important immediate effect: "From that day onward I took courage to emancipate myself from the fear of men, and whenever my inner convictions were at stake I let other people's opinions weigh less heavily with me than they had done previously. I also tried to unlearn my former dread of being laughed at by my schoolfellows."

During his teens Schweitzer went through what he described as "an unpleasant ferment" during which he became "a nuisance to everybody through a passion for discussion". He inflicted on everyone he met thoroughgoing closely reasoned considerations concerning all current questions "in order to expose the errors of conventional views". He remarked that his motive was not that of egotistical disputatiousness but rather "a passionate need of thinking, and of seeking the help of others for the truth". This led to inward rebellion against vacuous chatter, and he wondered "how far we can carry this good breeding without harm to our integrity".

In later life he also displayed a cavalier disregard for some of the more gushing social niceties. Erica Anderson relates Schweitzer saying amusingly on their second morning at Lambarene, "You probably expect me to ask how you slept last night ... but I won't ... I gave that up long ago. If you ask such questions you get interminable answers: 'Oh, I was still awake at three in the morning, docteur. At four I heard an owl screech, at five a frog croak, and so on ...'" Similarly, Frederic Franck learned not to offer excuses for arriving late at meals. "It is a rational procedure," Schweitzer explained, "otherwise I have to go through this boring routine of 'I'm sorry—it does not matter, don't mention it—yes that I could not help it, I hate to be late, and so on ad infinitum.'" So much for mimicry of refinements.

A resolution

In 1896, at the age of twenty-one, Schweitzer came to an important resolution—"There came to me ... the thought but I must not accept this happiness as a matter of course, but must give something in return for it ... I would consider myself justified in living till I was 30 for science and art, in order to devote myself from that time forward to the direct service of humanity." He counted on learning the nature of that service in the interval. Meanwhile Schweitzer pursued his doctoral studies of Kant and the eschatology of the New Testament. He published two doctoral theses, and his *Quest for the Historical Jesus* burst on the theological world in 1906. He was ordained curate in 1900, appointed lecturer in theology in 1902, and principal of the theological seminary in 1903. His prodigious energy was able to match the scope and intensity of his activities, which frequently left little time for sleep. He claimed that one could burn the candle at both ends, provided that the candle was long enough!

Musical studies

During this time Schweitzer was also developing his reputation as an organist and had taken lessons in Paris with Widor, with whom he later worked on a complete edition of Bach's works. The young man, when asked what he wanted to play on meeting the composer for the first time, had replied without hesitation, "Bach, of course." His book on Bach appeared in 1905 in French, and he completely rewrote it for the German edition some years later. When they were sitting up in the loft in Notre Dame with the light streaming through the Rose window, Widor gave his definition of organ playing as "the manifestation of a will filled with a vision of eternity".

This formulation appealed deeply to Schweitzer, who saw the organ as the "rapprochement of the human spirit to the eternal, imperishable spirit". Through the performer, Bach is able to transport us from a world of unrest to a world of peace; but the interpreter himself must be in a consecrated frame of mind, for Schweitzer asserts, "Bach's music depends for its effect not on the perfection, but on the spirit of the performance." For Schweitzer, Bach was an anchor of tranquillity. The reader can still share this experience, as many of his recordings on the Gunsbach village organ from 1950 are still available.

His resolution fulfilled

In the autumn of 1904, Schweitzer found an appeal for doctors in the Congo from the Paris Missionary Society. His search for a path of service was over, but his relatives and friends joined together in expostulating with him over the folly of his enterprise. He had a secure post and a growing reputation as a philosopher, theologian, and organist; he was burying his talents: his plan was a perverted form of pride, or the result of some secret disappointment. However, Schweitzer had carefully considered the plan and his talents, and was even able to envisage its ultimate failure. He wryly observed that "Anyone who proposes to do good must not expect people to roll stones out of his way, but must accept his lot calmly if they even roll a few more upon it. A strength that becomes clearer and stronger through its experience of such obstacles is the only strength that can conquer them." Schweitzer enrolled at his old university as a medical student, while continuing most of his other multifarious activities. He embarked for Africa with his wife in 1913, and divided the rest of his life between medical work at Lambarene and fundraising tours in Europe—lecturing and giving organ recitals.

The regeneration of society

In his essay *The Undiscovered Self*, C. G. Jung wrote:

> What we need is the development of the inner spiritual man, the unique individual whose treasure is hidden on the one hand in the

symbols of our mythological tradition, and on the other hand in man's unconscious psyche ... if the individual could be improved, it seems to me that a foundation would be laid for the improvement of the whole. Even a million noughts do not add up to one. I therefore espouse the unpopular review that a better understanding in the world can only come from the individual and be promoted only by him.

Schweitzer echoes these words:

The renewal of civilisation has nothing to do with the character of experiences of the crowd; these are never anything but reactions to external happenings. But civilisation can only revive when there shall come into being in a number of individuals a new turn of mind independent of the prevalent one among the crowd and in opposition to it, the tone of mind that will gradually win influence over the collective one, and in the end determine its character. It is only an ethical movement that can rescue us from the slough of barbarism, and the ethical comes into existence only in individuals.

Radhakrishnan, the philosopher president of India, expressed himself in similar terms:

The great ideas that move the world and exalt character ... come from the poets and thinkers ... thought is the essence of action ... life governed by ideals and philosophies are at the back of all revolutionary movements ... what we are is the result of what we think ... we cannot change the social order unless we change ourselves ... a more effective social order means a different quality of men ...

Schweitzer explains the divergence of individual and collective values as an unavoidable conflict:

Modern utilitarianism loses its sensitiveness to the duty of humanity in proportion to the consistency with which it develops into the ethics of organised society. It cannot be otherwise. The essence of humanity consists in individuals never allowing themselves to think impersonally in terms of expediency as society does, or to sacrifice individual existences in order to gain their object.

He argues that the great mistake of ethical thought has been in failing to admit the essential difference between the morality of an ethical personality and that which is established from the standpoint of society. As a result, the former is sacrificed to the latter, but the dichotomy remains: "Either the moral standard of personality raises the moral standard of society, so far as it is possible, to its own level, or it is dragged down by it."

The prevailing level of humaneness is thus a matter of individual responsibility, the voicing of the convictions of conscience. Such convictions of conscience can only be arrived at through elemental force, which implies inward spiritual emancipation rather than subservience to the interests of the group. Scepticism has sapped confidence in our own thinking, so that the individual view is dismissed as "merely subjective" by the conventional authority holding its own view as "objective".

Unfortunately, as outlined above, acquiescence to authority can only result in the annihilation not the transcendence of individuality—the submergence of the individual in the unconscious mass. It is important to realise that elemental force does not mean abstract theorising or lack of concern: on the contrary, it leads to a realisation of the interdependence of life, the oneness of being, to a sympathetic concern for all forms of life. This is Schweitzer's ethic of reverence for life fulfilled in action: "Whenever my life devotes itself in any way to life, my finite will to live experiences union with the infinite will in which all life is one, and I enjoy a feeling of refreshment that prevents me from pining away in the desert of life."

Schweitzer quotes Goethe in a similar context (he was awarded the Goethe Prize in 1932 and wrote a couple of wonderful essays about him):

> Be true to yourself and true to others,
> And let thy striving be in love,
> And thy life be an act.

"The great enemy of ethics is insensitivity," contended Schweitzer in one of his sermons. On the intellectual plane, loss of sensitivity is equivalent to what he called "resigned reasonableness", which a man acquires by modelling himself on others and abandoning his youthful ideals and concern. He once believed in the victory of truth, in humanity, in the good, in justice, and in the power of kindness and peaceableness. But these high-minded impulses have been inexorably dissolved by a corrosive cynicism. Schweitzer does not underestimate the difficulty of holding to such ideals. Writing at the end of *My Childhood and Youth* he observes: "We must all be prepared to find that life tries to take from us our belief in the good and true, and our enthusiasm for them, but we need not surrender them." If we do so, then our ideals are not strong enough; they must be experienced and transmitted through ourselves: "Grow into your ideals", he advises, "so that life can never rob you of them."

The individual is called upon to cultivate contrasting qualities of sensitivity and peaceableness on the one hand, and courage and independence of thought on the other. In our own radius, we can use kindness to heal misunderstanding, mistrust, and hostility, but we must stand firm and speak out in the face of temptations to inhumanity. The light must radiate without, the seed must be sown, as Goethe put it, "without worrying as to how large the harvest will be or where it will come up". Using Schweitzer's phrase, we must have "the soul of a dove in the hide of an elephant".

The Ethic of "Reverence for Life" and the Problem of Peace

In the 1980s, I was part of the British Council of the University for Peace (www.upeace.org), set up through the UN General Assembly in Costa Rica in 1980 by the then President Rodrigo Carazo Odio, who attended one of our meetings. Since that time UPeace has trained 2,000 leaders from more than 120 nations in master's and doctoral programmes—this is probably the first time you have read about it, which is symptomatic of our time. Another extraordinary man I came across in the same context was Dr Robert Muller (1923–2010, www.robertmuller.org), a charismatic assistant secretary-general of the UN, who was also chancellor of the University for Peace. He had unquenchable optimism and radiated joy and energy—he was also the creator of the world core curriculum. In our current turbulent times, it is easy to fall prey to pessimism and even despair, but these prophetic human beings remind us that visions and ideals are key components in co-creating a peaceful and sustainable future. They also emphasise, as do other thinkers quoted below, the inherent relationship between inner and outer peace—the chaos we see is an outer reflection of our collective inner states. This is where we as individuals need to start while initiating corresponding ethical actions to help realise our ideals. Contrary to the usual adage, if you want peace, prepare for war, UPeace proposes that if you want peace, prepare for peace.

"Only to the extent that the peoples of the world foster within themselves the ideal of peace will those institutions whose object is the preservation of that peace be able to function as we expect, and hope, that they will."
—Dr Albert Schweitzer, Nobel Peace Prize address

Readers of my previous article may recall the inscription under the commemorative statue of Albert Schweitzer in Kaysersberg: it simply ran "Prix Nobel de la Paix", an honour bestowed on a man who was passionately concerned with the problem of peace in the world, and whose philosophy of "Reverence for Life" can represent an ethical starting point from which to approach the problem of peace.

The German formulation of the ethic—*Ehrfurcht vor dem Leben*—is more explicit in its associations than the English Reverence, which unfailingly conjures up images of priests and perhaps altars; its roots are in the words honour and fear—honour in the sense of the old Testament commandment, and fear in the sense of awe in the face of the phenomenon of life, in its mystery and astonishing diversity.

Reverence for Life

Schweitzer describes the flash of insight which brought the phase Reverence for Life to his mind. For three days he had been on board a boat in tropical Africa, and had been struggling to find the elementary and universal conception of the ethical which as yet he had not discovered in any philosophy. He kept himself concentrated on the problem by covering sheet after sheet with disconnected ramblings, and it was only late on the third day that the formula which he had been seeking sprang as if spontaneously into his mind—Reverence for Life—the iron door had yielded "the path in the thicket had become visible". He now had an idea which enabled him to affirm the world and life in an ethical framework.

This terminology perhaps requires some explanation: Schweitzer felt that a *Weltanschauung* (world view) which renounced the world to concentrate on the perfection of the self in isolation was not helpful to life, and was in fact amoral. He therefore dismissed the ascetic rejection of the world advocated by some Buddhists, although he had more sympathy with the idea of the Bodhisattva, the sage who would not enter Nirvana himself before the last person had attained it. Perfection of the self in isolation was not, according to Schweitzer, the highest form of development, which must also involve some kind of devotion to the welfare of others. This in turn means accepting to work in the world, without, however, necessarily accepting the world's values. Thus Schweitzer was following Jesus's advice to be in the world but not of it, which implies some form of action, not retreat and quietism. We have already seen how Schweitzer applied this to his own life.

Schweitzer had his own characteristic formulation of the Cartesian *cogito ergo sum*—he claims that the most immediate fact of man's consciousness is the assertion, "I am life which wills to live in the midst of life which wills to live." It is immediately apparent that Descartes's formula has taken on a new orientation: it is no longer confined to thinking beings to whom the reality of thought is paramount, but has been extended to cover a much wider conception of life. The will to live or to survive is inherent in any living organism. Moreover, it emphasises that humans are only one of many forms of life, thus implying that our special status may be self-appointed and not intrinsic. However, insight is the gift of thought, of that special mode of thinking which was referred to in the previous article as "elemental", that is, concerned directly with the problems of existence, in contrast to refined philosophical hair-splitting.

Schweitzer defines deepened world—and life—affirmation as follows: "that we have the will to maintain our own life and every kind of existence that we can in any way influence, and to bring them to their highest value". There are obvious cases where one form of life needs to be sacrificed to another, but the principle nevertheless provides a criterion by which decisions can be made. Schweitzer sees his ethical formulation as an extension or universalisation of Jesus's ethic of love; compassion is not to be shown merely to members of one's family, race, or species, but is extended to all forms of life, including the planet itself. The edict of reverence for life is, according to Schweitzer, the rule of universal love, a love which confers value and meaning on the actions of life.

Ethical mysticism

For individuals who have grasped this principle with their whole mind, the result can only be an elemental responsibility towards all forms of life which cross our path; a responsibility which is constantly asking questions about thoughts and behaviour, and which is constantly urging the individual to act in accordance with the principles which they have apprehended. Schweitzer insists that this involves a rejection of relativism. The principle "recognises as good only the preserving and benefiting of life: any injury to, and destruction of, life, unless it is imposed on us by fate, is regarded as evil. It does not have a large stock of compromises between ethics and necessity." If we now revert to the idea of world-affirmation in relation to the individual's sense of elemental responsibility while bearing in mind the saying of Jesus that a man must be prepared to lose his self in order to find his soul, we can see the logic of what Schweitzer calls "ethical mysticism", in contrast to the intellectual mysticism of ascetic self-perfection.

On the one hand ethical mysticism admits that the world and life are absolutely mysterious and unfathomable, but on the other it knows that all Being is life "and that in loving self-devotion to other life we realise our spiritual union with infinite Being". In spite of the metaphysical nature of the language—and therefore the questions of defining exactly what is meant by being and spiritual union—the importance of this message can scarcely be overestimated: the individual secures the inner perfection of their personality by loving devotion to other forms of life, thus balancing and satisfying the demands of the internal and the external. It is interesting to note that a similar formulation was advanced by the historian Arnold Toynbee (1889–1975): he pointed out that life and egoism are interchangeable terms—"Altruism, alias love, is an attempt to reverse the natural effort of a living being to organise the universe round itself. Love is a counter attempt, on the living being's part, to devote itself to the universe instead of exploiting the universe. Self-devotion and self-sacrifice means orienting oneself towards some centre of the universe that is not oneself." Elsewhere he adds, "Love is the spiritual impulse to give instead of take. It is the impulse to bring the self back into harmony with the universe, from which it has been estranged by its innate, but not unconquerable self-centredness." Thus he is also arguing that the harmony and therefore fulfilment of the individuality involves devotion to and not exploitation of the universe and life.

Indian philosopher-president Sarvepalli Radhakrishnan describes the goal of civilised society as a state of non-violence and unselfishness which emerges from the earlier stages of the law of the jungle and the impartial rule of law, where moral responsibility was as yet insufficiently developed to exercise self-discipline. One does not have to look very far in order to appreciate how far removed we still are from this state: indeed, Radhakrishnan himself hints that such a state is unattainable when he asserts that life at best is a long second best, the perpetual compromise between the ideal and the possible. It goes without saying that this is not a reason for downing one's tools and throwing up one's hands in despair, but rather a cautionary note of realism for the benefit of those who think Utopia is just round the corner; the struggle has to be renewed daily.

In turn, Schweitzer considers that there are three kinds of progress significant for culture: "Progress in knowledge and technology; progress in the socialisation of man; progress in spirituality. The last is the most important." Elsewhere, he observes that technical progress and extension of knowledge do indeed represent progress, but not in fundamentals: *"The essential thing is that we become more finely and deeply human"* (my italics). Progress of the first kind has made man into a superman; he is now able to harness and control many of the latent forces of nature. We have also achieved a certain amount in the area of socialisation, but progress in this sphere has been limited by conflict between large socialised groups, even if there exists some degree of coherence and unity within the groups. The third kind of progress is now a pressing necessity: "This superman suffers from a fatal imperfection of mind. He has not raised himself to that superhuman level of reason which should correspond to the possession of superhuman strength." As an example Schweitzer quotes the conquest of the air as a decisive step forward for humanity, "but mankind at once took advantage of it to kill and destroy from a height. This invention forces us to acknowledge something which we had previously refused to admit: that the superman is impoverished, not enriched, by the increase in his powers." We have now reached the stage where the danger is not merely that of impoverishment through increase of powers, but rather the continued survival of the human race: as Jung pointed out, we now have the power to impose a new deluge on ourselves, and are thus directly responsible for the survival or destruction of life on the planet.

Nationalism

One of the greatest obstacles to reaching agreement on the common interests of humanity is the existence of the kind of nationalism which attributes only semi-human status to those outside the group: as Bertrand Russell put it—'It is difficult to resist the conclusion that most of the makers of opinion consider it more important to secure defeat of the 'enemy', than to safeguard the continued existence of our species." Fear and mistrust are still rampant, the enemy is seen as malicious and threatening; we must therefore defend ourselves against this monster. Meanwhile corresponding arguments are voiced on the other side, and the vicious circle is perpetuated. As Reinhold Niebuhr indicated, one of the apparently insurmountable problems is that the personal egoism of individual members of a nation may be sublimated into a national egoism of individual members of a nation, and the politicians are first and foremost defenders of the national interest and therefore of the national self-respect and pride.

Writing in 1946 Jung commented that "It is self-evident that it would be highly desirable to humanise humanity, but one sees the struggle the great powers have in order to reach agreement on apparently the most reasonable measures for the well-being of the world, and how they fail because one or the other refuses to be talked to or cannot give way." Russell is equally pessimistic about the obstacle of national pride: "The love of national independence is so strong in every state so that public opinion prefers the risk of war, however appalling, to being at the mercy of an international force. Much terrible experience will be necessary before mankind prefers an international state to death and destruction." Both Russell and Jung feel that it is too much to hope that we will be dissuaded from waging war by the atrocities associated with our previous experience of the phenomenon.

There has as yet been no war to end war (that was the hope after World War I), even though our current nuclear capabilities enable us to put an end to life, not just war. Einstein is said to have declared that a fourth world war would be fought with bows and arrows. War violates the oneness of humanity and sanctions atrocious acts of inhumanity. The crux of this issue is whether and when we will become capable of putting the universal interest of humanity ahead of the sectarian interest of nationalism. In normal political terms, as we have seen, this seems to be practically impossible; but nevertheless it must be made possible somehow or other if we are not prepared to run the risk of extinction of humanity and civilisation: neither individual human beings, nor the masterpieces of Chartres Cathedral or Bach's St Matthew Passion can be recreated.

Even if the problem of peace were ostensibly resolved on the political level, the outcome would be little more than a suspension of hostilities if it were not accompanied by a corresponding change of attitude in individual human beings. Krishnamurti calls war the spectacular and bloody projection of everyday life; and Radhakrishnan defines war as the effort of one group of men to impose its will by inflicting death and destruction on another group of men. The roots of war lie in our hearts, in pride and fear, in envy and greed, even though the weaknesses assume national dress. We ourselves may not be directly implicated in warfare, but we participate indirectly through projection of fear and suspicion onto the enemy, and in times of war we are probably guilty of an ambivalent attitude to killing; as Russell pointed out—"Everyone thinks of the enemy as the people who kill, and of our own soldiers as those who face death: the one is brutal, the other heroic." He concludes that because killing is of the essence of war, no one should uphold war who is not himself prepared to kill. The other way in which we are implicated is through our silent acquiescence and resignation in the face of the apparently insurmountable existence of war: to the extent that we resign ourselves to these conditions, we too become guilty of inhumanity.

Nuclear weapons

Nowadays it is impossible to talk of putting an end to war without considering the question of nuclear weapons. Schweitzer calls the Hiroshima bomb a foretaste of the ravages and human misery that the widespread use of such weapons would produce, and adds that to consider waging war with such weapons presupposes an utterly inhuman ideology. The acts of inhumanity perpetrated until now in conventional warfare would be extended potentially to the entire human race. In the event of mutual destruction there would be no one left to celebrate the "victory", no subjugated people to rule, no future. "Victory is no cause for rejoicing," writes Lao Tsu in the Tao te Ching, and he adds that war is conducted like a funeral—"When many people are being killed, they should be mourned in heartfelt sorrow. A victory must be observed like a funeral." In the event of nuclear destruction the funeral might be universal, with no one left to mourn. This possibility seems to be beyond the imagination of many people, who consider that because the effects would be so devastating, the weapons would never be used, but they fail to pursue the line of thought to the logical conclusion that if the weapons are too atrocious to use, then they should not be allowed to exist at all. My friend the visionary psychologist and historian Anne Baring has spoken out passionately against these weapons (see www. annebaring.com and YouTube) and Mikhail Gorbachev has also raised his voice. Our current focus on environmental issues has led us to neglect this crucial issue.

What can be done?

So far, as indicated above, purely political and military approaches to the problem have proved fruitless, so it is essential that another line should be taken, one which can only be initiated on an individual level. We shall consider first the possibilities for organised groups of individuals, and second what individuals can achieve in terms of direct interaction with their surroundings; both of these lines presuppose application of the principle of reverence for life outlined above, namely that the duty and fulfilment of the human being lies in devotion to other forms of life.

"The most crucial key to world peace", writes Arnold Toynbee, "is the promotion of understanding among peoples ... lack of mutual understanding, by creating an endless succession of hatred and fear, eventually leads to destructive consequences."

This calls for an education of both children and public opinion to extend their sympathies beyond neighbourhood and nation, and to try to grasp the interest of humanity as a whole, the humanitarian ideal, rather than their own particular advantage at the expense of another nation or group, as Martin Buber puts it—"Real peace is organic peace. A great peace means cooperation, and nothing else. Anything less than this is nothing." It would be naïve to suppose that such cooperation could emerge overnight over a whole range of issues, but without the belief that such cooperation is possible and a faith in the goodwill which might bring it about, such a scheme could never even get off the ground.

This leads to Schweitzer's proposals that "The command of the hour is that the people of the countries possessing atomic weapons make their voices heard. They must take over responsibility and prove capable of the spiritual act of commitment to humanitarianism. The salvation of mankind depends on such a policy. Lacking it, we are doomed to living in deepening misery, or to final annihilation." He urges public opinion to declare whether it is to stay caught in the ideology of inhumanity, or whether it wishes to adopt the ideology of humanitarianism and demand the abolition of such weapons. Such a policy has in fact been advocated by the Multilateral World Disarmament Campaign, which was set up following the UN Special Session on Disarmament in 1978. This organisation is now attempting to mobilise public opinion and mass support for its petition, which it hopes to present at the 1982 UN Special Session. The 1978 final document deplored the waste of resources on armaments, resources which might be diverted towards more pressing needs. It pointed out that modern armaments no longer defend a nation but threaten the extinction of humankind, and that in order to achieve disarmament "[T]he conscience of mankind must be aroused; the necessary 'political will' must be created to ensure that governments promote meaningful disarmament policies ... world public opinion must be mobilised to the dangers and waste of the arms race."

Those who have the interests of humanity at heart cannot simply stand back in helplessness and despair: they must act themselves and arouse those around them to similar action or else abdicate their humanity by not shouldering this responsibility. As Schweitzer expressed it (in 1923!), "At the present time when violence dominates the world more cruelly than it ever has before, I still remain convinced that truth, love, peaceableness, and kindness are the violence which can master all other violence. The world will be theirs as soon as ever a sufficient number of men with purity of heart, with strength, and with perseverance think and live out the thoughts of love and truth, of meekness and peaceableness." The reader will notice that the emphasis is on the individual, but that the precondition for the success of such a scheme is that a sufficient number of people act in this way. This in turn demands a spiritual commitment and an initial step of faith or confidence, which the person who wishes to devote him- and herself to humanity cannot afford not to make.

"What we can and should change is ourselves," wrote Herman Hesse, "our impatience, our egoism (including intellectual egoism), our sense of injury, our lack of love and forbearance. I regard every other attempt to change the world, even if it springs from the best motives, as futile." I have already quoted Toynbee's form of the same prescription; Dr Winifred Rushforth—a doctor who worked in Edinburgh and corresponded with Jung—expresses it as "the deliverance from fear into a life of creative love and sanity"; and Radhakrishnan talks of non-violence as being not a physical condition "but a mental state of love ... absence of malice and hatred (the inner violence)". He urges that "While we need not lose ourselves in the pursuit of an impossible perfection, we must strive perpetually to eliminate imperfection, and grow towards the ideal."

Apart from the vices and qualities already mentioned, Schweitzer singles out one quality which we can all cultivate, that of kindness. He contends that "All the kindness which a man puts out into the world works on the heart and thoughts of mankind, but we are so foolishly indifferent that we are never in earnest in the matter of kindness. We want to topple a great load over, and yet will not avail ourselves of a lever which would multiply our power a hundredfold." But in order to express such kindness, we must first of all make peace with ourselves and our own destructive impulses, so that we can become beacons of kindness to others: this should not be impossible for any of us, at least in some degree—as Emperor Marcus Aurelius said—"Wherever it is possible to live, it is possible to live well."

In his book *On the Edge of the Primeval Forest*, Schweitzer relates a story from the First World War, which reads even more ironically today than it did then: "About this time it became known that of the Whites who had gone home to fulfil their military duties ten had already been killed, and it made a great impression on the natives. 'Ten men killed already in the war!' said an old Pahouin. 'Why, then, don't the tribes meet for a palaver? How can they pay for all these dead men?' For, with the natives, it is a rule that all who fall in a war, whether on the victorious or on the defeated side, must be paid for by the other side." The implication is that the victor will probably find the payment more expensive than the vanquished. The modern sensibility is no longer shaken at the death of ten men, and seems almost able, or at any rate resigned, to face the possibility of the death of millions. This resignation is a waiving of moral responsibility and can only contribute to the chances of the disaster supervening. As Schweitzer put it in his Nobel Peace Prize address: "In so resigning ourselves, without any further resistance, we ourselves become guilty of inhumanity."

Schweitzer observed that many people to whom he had talked looked back wistfully on the idealism and capacity for enthusiasm of their youth but regarded it as almost a law of nature that people became cynical, resigned, and pessimistic. Schweitzer's challenge on the problems facing the world of today is that although life attempts to remove one's belief in the good and the true, and our enthusiasm for them, we need not surrender them—"That ideals, when they are brought into contact with reality, are usually crushed by facts does not mean that they are bound from the very beginning to capitulate to the facts, but merely that our ideals are not strong enough ... or stable enough in ourselves." The ethic of Reverence for Life imposes on us a limitless responsibility towards other forms of life; in the context of the ideal of world peace, the individual who is aware of this elemental responsibility is obliged to do all in their power to promote the welfare of humanity through cultivation of the humanitarian ideal within their own circle, and through opposition to the atrocious inhumanity of war, violence and the use of nuclear weapons. Conscientious sowers must sow in faith even if they doubt whether the soil will yield a harvest.

The Ethical Mysticism of Dag Hammarskjöld

My copy of Markings *is dated September 1981, when I was just starting my second year teaching at Winchester College (this essay was published in 1983). It is an extraordinary book, revealing as Dag Hammarskjöld (1905–1961*) puts it, "my negotiations with myself—and with God". As his career developed from being chairman of the National Bank of Sweden aged thirty-six to becoming the youngest person to hold the post of secretary-general of the UN, Hammarskjöld realised that the contents of his private diary in terms of a true personal profile might be of interest after his death—and so it has abundantly proved. The book came out in 1964, edited and with an introduction by W. H. Auden, and has regularly been reprinted since that time. It is a unique record of the struggles and insights of a mystical man of action, hence the title of this essay. However, the negotiations to which he refers are those of life itself in which we are all necessarily engaged.*

*Hammarskjöld died in an inexplicable plane crash on September 18, 1961, along with fifteen other passengers. Former US president Harry Truman is reported to have said in a New York Times *article published on September 20, 1961 that "Dag Hammarskjöld was on the point of getting something done when they killed him. Notice I said 'when they killed him.'"*

"In our era, the road to holiness necessarily passes through the world of action."

The reader might be excused for attributing the above quotation of Hammarskjöld's to Albert Schweitzer, whose ethical ideals, in Hammarskjöld's opinion, "were harmonised and adjusted to the world of today", the ideal of service being supported by, and supporting, the basic attitude set forth in the Gospels. When he was installed as secretary-general of the United Nations, Hammarskjöld made the following pledge, to which he was deeply committed: "I solemnly swear to exercise in all loyalty, discretion and conscience the functions entrusted to me as Secretary General of the United Nations, to discharge these functions and regulate my conduct with the interests of the UN only in view, and not to seek or accept instructions in regard to the performance of my duties from any government or authority external to the Organisation." From his father's family, Hammarskjöld had inherited a conviction of the ideal of selfless service to one's country or humanity; such service, he claimed, "required a sacrifice of all personal interests, but likewise the courage to stand up unflinchingly for your convictions". The private man should disappear behind the international public servant. What emerges from Hammarskjöld's *Markings*, published after his untimely death, is his concern, not merely for political impartiality, but also for transcendence of any selfish interests in devoting his talents to the welfare of his fellows.

Building trust

"One of the most curious and most upsetting features about the present world situation is that everybody is afraid of everybody—hence the difficulty of creating trust at an international level." Sadly, Hammarskjöld's remark is no less true some thirty years later. He stressed that there was no alternative to peacefully negotiated agreements, the issue being between "civilisation and the cudgel, between the human and subhuman". He sensed the dangers of ideologies claiming a monopoly on rightness, liberty, and human dignity; this could only lead to self-righteousness and hypocrisy, and had to be combatted by establishing a network of human contacts and communications across geographical and political boundaries—only thus would there be any hope of a true world community coming into existence.

As a negotiator, Hammarskjöld was reputed to be a master of "calculated imprecision" in his efforts to bring two sides to an agreement. A lasting solution, he claimed, could only be achieved "if you have learned to see the other objectively, but, at the same time, to experience his difficulties subjectively". The objectivity required was "a heightened awareness combined with an inner quiet", and the experiencing of the other's difficulties subjectively entailed a kind of humility which suspended judgment. The hazard of this manoeuvre was that, by becoming a chameleon, he thus aroused the suspicions of both parties.

A lonely mountaineer

On one occasion, he characterised the qualities needed in his job as those of a mountaineer: "perseverance and patience, a firm grip on realities, careful but imaginative planning, a clear awareness of the dangers, but also of the fact that fate is what we make it, and that the safest climber is he who never questions his ability to overcome all difficulties". There are in fact, few distinctions between the political and spiritual mountaineer: faith and courage are required in both undertakings. Since, as we have seen, impartiality was of the essence of Hammarskjöld's position, he had to weigh up any advice very circumspectly and arrive at the most dispassionate possible judgment or decision; in this he realised that ultimate responsibility meant ultimate loneliness and isolation. Moreover, Hammarskjöld never married (he claimed he would not have had the time), and suffered acutely from a sense of loneliness. In a poem describing the experience of being awoken by his own scream, he characterises it as "the voice of loneliness screaming for love". Yet it would be misleading to imagine that Hammarskjöld's dreams were only nightmares. Elsewhere, he describes a vision of paradise: "In a dream, I walked with God through the deep places of creation: past walls that receded and gates that opened, through hall after hall of silence, darkness, and refreshment—the dwelling place of souls acquainted with light and warmth—until, around me, was an infinity into which we all flowed together and lived anew, like the rings made by raindrops falling upon wide expanses of calm, dark waters."

Such a harmony of vision was attainable for Hammarskjöld only at the end of a long and arduous trail. The search and the effort are described in the following poem:

Echoing silence

Darkness lit up by beams
Light
Seeking its counterpart

In melody
Stillness
Striving for liberation
In a word
Life
In dust
In shadow
How seldom growth and blossom
How seldom fruit

A disconsolate tone, but an eternal inspiration. The theme of striving is taken up again in one of Hammarskjöld's poems, the first sentence of which is often quoted on its own:

The longest journey
Is the journey inwards.
Of him who has chosen his destiny,
Who has started on his quest
For the source of his being
(Is there a source?)
He is still with you,
But without relation,
Isolated in your feeling
Like one condemned to death
Or one whom imminent farewell
Prematurely dedicates
To the loneliness which is the final lot of all.

The last line contradicts his vision of heaven. Here he is without relation, while above he talked of an infinity "into which we all flowed together and lived anew"; but, without the possibility of the pendulum swinging to despair, neither can there be hope. He reaches out from his isolation, and senses a force beyond himself beckoning him on, transcending his feeling of isolation:

Now. When I have overcome my fears—of others, of myself, of the underlying darkness—at the frontier of the unheard-of:
Here ends the known. But, from a source beyond it, something fills my being with its possibilities.

He is not alone; but the striving to overcome the isolation opens up new challenges involving freedom from fear, openness to life, and love. Once the negative blockages are removed, the self is freed to become the creative instrument of a positive and outflowing love. The following two prayers express the wishes and the qualities required to bring them about:

> Hallowed by Thy Name, *not mine*
> Thy kingdom come, *not mine*
> Thy will be done, *not mine*
> Give us peace with Thee,
> Peace with men,
> Peace with ourselves,
> And free us from all fear.

* * *

> Thou who art over us,
> Thou who art one of us,
> Thou who *art*—
> Also within us
> May all see thee—in me also
> May I prepare the way for Thee,
> May I thank Thee for all that shall fall to my lot,
> May I not forget the needs of others;
> Keep me in Thy love
> As Thou wouldest that all should be kept in mine.
> May everything in this my being be directed to Thy glory,
> And may I never despair,
> For I am under Thy hand,
> And in Thee all power and goodness.

> Give me a pure heart—that I may see Thee,
> A humble heart—that I may hear Thee,
> A heart of Love—that I may serve Thee,
> A heart of faith—that I may abide in Thee.

Dag Hammarskjöld defines faith as a state of the mind or soul, not something to be apprehended rationally. He claims that, "Only through the self-knowledge we gain by pursuing the fleeting light in the depth of our being, do we reach the point where we can grasp what faith is." The kind of self-knowledge referred to above, he found in the writings of the mediaeval mystics, "for whom self-surrender had been the way of self-realisation". Their faith enabled them to live out a constant affirmation of the demands of life, so that Love (which Hammarskjöld comments is a much misused word) "for them meant simply an overflowing of the strength with which they felt themselves filled when living in true self-oblivion. And this love found natural expression in an unhesitant fulfilment of duty and an unreserved acceptance of life, whatever it brought them personally of toil, suffering—or happiness."

Hammarskjöld's description of the mediaeval mystics embodies his own aspirations and ideals, a "life of active social service in full harmony with himself as a member of the community of the spirit". This creative self-effacement is the dominating fugal theme running through *Markings*; the varieties of its expression make it difficult to harmonise all the appropriate aspects without some degree of repetition.

Self-effacement

We shall start by citing some of the more comprehensive statements, moving on to a consideration of some of the qualities acquired and required in self-effacement, finally seeing how these qualities can be expressed in action. Hammarskjöld's starting point is the assertion referred to in connection with the mystics: that self-realisation can only be achieved through self-surrender, the "self" finding its true nature in the "Self":

> Clad in this "self", the creation of irresponsible and ignorant persons, meaningless honours and catalogued acts—strapped into the strait-jacket of the immediate.
> To step out of all this, and stand naked on the precipice of dawn—acceptable, invulnerable, free: in the Light, with the Light, of the Light. *Whole*, real in the Whole.
> Out of myself as a stumbling block, into myself as a fulfilment.

An interesting echo of this sentiment can be found in a letter written by Jung in his old age to the Earl of Sandwich:

> Old age is only half as funny as one is inclined to think. It is at all events the gradual breaking down of the bodily machine, with

which foolishness identifies ourselves. It is indeed a major effort—
the *magnum opus* in fact—to escape in time from the narrowness of
its embrace and to liberate our mind to the vision of the immensity
of the world, of which we form an infinitesimal part.

Both men speak of the limitations of identifying oneself with one's
bodily entity, and yearn for the freedom of the limitless, expressed by
Hammarskjöld in terms of light (the central symbol in *The Secret of the
Golden Flower*, for which Jung wrote a commentary). The image is developed as follows:

> You are not the oil, you are not the air—merely the point of combus-
> tion, the flash point where the Light is born.
>   You are merely the lens in the beam. You can only receive, give
> and possess the Light as a lens does.
>   You seek yourself, "your rights", you prevent the oil and air
> from meeting in the flame, you rob the lens of its transparency.
>   Sanctity—either to be the Light, or to be self-effaced in the Light,
> so that it may be born, self-effaced so that it may be focused or
> spread wider.

In this context, the self as a channel is both filter and obstruction; as a
manifestation of the Light, the interference must if possible be eliminated.
Brother Roger of Taizé writes in similar terms. For him the unity of the
personality is the reconciliation of the self with God, an insight grasped
only in fleeting moments, and one which must be "returned to, tirelessly".
The "transparency" to which he aspires takes years and years to acquire
(he also uses the term "limpidity"). He does, however, add that, "for anyone who renews this transparency day after day, times of peace come,
and, with them, such joy"; and that "The more we live in transparency,
the more we become a source of peace for those around us."

Dag Hammarskjöld, Brother Roger of Taizé and C. G. Jung are all
acutely aware of reaching towards transcendence, but equally that
the distractions of time and changing circumstances are constantly
diverting or diluting our energies. Some of the principal qualities
which Hammarskjöld himself strove to cultivate in his efforts towards
self-effacing transparency were stillness, equanimity, humility, and
the capacity to forgive; all these found their eventual overflow into
love, in which the self remains as a means while vanishing as an end,

202 A QUEST FOR WISDOM

finding its fulfilment and meaning in a sense of what Hammarskjöld calls "co-inherence".

Stillness

Amid the bustle and pressure at the UN, Hammarskjöld must have regarded stillness as an essential requirement for the maintenance of internal equilibrium and proportion. Two entries illustrate his feelings: "To preserve the silence within—amid all the noise. To remain open and quiet, a moist humus in the fertile darkness where the rain falls and the grain ripens—no matter how many tramp across the parade-ground in whirling dust under an arid sky."

> Understand—through the stillness,
> Act—out of the stillness,
> Conquer—in the stillness.
> In order for the eye to perceive colour, it must divest itself of all colours.

The last quotation related the stillness back to the image of light. The stillness is Eliot's "still point of the turning world", at once a place of refuge and restoration, and the point of clear perspective.

For Hammarskjöld stillness and equanimity were linked: "We have to acquire a peace and balance of mind, such that we can give every word of criticism its due weight, and humble ourselves before every word of praise."

Detachment

This is undoubtedly a counsel of perfection in a society which so consciously cultivates the external image. The deliberate adjustment, which Hammarskjöld was attempting to make, corresponds in some ways with the state of mind recommended by the Taoist sage, who remains "unattached and calm" in his conviction that tranquillity cannot be achieved through the dependency of desire. Lao Tsu asks:

> Fame or self: which matters more?
> Self or wealth; which is more precious?
> Gain or loss; which is more painful?

> He who is attached to things will suffer much.
> He who saves will suffer heavy loss.
> A contented man is never disappointed.

He urges people to accept disgrace and favour willingly, to accept being unimportant, and not to be concerned with loss or gain. Chuang Tsu takes this further in a passage which he attributes to Confucius, where acceptance results from insight into the nature of change, of alternation between the principles of yin and yang:

> Life and death, profit and loss, failure and success, poverty and wealth, value and worthlessness, praise and blame, hunger and thirst, cold and heat—these are natural changes in the order of things. They alternate with one another like day and night. No one knows where one ends and the other begins. Therefore they should not disturb our peace, nor enter into our souls. Live so that you are at ease, in harmony with the world, and full of joy. Day and night, share the springtime with all things, thus creating the seasons of your own heart. This is called achieving full harmony.

Hammarskjöld recognises the reality of mixed motives in decision-making, for every side of our characters plays an important part in the process. In spiritual striving, the dilemma is poignantly expressed by Becket in Eliot's *Murder in the Cathedral*:

> Is there no way, in my soul's sickness,
> Does not lead to damnation in pride?

Humility

Hammarskjöld declares that, even as Mephisto smilingly declares himself the winner, "He can still be defeated by the manner in which we accept the consequences of our action." He exhorts himself never to "let success hide its emptiness from you, achievement its nothing-ness, toil its desolation. And so keep alive the incentive to push fur-ther, that pain in the soul which drives us beyond ourselves. Whither? That I don't know. That I don't ask to know." This last sentence brings us back to his idea of faith, for him a precondition of the next quality, humility.

Humility is just as much the opposite of self-abasement as it is of self-exaltation. To be humble *is not to make comparisons*. Secure in its reality, the self is neither better nor worse, bigger nor smaller, than everything else in the universe. It *is*—is nothing, yet at the same time one with everything. It is in this sense that humility is absolute self-effacement.

To be nothing in the self-effacement of humility, yet, for the sake of the task, to embody *its* whole weight and importance in your bearing, as the one who has been called to undertake it: To give to people, works, art, what the self can contribute, and to state, simply and freely, what belongs to it by reason of its identity: Praise and blame, the winds of success and adversity, blow over such a life without leaving a trace or upsetting its balance:

Toward this, so help me, God.

The passage shows the links in Hammarskjöld's mind between self-effacement and the qualities of humility and equanimity; significantly, he transforms the commentary into a prayer. He makes another connection between humility and the stillness necessary for undistorted perception:

To have humility is to experience reality, *not in relation to ourselves*, but in its sacred independence. It is to see, judge, and act from the point of rest in ourselves. Then, how much disappears, and all that remains falls into place.

In the point of rest at the centre of our being, we encounter a world where all things are at rest in the same way. Then a tree becomes a mystery, a cloud a revelation, each man a cosmos of whose riches we can only catch glimpses. The life of simplicity is simple, but it opens to us a book in which we never get beyond the first syllable.

Many other writers have shared and appropriated the same insight. Blake claimed that "If the doors of perception were cleansed, everything would appear as it is, infinite." Chuang Tsu likens the mind of a perfect man to a mirror which grasps nothing, expects nothing, reflects but does not hold; thus he can be aware of all that is, and "dwell in the infinite". Arnold Toynbee held that the intellectual goal of human nature was to transcend those intellectual limitations imposed by its relativity, thus "to see the Universe as it is in the sight of God, instead of seeing it with the distorted vision of one of God's self-centred creatures".

> Finally, his son Philip Toynbee records the first occasion on which he really contemplated a tree on one of his walks: "The tree was there and now, in its own immediate and peculiar right: *that* tree and no other. And I was acutely here-and-now as I stared at it, unhampered by past or future: freed from the corruption of the ever-intrusive ME. Intense happiness."

Philip Toynbee's perception was unfiltered by a sense of space-time, and uninterrupted by self-awareness. He saw reality in what Hammar-skjöld called "sacred independence": humility extended to perception.

Forgiveness

Dag Hammarskjöld speaks of forgiveness in relation to freedom, both for himself and for the other. In his own life, he must detach himself "from all that was unjust in my past and all that is petty in my present", thus forgiving himself daily. He claims that we *are* forgiven in the presence of God, but that we cannot feel His presence if anything is allowed to stand between ourselves and others:

> Forgiveness breaks the chain of causality, because he who "forgives" you—out of love—takes upon himself the consequences of what *you* have done. Forgiveness, therefore, always entails a sacrifice. The price you must pay for your own liberation through another's sacrifice, is that you in turn must be willing to liberate in the same way, irrespective of the consequences to yourself.

In this way, forgiveness also involves self-effacement. Schweitzer goes further, by claiming that forgiveness is a moral obligation resulting from self-knowledge:

> I am obliged to exercise unlimited forgiveness, because, if I did not forgive, I should be untrue to myself, in that I should thus act as if I were not guilty in the same way as the other has been guilty

with regard to me. I must forgive the lies directed against myself, because my own life has so often been blotted by lies; I must forgive the lovelessness, the hatred, the slander, the fraud, the arrogance which I encounter, since myself have so often lacked love, hated, slandered, defrauded, and been arrogant. I must forgive without noise or fuss.

This is forgiveness as a sign of humility.

Arnold Toynbee defines the moral goal of human nature as being "to make the self's will coincide with God's will, instead of pursuing self-regarding purposes of its own". This goal complements the intellectual aim previously cited, translating it into the moral dimension. Readers of my earlier articles on Schweitzer (see above) may recall that he defined ethical mysticism as the insight that "All Being is life, and that, in loving self-devotion to other life, we realise our spiritual union with infinite Being." Earlier, we saw how Hammarskjöld regarded the love manifested by the mediaeval mystics as an overflowing of the strength with which self-oblivion had filled them: "an outflowing of a power released by self-surrender", as he puts it; such hourly self-surrender, he claims, "gives to your experience of reality the purity and clarity which signify 'self-realisation'"—and, he might have added, the answer to the question of meaning in life. The question actually dissolves in the experience.

Hammarskjöld's ethical aim was to treat himself as an end only in his capacity as a means; to live his individuality to the full, but for the good of others; to make his whole being an instrument of something greater than himself. In transparency, he hoped to vanish as an end, remaining only as a means expressing itself through love:

> When you have reached a point where you no longer expect a response, you will at last be able to give, in such a way that the other is able to receive, and be grateful. When Love has matured and, through a dissolution of the self into light, become a radiance, then shall the Lover be liberated from dependence upon the Beloved, and the Beloved also made perfect by being liberated from the Lover.

The perfect expression of love is in creative freedom. Here, and in this next poem, we catch an echo of Hammarskjöld's earlier vision of paradise, where "all flowed together and lived anew", where self-forged chains melt away:

> The chooser's happiness lies in his congruence with the chosen,
> The peace of iron-filings, obedient to the forces of the magnetic field—
> Calm is the soul that is emptied of all self,
> In a restful harmony—
> This happiness is here and now,
> In the eternal moment of co-inherence.
> A happiness within you—but not yours.

The self is still aware in this co-inherence, inter-penetrated with a happiness flowing through it. Such happiness can be felt as a "freedom in the midst of action, a stillness in the midst of other human beings", but only as a constant reality "to him who, in this world, is free from self-concern" and therefore receptive to the inflow. Time precludes full realisation of this ideal. The most we can hope for is that some partial illumination may radiate from our lives in love and sensitive awareness, faculties all too often eclipsed by daily pressures. What we have to pray for, asserted Hammarskjöld, is to become "a mirror in which, according to the degree of purity of heart you have attained, the greatness of life will be reflected". A spiritual message for the individual and the age.

Religion, Society and Spiritual Renewal in Radhakrishnan

I *already described how I first came across the work of Radhakrishnan in Foyles bookshop in 1974. Subsequently, I acquired quite a few more volumes on various visits to second-hand bookshops, including* Religion and Society, *on which I draw here in this essay dating from 1983. My copy is dated 1978, and it cost 75p, reduced from £1 as it was "pencilled"—it is now much more so than when I bought it ... and still well worth studying for its brilliant spiritual insights. Reading the biography of his father by Sarvepalli Gopal, I remember being struck by three stories about Radhakrishnan. While he was Indian ambassador in Moscow (he only agreed with Nehru to go if he could spend six months of the year in Oxford and continue his scholarly work) he was asked to give a lecture to the atheistic faculty of philosophy in the University of Moscow. At the end of the lecture, one of the professors asked him how he could believe what he had said about God. Radhakrishnan responded: do you believe in the good, the beautiful, and the true? After some hesitation, the interlocutor replied that he did—"That, said Radhakrishnan, is what I've been talking about." When he took his leave from Stalin, the dictator movingly told Radhakrishnan that he was the only person who had ever treated him as a human being. The final story comes from his period of office as president of India. A senior politician friend complained that he was always being misreported by the press. Radhakrishnan responded that he was never misreported as*

209

he always gave more or less the same speech about the good, the beautiful, and the true, so the press knew the speech by heart. Besides, he added, one cannot say these things too often.

> *If our civilisation perishes it will not be due to ignorance of what is needed to save it. It will be due to resistance to adopting the remedy, even when the patient appears to be dying.*
>
> —Radhakrishnan

Among the portraits I noticed adorning the dining room of All Soul's College, Oxford when I visited my friend Iain McGilchrist in 1981, there was one that was immediately striking on account of its simplicity. The figure is not smothered in red academic robes, but stands unaffectedly in a white tunic with his hands clasped in front of him. Sir Sarvepalli Radhakrishnan was one of the most remarkable men of his generation. Born in 1888, he held a number of chairs of philosophy in India before being appointed the first Spalding Professor of Eastern Religions and Ethics at Oxford in 1938, a chair which he held until 1952. He subsequently became vice-president of India, ambassador to Moscow, and finally president of India from 1962–1967.

Shortly before his death in 1975 he received the Templeton Prize for his outstanding contribution to religion: we shall see that his basic attitudes have much in common with this year's winner of the same prize, Alexander Solzhenitsyn. Radhakrishnan's major works include a two-volume *History of Indian Philosophy, An Idealist View of Life, Eastern Religions and Western Thought*, and standard editions of the *Bhagavad Gita*, the *Brahma Sutra*, and the *Upanishads*. The range and clarity of his thought is astounding, and his style a model of limpid exposition—I even used it as an example in a class on prose style at Winchester alongside Edward Gibbon, Lord Macaulay, Arnold Toynbee, and Bertrand Russell. In this article I shall consider Radhakrishnan's analysis of the crisis of our time and the challenge which it represents, his view of the role of religion and the spiritual life in relation to society, and the change of heart which he considered to be essential to the long-term survival and stability of the world.

Following the Hindu tradition, Radhakrishnan considered that man was an embodied spirit, and that his innermost being was divine. He therefore made a stand against a purely materialist assessment of human nature and motivation. The body is seen as the instrument through which we register and enjoy the world—"We need not pluck out our eyes to see better," as he puts it. In other words, we must neither abuse nor despise the body if we want to contribute effectively to the work of the world. Eternal truths must be translated into the social and temporal dimension through contemplation and ethical conduct—"Sanctity and love go together." The Hindu view recognises four ends of life in the ethical, the economic, the artistic, and the spiritual, which means that work in the world is stressed along with contemplation. Neither is sufficient without the other. The contemplation provides the quality of the action, and the action the embodiment of the contemplation—another formulation of Schweitzer's ethical mysticism in a life dedicated to service.

Towards a planetary patriotism

Radhakrishnan repudiates the Marxist contention that human progress is inevitable; but equally, nor is the decline of a society or civilisation—"History is an uninterrupted becoming, a ceaseless stream of which no one knows either the beginning or the end." Nothing is predetermined in this sense; there are only possibilities and probabilities which we may attempt to avert or bring about. Radhakrishnan's social starting point is that "Our planet has grown too small for parochial patriotism." He then argues that one of the recognised tests of an advance in civilisations is the gradual extension of the boundaries of the group, so that ultimately one comes to think and act in terms of the human race, not simply on an individual basis or according to the interests of a particular group. It is clear that the urge of nationalism and its ideals still dominates the thoughts and ideals of peoples of the world, whether in terms of power blocs, EU squabbles, or wars of "liberation".

However, this state of affairs is more induced than natural—"Nationalism ... is not an instinct. It is an acquired and artificial emotion." Baseness, brutality, and violence are considered to be quite normal if associated with a nation's cause. Nationalism or patriotism, however, with its love of one's native soil and loyalty to regional traditions, does not automatically entail violent hostility towards one's neighbours. Radhakrishnan regrets that "Patriotism has killed piety, and passion logic." Even if this statement reflects the surface situation, "Human roots go deeper than the fibres of race and nationality," so that the potential to extend social sympathies and instincts does exist.

Such potential can only be developed when we reach the insight that life in oneself and in others is sacred, that each person is an end in themselves and must not be crushed by the centralised machinery of mass propaganda; we must not allow ourselves to be persuaded that our only value lies in relation to the state, whose interest must be defended with our lives. Radhakrishnan sees true patriotism not as a local, racial, or national attachment, but rather as a human one.

Fanatical patriotism, a blind will for power, and unscrupulous opportunism form part of national foreign policy in all countries, even if in different degrees. These qualities are readily perceived in the "enemy", but usually renamed when applied to ourselves—after all, we are only defending our legitimate interests against the foreign antagonist. When violence erupts into war, this cannot simply be ascribed to circumstances. Wars are not "what insurance companies call acts of God. These are acts of men." The continued existence of war is a verdict on mankind: that respect for man and brotherhood is trampled on, resulting in confusion, hatred, and fear; that human life is not universally recognised as sacred; and that we have not yet acquired the wisdom to refrain from using our immense technological power for destructive ends. The verdict is also a challenge to analyse the nature of the conflicts and destructive impulses and to formulate ideals towards which we can strive.

"Civilisation consists in the gradual subordination of the instinctive life to the sway of reason." This is another call for extended social sympathies. By civilisation Radhakrishnan means a way of life, a movement of the human spirit—its essence lies not in any biological unity of race, or in political arrangements, but in the values that create and sustain them. He suggests that if the world is now in a perilous condition, it is because the central questions of the values of life, of philosophy and religion, are brushed aside to empty notions and mere fancies. They are considered to be so secondary to immediate material considerations as to be virtually irrelevant. This perspective is all the more lamentable because the relative nature of material value and well-being is not even perceived.

It is as if one had grown so accustomed to wearing tinted contact lenses that one no longer realised that one's perception was coloured. If every civilisation is the expression of a religion, the predominant world view of the West is secular humanism. In turn, this affects our prevalent conception of human nature and destiny. If we regard ourselves as the most cunning of animals, economic beings controlled by the laws of supply and demand and class conflicts, or even as a political manipulator, then our values will be those of anarchic jungle warfare and the competitive survival of the fittest. If, on the other hand, we share Radhakrishnan's conviction that humans have a spiritual element requiring them to "subordinate the temporal and the expedient to the eternal and the true", then this spiritual element must be respected and cultivated: political institutions must also be based on spiritual, not on purely material premises; and world leaders must see beyond the pride of the intellect if they are to avoid falling into the pit of destruction and dragging the rest of humankind down after them. Radhakrishnan sums up our situation as follows:

> There must be a change in the ideals we cherish, in the values we adopt, before we can give social expression to them. We help to secure the future only to the extent to which we ourselves are changed. What is missing in our age is the soul; there is nothing wrong with the body. We suffer from sickness of spirit. We must discover our roots in the eternal and regain faith in the transcendent truth which will order life, discipline discordant elements, and bring unity and purpose to it. If not, when the floods come and the winds blow and beat upon our house, it will fall.

Transcending religious limits

"If the world is in search of its soul, religions as they have come down to us cannot supply that soul," argues Radhakrishnan. Why not? Principally because they divide humanity into hostile camps, and emphasise their differences in order to assert their separate identities. All creeds, however, "are attempts of the finite mind to grasp the infinite". They arise from and are adapted to different needs of different people at different times. Being finite, all creeds are tentative, so that there is no justification for intolerance. Religions which have regarded themselves as final and absolute have encouraged their adherents to impose their opinions on the rest of the world, with disastrous consequences—oppression, injustice, and cruelty being the very negation of the spiritual wisdom at the heart of the higher religions. Because religion has been confused with the profession of a revealed truth, outward machinery and institutions have submerged the concerns of the heart and the spirit; individuals are subordinated to the authority of priest or Church, to whom we abdicate our responsibility in return for protection and some kind of guarantee of salvation.

If we remain at the level of dogmas and definitions, we are divided and argue; but in the spiritual life of inward prayer and contemplation we are united, both with each other and with the Supreme. This insight leads Radhakrishnan to distinguish between religion as identified with adherence to dogmas and observance of ceremonies, and the spiritual life "which insists on a change of consciousness for which all else is the means". The reason why organised religion has failed to transform the human race is that "It has not sufficiently emphasised that its sole justification is to open the way to spiritual existence"—human nature is not transformed merely by tinkering with ideas and formulations on the surface, but by means of radical changes in consciousness. Such changes in consciousness cannot be a mass affair, but can only take place in the individual: then the aggregate of all individual changes may have a profound impact on society.

In contacting the unity of spirit within themselves, individuals are then enabled to perceive the unity of humankind; and in apprehending the perennial philosophy at the heart of religion, we can appreciate the qualities of its various manifestations without insisting that any one historical vehicle has a monopoly of truth. It is Radhakrishnan's belief that "When the human being perceives that he belongs to a higher order of reality than brute nature, he cannot be satisfied by worldly success or the triumphs of materialistic science." We become capable of sacrifice for this ideal. This leads to a redefinition of religion in practical terms as "the discipline which touches the conscience and helps to struggle with evil and sordidness, saves us from greed, lust and hatred, releases moral power, and imparts courage in the enterprise of saving the world". The religion of the truly religious is not shackled by creeds, dogmatic sentiments: it is "to do justly, to love beauty, and to walk humbly with the spirit of truth". Such is the way of a true religious life. It represents a creative response to the challenge posed by the crisis of our times, and demands the cooperation of each individual.

Education in human values

In a section entitled "Education in Values", Radhakrishnan maintains that *"If our civilisation perishes it will not be due to ignorance of what is needed to save it. It will be due to resistance to adopting the remedy, even when the patient appears to be dying."* He complains that much of what now passes for education succeeds in anaesthetising the soul. We are moulded into approved patterns instead of developing our creative and critical powers in tandem.

Thinking in herds is more a question of instinct than thought: "We become mass men hermetically sealed, repeating parrot-like set views on society, state, custom, law and individual." We are unaware of the true significance of human life, we become "greedy for sensations, obscurely resentful and eager for something to blame and hate". Any unity which is achieved is unconscious or restricted and militates against the realisation of the underlying unity of humanity. But until we foster a social consciousness and sense of responsibility which transcend the limits of our political community, we cannot hope for the ultimate success and stability of supra-national organisations—they will remain dependent on the powers and caprices of a few influential nations. As Dr Robert Muller proposed, the UN charter of human rights should be studied and discussed in every school, and strenuous efforts should be made to deepen mutual understanding and emphasise our common humanity and universal spiritual destiny.

On a practical basis, Radhakrishnan offers some advice to individuals on their role and possibilities. We know that the present time is of crucial importance in human history, but there is no need for fatalistic resignation and despair. Each of us can work so as to ensure that our influence is for the good, something which is only possible if we remake ourselves. He offers five guidelines:

1. Reverence for life and respect for fellow men (*ahimsa*): we should not consciously inflict sorrow or suffering.
2. We should not be attracted by love of power or greed for other people's possessions.
3. Self-control, and the acquisition of a balanced view and serenity.
4. Speaking the truth—without malice or fear, and even to people who do not wish to hear it.

5. Abstinence from intoxication, including fanatical adherence to dogmas and doctrines.

These five principles are intended to develop in us wisdom, humility, and selflessness. Being centred in the spiritual reality we will find ourselves free of the all-pervasive greed and fear in the world. Through the quality of our being, we will be contributing towards that essential profound shift of consciousness which clothes the future with hope instead of obliterating it in a moment of confused desperation.

Ethics and the Nature of the Human

*T*he basic question discussed in this 1983 essay is the relationship between metaphysics and ethics and the implications of a transcendent basis for ethics for everyday life. Just this morning I have been reading a section in French of a book by Peter Deunov on La Vie pour le TOUT—Life for the Whole where he explains that the universe is a unity in diversity, that the part cannot detach itself from the whole or even exist outside the whole (think of the vine and branches in John)—and that since we are part of this Whole, we should live in and for the Whole on the basis of love. He goes on to say that there are three kinds of life: the life for oneself, the life for society, and the life for the Sublime Principle, for the Whole. Corresponding to this is the law of the part, the law of oneself; the law of the majority or the law of the neighbour; and finally, the law of the Whole where we devote ourselves to the Whole. By doing so, we also live for our neighbours and for ourselves, because the law of the Whole embraces these other levels. Metaphysically, this is expressed in Emerson's idea of the Oversoul and Paul Brunton's Overself, a formulation one also finds in the subtle gnosis of Plotinus: "Thus each one of them sees the things in its own being and in the being of its neighbour, and therefore they are all inside all of them, and the whole is in the one and the one of them is the whole"—in short, ethically we are one another.

Fritjof Capra has suggested that the twentieth-century crisis of values is a crisis of perception; that the way in which we look at the world and ourselves profoundly influences our outlook and behaviour. In this article I propose to discuss the connection between world views (incorporating views on God, humanity, and nature) and ethics as systems of morals or rules of behaviour. After a few preliminary remarks I shall look at the Christian ethic and its system of rewards and punishments, moving on to consider the rise of the mechanical view of humanity and nature and its consequences. Analytical psychology and modern physics have played a crucial role in extending our knowledge of the human and the material universe respectively; they have also undermined some of the assumptions of the mechanistic outlook. I shall then examine the near-death experience (NDE) and compare some of the findings with similar reports ostensibly originating from discarnate human beings. It will be found that the NDE shares certain features with mystical experience, and that together they provide a clue to an extended definition of identity and self. Before concluding, I shall compare the ideas of post-mortem spiritual gravitation and karma in relation to release and enlightenment.

The human situation

The vast majority of human beings find themselves in the context of a state and of smaller institutions and groups which impose certain norms and expectations on their members: relationships with family, workplace, and country. The cohesion and perpetuation of each of these groups require a degree of obedience and submission on the part of the individual as well as free cooperation with those encountered in the course of the day. The individual is a unit in each of these contexts, and from the point of view of the group or state, its own continued existence is more important than that of any individual (a point which is elaborated below). The person is subject to social and political demands which constitute a social and political ethic. In addition, humans stand related to nature, which they attempt to exploit or with which they cooperate; from this one could deduce an ecological ethic. Finally, there is the transcendental framework of the religious ethic. If the transcendental dimension is not taken into account, then this category is frequently subsumed under the political ethic, which for the spiritual perspective is an aberration, an inversion of values: the transcendental should contain the political, not the political strangle the transcendental. The religious ethic relates to human behaviour. The inner disposition and tendencies, the purity of motivation, in short, the *being* of the individual is central. A complete ethic would have to account for these various levels and dimensions. Our concern here will be primarily for the religious ethic and its relationship to the social, political, and ecological factors.

The Christian ethic

The teaching of the Sermon on the Mount, which so inspired the Hindu Gandhi (strongly influenced by Tolstoy) in our own century, has never been applied on a large scale, even, alas, among Christians themselves. The injunctions are of unsurpassable sublimity, often regarded as "unrealistic" in practice. The one who loved their enemies might be considered politically naïve, if not actually treacherous to their own country. It is beyond the scope of this article to undertake a detailed consideration of all aspects of Christian ethics. The core, however, can uncontroversially be expressed in the commandments to love God and one's neighbour, exhibited in the parable of the Good Samaritan; and in the story of the Last Judgment in Matthew 25 we are encouraged to recognise Christ in our neighbour, like the Benedictine reception of visitors. The metaphysical framework of Christianity includes the doctrine of original sin, and redemption through the death of Christ on the cross.

The expectation of the impending advent of the Kingdom of God made the original Christian orientation an otherworldly one which tended to devalue physical life in relation to eternal life. The dead were meant to sleep until the resurrection of the flesh followed by the Last Judgment, after which there would be an irreversible consignment to heaven or hell (the doctrine of purgatory was a later Catholic extension when it was thought that most people did not deserve either state immediately and permanently). Inquisitorial persecutions were pursued against heretics who deviated from the "true faith", leading in some cases to wars of religion which repelled many of the rationalists of the seventeenth and eighteenth centuries. During the Middle Ages, lurid descriptions in sermons of the torments in prospect for the damned kept many of the faithful in fear and trembling about their ultimate fate; especially when such tirades were reinforced by the doctrine of predestination, whereby an omniscient and omnipotent God willed (arbitrarily, as it seemed to the rationalists) that certain people should enjoy everlasting bliss while others, unwittingly less fortunate, were relegated to the nether regions.

If persecution, wars of religion, and certain doctrines rendered Christianity less acceptable to many thinking individuals, perhaps the most potent factor in the decline of traditional religion and in belief in an afterlife was the teaching of everlasting punishment in hell. Hell became a more and more embarrassing scar to the liberal theologian who asserted that God is love—could a beneficent creator, even allowing for the perversity of human free will, seriously condemn any of his creatures to eternal torment?

The mechanistic outlook

Something had to give: either the idea or existence of God, and/or the notion of hell. In contemporary polls many fewer respondents believe in hell than in heaven, and between thirty and forty per cent do not believe in an afterlife of any kind. This state of affairs is not simply due to the inherent decline of traditional Christianity, but also to the widespread influence of the mechanistic outlook, to which we must turn our attention, after this necessarily sketchy coverage of some aspects of Christianity.

Descartes based his philosophy on the proposition "I think, therefore I am". In doing so he made a radical departure from the theological tradition by placing humans, not God, at the centre. He also started from a position of doubt or scepticism about the status of information derived from the senses. The body he regarded as a machine, and animals as automata; humans were distinguished from animals by rationality and the ensuing conception of the soul. Descartes's scepticism and his theory that animals were machines had consequences which he himself might not have foreseen: the scepticism was translated into a general attack on religious authority in the name of the scientific verification method of observation, induction, and experiment; while his theory of animals as automata was extended to man as evolution and behaviourist psychology blurred the distinction between human and animal, treating both in terms of a crude model of stimulus and response.

Such a view represents a devaluing of our humanity, leading to a tendency to regard humans as nothing more than mass particles. At best, this is only a biological half-truth. At the same time, the concept of the soul was being squeezed out by mechanistic approaches in physics, then in biology and psychology (humans explained in terms of physico-chemical constituents), and the absolute values grounded in traditional Christianity were decaying. The focus moved away from a concern with salvation in the next world towards the future of humankind on earth. Although in some ways it was a necessary shift away from the otherworldly orientation, the compensation was so drastic that material welfare came to dominate the ethical scene.

The doctrine of original sin was repudiated and replaced by a belief in the fundamental goodness and perfectibility of the human; the goal was no longer transcendence of the world but fulfilment in it, now or in the future. The characteristic ethic was utilitarianism, the greatest happiness of the greatest number. For happiness we can, broadly speaking, read material goods: the aim is maximum consumption of material goods, which should theoretically lead to maximum happiness (or satisfaction, as the economists would put it). From this it follows that individual and group material interests are the most important criteria. The economist Adam Smith argued that the general interest was best served by "the invisible hand", each pursuing their own interest, while in reaction to this Marx contended that the impulses of private concern must be curbed by the common ownership of the means of production; these poles represent market- and the state-controlled economies respectively. It is important to note, however, that each system professes to bring about the material welfare of the individual; they are heading towards the same goal on different roads.

Trends and implications

What is the significance of these trends for ethics? Technological progress, especially in communications, enables a far greater degree of control to be exercised by governments; tyranny can be practically all-pervasive (now all the more so than in the 1980s). Society or the state become the supreme criteria within a materialistic framework. Humans are cogs, tiny particles in this immense engine; they are relieved of their moral responsibility, provided that they submit to authority, as proposed by Dostoevsky's Grand Inquisitor. The political and social ethic is now paramount in a totalitarian regime; it has swallowed up the religious impulse in a wave of revolutionary fervour, often cashing in on nationalism for reinforcement. Social and political conformity is rewarded, the future is the only transcendence, and humanity is forgotten in the name of the idea. Spirituality deprived, we lose our sense of direction.

Analytical psychology has pointed out some of the dangers of the present situation. Erich Neumann argues that "By identifying his personal ego with the transpersonal in the shape of the collective values, the limited individual loses contact with his own limitations and becomes inhuman." The atrocities perpetrated by the political fanatic testify to the truth of this statement; and in such cases, individual moral responsibility is handed over to the cause: the individual is "just following orders". This psychology also reinstates the Christian doctrine of original sin in the shape of the "shadow", the unconscious evil side in human nature (only too apparent in the atrocities referred to above). One of the primary dangers of the shadow is that we fail to recognise it in ourselves and project it onto our enemies: "The fight against heretics, political opponents and national enemies is actually the fight against our own religious doubts, the insecurity of our own political position, and the one-sidedness of our own national viewpoint," argues Neumann.

The mutual suspicions and recriminations of the superpowers provide a classic illustration of the thesis; each recognises the threat of the other (evil intentioned) side without perceiving the menace represented by their own weapons. Analytical psychology stresses the crucial importance of individual development and moral responsibility. The unconscious evil in oneself must be faced and worked through, not unconsciously projected onto an "enemy" as an excuse for self-righteous complacency. Widening of consciousness leads in turn to a broadening of sympathies, so that psychological development and ethical evolution can proceed hand in hand.

Modern physics has undermined some of the assumptions of the mechanistic outlook. Quantum theory has demonstrated that determinism and causality are only useful categories when large numbers are being considered: they vanish at the subatomic level. The boundaries of space and time have melted away. The observer can no longer be excluded from any statement about the universe: observer and observed are relative and interdependent. Matter has been shown to be convertible into energy; it sometimes behaves like a particle, sometimes like a wave, depending on the kind of question asked. Finally, David Bohm has argued that separation exists only in appearance, behind which there is unity; it makes as much sense to say that space unites us as divides. The matter of our bodies is a condensation in the physical field. The mass particle is no longer an appropriate image of the human being; we are closer to being a wave in the ocean of Being.

NDEs and transformation—the overself

Over the past ten years an immense amount of interest has been generated in the NDE. What concerns us here is not so much the details of the experiences as their after-effects. There is, according to Grof "a realisation of the absurdity and futility of exaggerated ambitions, attachment to money, status, fame, and power, or pursuit of other temporal values". The present becomes more important than the future, and there is a distinct increase of interest in spiritual and religious matters. Life, nature, and people are more deeply appreciated, with an emphasis on love, compassion, and giving; furthermore, the love is not so much the conditional type hingeing on self-interest so much as the kind which unconditionally accepts oneself and the other. It seems to me that those who have had experiences close to death have returned with an insight into their true natures and into real, rather than illusory and temporal values. They hold a lesson for us all.

One of the most significant experiences undergone by some of those with an NDE is the so-called "life review"; such an experience is also reported by the discarnate through mediums, and is referred to in the *Tibetan Book of the Dead.* One of Kenneth Ring's respondents describes the experience as follows:

> I experienced what I call a judgment, a total review of my life. It was experienced in its essence and totality. It was surveyed in one clump, as it were (others do describe a series of vivid memory-images). You could say the creator judged me, and be correct. I felt it was that, but even more, it was the totality of my Self, my larger SELF, my true Self, judging my little self, the ego, the habits and patterns and tendencies of J.T. (the respondent) within the context of the twentieth century.

Paul Brunton describes the same process. At death the individual becomes aware of a hidden "I", in his terms the Overself, the infinite spark at the centre of the human, the Hindu Atman or Self:

> Through his eyes he will gaze afresh at the total impression rather than the episodal detail of his earthly life. Through its revelatory

eyes he becomes his own incorruptible judge. The purely selfish, purely personal point of view deserts him. For the first time, perhaps, he sees himself not only as others see him but also as the impersonal power of karma sees him. During this time, he comes face to face with the *consequences* for other persons of his acts while on earth ...

The judge is a sort of conscience which perceives the implications not only of acts but also of thoughts. Does not Jesus say that a man who looks lustfully at a woman has already committed adultery in his heart? In the judgment, the person apparently *experiences* the effects on others of his actions and thoughts, whether positive or negative. We are much more responsible than we perhaps realised.

Our next clue is the nature of the mystical experience, also encountered by many near-death experiencers. During his experience of judgment, J.T. became aware of another Self, which he describes as "a larger sense of I or of another presence". Other similar formulations can be found: "I felt as though I were the centre of the universe and at the same time the centre was everywhere," and "The whole time I was in this state, it seemed infinite. It was timeless. I was just an infinite being in perfection." There is an expansion of self and identity far beyond normal limited conceptions of personality, an experience of infinity, eternity, love, and peace—total harmony. In Hindu terms this is explained as an experience of the Atman, the divine principle and centre at the core of the self. The physicist Schrödinger comes up with a similar conclusion on the basis of the one world concocted from the mental experience of many egos: "the unification of minds or consciousness. Their multiplicity is only apparent, in truth there is only one mind."

Paul Brunton's explanation, as we have seen in connection with judgment, is the individual Overself, the non-egoic root of personality— what Emerson called the Oversoul in an essay of the same title. This Overself, in turn, is a phase of the World-Mind: "This mystical meeting-point, the Overself, represents the utmost extent to which the finite self can consciously share in the ultimate existence. It is that fragment of God which dwells in and yet environs man, a fragment which has all the quality and grandeur of God but not all of the power and amplitude of God." It follows logically from this that "Each Overself *in itself* is exactly the same as and all one with another." In other words, each

Overself has a different relation to God and finite personality; the difference, however, is *not intrinsic*.

Each Overself is distinct but not separate, at one with all the others, but not identical. This subtle distinction is of cardinal importance: *at heart we all participate in the same being; we are one another* (see my book *Resonant Mind* for a more extensive and detailed argument). Seen from this angle, the welfare of the individual is inextricably connected to the welfare of all: in loving our neighbour we are loving ourselves, in hurting our neighbour we are hurting ourselves. It is this experience which we pass through in the life review or judgment. The conception of the oneness of being gives Schweitzer the starting point of his ethics. The At-Onement of our Overself provides a metaphysical basis for the commandment to love our neighbours as ourselves. Ultimately, suffering will arise when we fail to observe this law. The great religions all teach that the quality of post-mortem existence (whether or not it includes rebirth in another physical body) depends on the quality of the individual. In a mental post-mortem world, the desires and thoughts, the central concern of the individual, will be reflected in the quality of environment.

This state of affairs is explained by Brunton as the logical operation of a spiritual force of gravity, of mental affinity—Swedenborg's ideas discussed in a previous essay are similar. The individual naturally comes to associate with those in complete harmony with their inner self. States of paradise seem to reflect Unity, Light, and Love, qualities which decrease and are transformed into their opposites as one slides down the scale. Reincarnation is an extension of this principle of affinity or gravity. Such a scheme is described in the *Tibetan Book of the Dead*, in Brunton, and in Da Free John (*Easy Death*). At death the self is presented with an opportunity for transcendence, a surrender into the Light of Being and Bliss. The finite identity recoils from the possibility, preferring to cling to its familiar limitations; and it is the shape and tendency of these limitations that draw the individual back into the finite world of matter and space-time.

Conclusions

What conclusions can we draw from all this? First, that we must strive to realise our dual identity. Humans are what Koestler calls a holon; that is to say that, on the one hand, the finite individuality is relatively autonomous and separate, while on the other it participates in the Overself in which the finite melts into the infinite, and the sense of separation dissolves. At one level we are different from other people, while on the other we are identical. During earthly life we may have the impression of being able to hurt others without hurting ourselves, but we eventually come to realise that to hurt others *is* to hurt ourselves; that the expression of love and compassion is self-fulfilment and fulfilment of the law.

Furthermore, we must purify our motives if we are not to fall prey to self-righteousness and moral complacency. There must be no discrepancy between thought and action, between being and doing; each should mirror the other. As our consciousness and identity expand, so we are less likely to project our own evil onto some third party; our sympathy (literally, to feel with), our circle of compassion, is widened and deepened, our freedom and sense of responsibility enlarged. The religious ethic now naturally contains the political, social and ecological ethic, the inner rules the outer, values attain their proper divine hierarchy. The process of creating harmony within is radiated outwards in our sphere of influence as we courageously pursue our sometimes faltering quest towards loving unity and transcendence.

Beyond Fanaticism—the "Pneumatocratic" Perspective

*T*he essential thing to explain about this essay is the term "pneumato-cratic" or "pneumatocracy", meaning "rule of the soul", a term coined by Johan Quanjer (1934–2001), the Dutch editor of the journal New Humanity, in which many of the essays in this volume were first published. I met Johan at the 1981 Mystics and Scientists conference and he published my first article—on Albert Schweitzer—later that year. Pneumatocracy should not be confused with authoritarian theocracy since it is founded on individual liberty and conscience. The central point is the extent and depth of our sense of identity corresponding with the anchor of our ethics. And it seems to me desirable that this should go beyond the individual, social, and political to a transcendent ground that we all share. I elaborate these arguments in greater detail in terms of an ethic of interconnectedness in my book Resonant Mind. This essay was published in 1985.

> "It is time, high time, that civilised man turned his mind to fundamental things."
>
> —C. G. Jung

In the previous article I tried to outline some of the connections between ethics and human nature. In this article I would like to investigate in greater detail the possible relations between the individual and the group in the light of a spiritual understanding of the human. To do this one needs to analyse social psychology and its implications for individual fulfilment; then it helps to look closely at the past in order to understand the present, as well as possible future developments. We shall see that the next step in the evolution of consciousness and moral responsibility entails the individual becoming much more integrated within, and thus less dependent on external props for their identity and sense of purpose.

Holons

A helpful starting point is Arthur Koestler's idea of the "holon". He argues that everything has two aspects: it can be thought of as a part of a greater whole or as an autonomous whole in itself. Biologically the individual is a whole; yet, on another level, we are part of a family, a society, a nation, the human race, life on earth, etc. Equally, the organs of the body are in a sense autonomous wholes, while being part of the system in the body; they work together to ensure physical equilibrium, each playing a vital but different role. The two aspects of the holon have their typical behavioural patterns: in so far as individuals wish to express their part-ness, they are self-assertive, while the corresponding expression of wholeness lies in harmonious integration with the whole; either one's separate identity is asserted, or else one subsumes oneself into the identity of the group by attaching to oneself the appropriate label of family, tribe, party, or other organisation.

It is clear that society cannot operate stably unless there exists a balance between these two tendencies. At one extreme, the resulting diversity would be nothing short of anarchy, quite without any underlying cohesion; while the total abdication of individual self-assertion would produce an amorphous, tedious, and predictable human anthill—unless under the control of a powerful fanatical leader who would direct the ants towards the achievement of his own ends, while assuring them that they were performing a glorious and necessary service to their cause and country. The anarchist accepts no authority but himself, while those at the other end of the spectrum surrender their judgment to the powers that be and are prepared to be used as mere instruments.

The mediaeval view

In the Christian mediaeval world view, people understood their place in the scheme of the universe. The world was a bridge over which they passed on their way to an eternal destiny, whether damned or saved. The dictates of the Church provided milestones and signposts along the road, warning of snares, detours, temptations, and the deceptive appearance of the wide straight highway along which many an unwary traveller journeyed. The ways of the world were not to be trusted, a person's principal concern was the salvation of their soul, and their life and business dealings reflecting such an understanding. There was no sharp distinction between personal and commercial morality, since the authority of the Church's teaching (if not its practice) was all-pervasive.

There was no question of a double standard: one for private affairs and another in business. As the representative of God on earth, the Church claimed absolute authority and jurisdiction over the ethical conduct of the individual. Those who submitted gracefully were embraced with maternal love and forgiveness; they gained an emotional and spiritual security and sense of identity so long as they unquestioningly obeyed ecclesiastical edicts; if they sinned and confessed, forgiveness and abso-lution were open in order to assuage their sense of guilt and inadequacy: a safe institutional haven from the harsh storms raging outside.

If, however, believers began to doubt the efficacy of the scheme, it was not long before they felt the icy blast of intolerance blowing in their direction. There could be no salvation outside the Church (*extra ecclesia nulla salus*), and indeed it was presumptuous arrogance even to enter-tain such an outlandish notion. The dogma was reinforced with threats of the grim prospect of eternal damnation looming ahead, as depicted in so much lurid art and on the portals of the great French cathedrals. Fear might well drive the doubter to repentance and subsequent rein-corporation into the fold. But the persistent renegade might then be hounded as a heretic, brought to trial, and, in the absence of a last-minute recantation under duress, handed over to the civil authorities and put to death. Galileo's famous withdrawal of his scientific findings enabled him to escape the stake at which Giordano Bruno had perished not long before.

Considered in the light of Koestler's categories, we find that the heretic corresponds to individuals who assert their integrity and independence (the root word in Greek, *haerein* means to choose); they were not prepared to be absorbed into the womb of the Church; the unconditional forgiveness of the feminine side gave way to the rigorous chastisement of a masculine attitude; the shield of the believer became a menacing sword to the rebel. Those who submitted, on the other hand, enjoyed comparative security at the cost of their freedom and personal responsibility; they found a ready-made sense of identity and purpose which even sanctified persecution of those less orthodox than themselves.

Protestantism and modernism

The traditional scheme of Christian virtues is almost completely reversed in Puritan theology, according to R. H. Tawney in his classic book *Religion and the Rise of Capitalism*. While salvation is instigated by grace, this grace is not mediated through any earthly institution, but is rather the outcome of a direct and solitary encounter with God. These spiritual aristocrats imposed upon themselves a rigorous self-discipline that strengthened their wills, but at the same time they had scant compassion for the shortcomings of those less valiant than themselves. The conviction that character counts for everything and circumstances for nothing drove them to vigorous exertions, while rendering them correspondingly uncharitable towards those less disciplined than themselves.

If success is the result of effort and character, then failure (or poverty) can be regarded as the inevitable consequence of idleness and weakness. The most powerful influence stemming from this view is the emphasis on personal accountability, but its treatment of social problems takes no account of the influence of environmental factors, even if these have sometimes been overplayed in our own day. One further significant development in Puritanism was the demand that the Church should not interfere in the economic field; this marks the decline of its sphere of interest and the establishment of a separate standard; even if the first Puritans maintained scrupulous levels of behaviour, the door was now open to the proposal that norms of behaviour in business could be different from those of personal morality.

While many people remained nominally religious, the influence of Descartes, Newton and the rising sciences relying on observation and experiment rather than tradition and authority encouraged a trend towards a purely secular and mechanical view of the world and humanity. With the erosion of boundaries between animal and the human when understood in evolutionary terms, Descartes's contention that animals were automata was extended to include us: mind and soul came to be seen as by-products of the body which perished at physical death; there was no higher purpose to human existence—such views were written off as superstitious nonsense or deceptive desires for wish-fulfilment. Life was the end-product of countless chance combinations of molecules building up to greater complexity in the course of development. One logical extension of the Darwinian struggle towards the survival of the fittest was Nietzsche's Superman who emerged as the ultimate and triumphant specimen trampling on his numerous less well-endowed fellow creatures whose life was of small account when compared to the quality of his own. Another extension was the idea of a master race with the right to exploit weaker brethren; and a final possibility envisaged the rise and ascendancy of the industrial proletariat to a position of impregnable superiority—the fittest in this case, exactly the opposite of Nietzsche, being the most numerically numerous. All three extensions of Darwinism are based on the dominion of one individual, race or class over another; crushing of resistance is inevitable if supremacy (and therefore fitness to survive) is to be asserted and maintained.

This mechanical and industrial view underlies both capitalist and communist secular societies. Science and technology aim at prediction and control, and, if necessary, manipulation and exploitation of the individual. Quantification and abstraction have encouraged analyses of human beings as mass particles, cogs in a machine, pawns in a manoeuvre, or average consumers of a standardised product. If the behaviour of the worker, the soldier or the customer can be predicted and controlled, production targets, military tactics and marketing strategies can be more accurately and reliably planned.

Commercial and collective allegiances

The present structure of capitalist economies is geared towards more or less continuous economic growth. In order for demand, and therefore production, not to slacken, it is essential that consumers be stimulated to desire more and newer products, and that they be convinced that their happiness will be correspondingly enhanced by this increased consumption. Our status and identity are measured by the quality and quantity of our possessions, while our purpose in these narrow terms is the maximum accumulation of desirable items. If we are kept busy enough at this game, we may not even notice that it is bound to end in the disappointment of death. In our careers we naturally identify with the firm for which we work, using the first-person plural to describe our association and activities; a considerable part of our identity may be vested in our company. We rejoice in its successes as our own, lament its failures as personal setbacks, and fully assume the role which we are assigned by the organisation. This is all very well if the job is kept in perspective. But if it becomes one's chief source of identity and purpose, it has overreached itself by becoming a substitute for real religion, an opiate to divert one from the inner quest, only part of which can be expressed through work in the material world. In both the above cases the individual has surrendered to a greater whole: the consumer has succumbed to the marketing plan, while the working person has mortgaged their soul to the company.

The totalitarian state may be less open to devious commercialism, but it demands from the individual an uncritical acceptance of its belief system and an unquestioning obedience to its authority. The price of security and stability is abjuration of any forms of self-assertion which are not sanctioned by the party. It is an unrelenting patriarchal structure which exhibits none of the maternal elements of the mediaeval Church, while claiming absolute allegiance from its subjects. The value of the individual is defined solely in political and economic terms. The materialist world view prevents possible consideration of other levels of being and other avenues of fulfilment. The wholeness of the human being is largely discounted in favour of the conformity of the part. The sin of disobedience and dissidence is not lightly tolerated; the fires of eternity are replaced by the living hell of the mental hospital and labour camp; the penalties of disobedience are more immediate—sanctions which frighten the majority into abject acceptance or cowering apathy.

The same analysis can be applied to any group or organisation which requires unquestioning obedience to authority. Paradoxically, the act of integrating into a group identity may involve a noble altruism on the part of the individual concerned, but the resulting group may then behave in a collectively selfish manner towards other groups, as noted by Reinhold Niebuhr. In this way, the integrating tendency of the individual may be subordinated to the self-assertive tendency of the group.

The fanatic identifies himself completely with a cause to the extent that he feels no independent sense of purpose and identity; he is a mere instrument, his life only being of value in relation to the cause. It follows from this that the lives of others are to be similarly assessed: they are either valuable or detrimental; if valuable, then their services must be enlisted, if detrimental, then they must be "eliminated". The fanatic is prepared to die and prepared to kill. He is guilty of having forgotten and abandoned his humanity for an abstract idea considered more important than human life; he fails to realise that he is himself more than a unit, and moreover that he is personally responsible for the suffering which he inflicts. In treating himself as a means to an end, he is compelled to regard others in the same light; a resulting devaluation of human life is engendered by this devastating delusion.

Pneumatocratic people can only gaze aghast at this spectacle. Their starting point is the consideration of the human being in terms of a number of interrelated levels which include the material but which are not limited to it; political and economic concerns have their place, but are not allowed to become dominant. A hierarchy of values arises from a multidimensional view of the human, and a delicate balance is established in the flow and relationship between various levels. The vertical or inner axis is central: humankind's unity of being in God is apprehended in records of cosmic consciousness, or in direct personal experience. From this realisation emerge the following guidelines:

1. On a spiritual level, men and women are interdependent, interconnected holons. Their part-ness is represented by the image of God as transcending the individual, while their wholeness resides in the idea of immanence, of the God dwelling in each one, and able to recognise itself in and through each one. The transcendence of God makes the individual insignificant, while Divine immanence confers an infinite value; both complementary truths need to be appreciated.
2. Human beings should treat each other as ends in themselves, never as means to any end, however noble. Life is sacred, not ideas.
3. The underlying purpose of society is to provide the most favourable conditions for the evolution of consciousness, freedom and compassion. Extension of consciousness integrates the shadow side of our natures and prevents us from projecting our own evil and limitations onto other people or rival groups; freedom is extended with consciousness as we are less strongly driven by irrational drives and

more consciously steered by discerning wisdom; and compassion derives from our understanding of an identification with the difficulties of our neighbours.

4. It is a grave error to limit one's identity to some transient cause or idea, which is liable to deceive you into thinking of it as a whole rather than a part; blind fanatical devotion is the searing scourge of history.

5. The diverse ways in which humankind strives for unity are microcosmic patterns of the mystical quest for unity with God; as a result, any quest which stops at the individual or the collective is mistaking a part for the whole; the collective is only a mirage of the universal— our true identity.

6. The inner is a reflection of the outer and the outer of the inner (as above, so below). Changes in one must be accompanied by corresponding change in the other. In Koestler's terms, the yogi must work hand in hand with the commissar, inner transformation with outer transformation—regeneration of the individual with regeneration of society.

7. Self-assertive rights need to be balanced by integrative obligations in order to avoid destructive extremes; this applies just as much to nature as to society.

The psychological and spiritual challenge confronting pneumatocratic people is a formidable but not impossible task. Economics and politics must once again be brought within an overall spiritual ethic. Wisdom and compassion must be applied to our awe-inspiring technological prowess if we are not to allow ourselves to be destroyed by what we have created. We must work to dissolve the cloud of fear, suspicion and hatred which hang menacingly over us by recognising our common spiritual being and personal responsibility for our contribution towards such clouds. We must no longer rely for our security on submission to an external authority, but must strive for our own integration and wholeness, an essential microcosmic contribution open to each one of us. *It is too late and too dangerous to leave the tasks to experts and governments.* The clarion is sounding. Millions of individuals must wake up, speak out, radiate, and act in their own circles, calling for a colossal mobilisation of spiritual resources rising into irresistible floods of love and light to burst through the crumbling dams of materialism.

Voltaire and Russell—the Crusade against Dogma and Fanaticism

*A*n essay delivered to the Edinburgh Speculative Society during the session 1979–80. The Speculative Society was founded in 1764 "for the improvement of literary composition and public speaking". It was an expression of the Scottish Enlightenment and among the most famous members are Sir Walter Scott and Robert Louis Stevenson; also many prominent members of the Scottish Bench. My own great-grandfather, Professor James Lorimer FRSE, professor of international law at the University of Edinburgh from 1862 to 1890, was a member in the 1840s. His magnum opus in two volumes—The Institutes of the Law of Nations appeared in 1883 and foreshadowed the United Nations.

I read a good deal of Voltaire as an undergraduate at St Andrews and admired the way in which he campaigned for tolerance and against religious abuses, often at considerable personal cost. Although I disagree with Russell's atheistic philosophy, I do share his and Voltaire's repugnance for fanaticism in whatever form. I can't now remember how I came across Russell's essay on Voltaire but I found it fascinating and instructive. I do remember, though, burning the midnight oil in my turret quarters at Fettes College to finish this essay, and many friends I made at the "Spec" have been the most enduring—we try to attend at least once a year to spend an evening under candlelight in the Georgian Hall.

Mr President, Gentlemen—as research on this essay proceeded as an increasingly frantic rate, your essayist became uncomfortably aware that the scope of his subject could be enlarged upon almost indefinitely, and he was haunted by visions of members of the Society slumped on the benches in the early hours of the morning as he turned the final page of his epic ... I should like to preface the essay with two aphorisms:

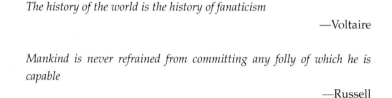

The history of the world is the history of fanaticism

—Voltaire

Mankind is never refrained from committing any folly of which he is capable

—Russell

In the dictionary "dogma" is defined as a principle, a settled opinion, a doctrine laid down by authority. So far as Russell and Voltaire are concerned, it is the last two definitions that illustrate what they were combating since, for them, authority is no substitute for careful observation. Fanaticism is derived from the Latin *fanaticus* which means "belonging to a temple" and is defined as "extravagant or unreasonable zealousness, especially in religion". It will, I hope, become clear that both men regard the combination of these two factors as responsible for most of the past and present miseries of the human race.

In this essay, I shall start by comparing the metaphysical scepticism of the two men and their views on the limits of reason; then I shall discuss their views on God and the pantheistic streak they share; on dogma and its relation to knowledge; on religion and its value; on war, fanaticism, and its relation to dogma and psychological uncertainty; and finally their views on ethics and its relation to reason.

In 1958, Bertrand Russell wrote an article entitled "Voltaire's Influence on Me". In it he was trying to steer a course "between the fanatic who does too much, and the sceptic who does too little". He explained that, while his views coincide with those of Voltaire on a number of issues, it was the tone rather than the content of the arguments that he found attractive. It was by reading Voltaire that he discovered the merit of ridicule in that "It suggests the absurdity of all dogmas in areas where only doubt or a confession of ignorance is rational" and he appreciated the quality of Voltaire's wit "which penetrates in a moment to the inner core of humbug beneath pretentious trappings". For instance his attacks—similar in vein to those of Moliere—on the medicine of his day: "The art of medicine consists of amusing the patient while nature effects the cure," or "Doctors pour drugs, of which they know little, to cure diseases of which they know less, into human beings of whom they know nothing"; in *Candide* he describes how "Owing to medicines and bleedings, the hero's illness became serious"; in another story he describes "one of those fashionable doctors which ladies call in when they are suffering from vapours, or nothing at all". People are naturally unwilling to be associated with anything or anybody ridiculous, hence the power of the *reductio ad absurdum* as a polemical weapon.

Both Russell and Voltaire acted as Socratic gadflies to their respective generations. They were passionate moralists, always ready to take a stand on an issue instead of confining themselves to the realms of theory, like so many of their contemporaries. Voltaire realised that nothing was to be gained by moderation, while Crawshay-Williams characterised Russell's attitude as one of "extreme feeling on a rational basis"—one incident relates how he interrupted a discussion on mathematical philosophy to get out of the car and fly into a rage at the incompetence of his builder and carpenter—when he got back into the car and immediately resumed the conversation in an apparently unruffled manner, the others were flabbergasted. He explained that it was only by flying into a rage and being unfair that either of the men would be goaded into action, and that within a few days they would have persuaded themselves that they were right anyway.

Historical examples of metaphysical scepticism are not hard to find: one of the earliest examples is the early Greek philosopher Xenophanes, quoted in Russell's *History of Western Philosophy*, who explained that:

> *The gods did not reveal, from the beginning, all things to us, but in the course of time through seeking we may learn and know things better. But as for certain truth, no man has known it, nor shall he know it, neither of the gods, nor yet of the things of which I speak. For even if by chance you were to utter the final truth, he would himself not know it. For all is but a web of guesses.*

The metaphysical mystery of the universe can never finally be solved, and seems to lie beyond the capacity of human reason. Numerous other writers expressed similar thoughts, for instance Omar Khayyam:

> *Into this universe and why not knowing,*
> *Nor whence like water willy-nilly flowing*
> *And out of it by wind upon the waste*
> *I know not whither, willy-nilly blowing.*

Or Pascal: "The final postulate of reason is to recognise that there are an infinite number of things which elude its grasp." Or, in our own day, Albert Camus: "The absurd is lucid reason noting its limits." Or, finally, Albert Schweitzer:

> All thinking must renounce the attempt to explain the universe. We cannot understand what happens in the universe ... what is full of meaning is united with what is senseless. The spirit of the universe is at once creative and destructive ... therefore it remains to us a riddle.

Voltaire prefers to invert Montaigne's question, "What do I know?" and ask, "What don't I know?" He confesses his inability to understand the nature of matter, still less of spirit, and asserts that the first principles of existence are impenetrable. Thus he conforms, by implication, to the advice of the Buddha not to indulge in fruitless speculation, but rather to strive for liberation; in Voltaire's case, this meant concentrating on ethics rather than metaphysics. He claims that Zadig was familiar with the laws of nature but "savait de la metaphysique ce qu'on en a su dans tous les ages, c'est-a-dire fort peu de choses" (knew of metaphysics what has been known in all ages, that is to say very little). In *Micromégas* he declares that "Our existence is a point, our duration an instant, our global an atom," thus foreshadowing the now familiar vast timescales posited by geology and theories of evolution. In addition to the above factors, Russell flourished at a time when metaphysical statements were considered meaningless by many philosophers, and where doubts about the meaning and value of existence were reinforced by stressing the impersonal nature of cosmic processes—human beings are seen as "the product of causes which had no prevision of the end they were achieving", human life is described as brief and powerless, and he thought the only firm foundation to be one of unyielding despair.

God, religion, and dogma

A comparison of the two men's views on God may throw some light on how the affirmation of the mystery of existence may lead to a declaration of its meaninglessness. While Russell rejects all proofs for the existence of God, Voltaire rejects only the ontological argument. He maintains that we know God only by His effects, we cannot know Him by his nature, which is inscrutable to human reason; thus he urges men to adore God without wishing to "pierce the obscurity of His mysteries". While rejecting revealed religion, he claims that the rational man need only open his eyes to nature to perceive God for "All is art in the universe, and art announces an Artisan." This is a classic statement of the teleological argument subscribed to by Newton and Locke, men greatly admired by Voltaire as pioneers of the empirical method and natural religion. Russell points out that this argument can easily be parodied by claiming that rabbits have white tails in order that they may be less difficult to shoot, and goes on to claim that Darwin's natural selection is sufficient to account for so-called design; moreover, he claims that judging from the world and the seedier specimens of humanity, an omnipotent and omniscient God could have done a better job. This brings me into areas which are beyond the scope of this article, so I shall pass on to the moral argument.

Had he lived to read it, Voltaire would almost certainly have approved of Kant's moral argument for the existence of God in the light of his maxim that if God did not exist one would have to invent him. The need for justice and the need for God are closely bound up, hence atheism is "a frightful moral mistake, incompatible with wise government". The belief in a God who rewards good actions and punishes evil ones is seen as "the belief most useful to human beings" as it acts as a curb on the worst secret vices of society, those which human schemes of justice fail to bring to light. Russell dismisses this argument as sentimental subjectivism and sees no need for this kind of social sanction based on a form of superstitious fear. He simply accepts the existence of injustice and does his best to combat it. Voltaire sees God as the guarantor of absolute moral values, while for Russell, as for many other writers since Nietzsche, the non-existence of God implies the non-existence of absolute values; hence we are driven back to a form of relativistic humanism, where we become responsible for the creation of our own values and meaning. Thus metaphysical scepticism combined with agnostic views on God and morals deprive life of any transcendent significance.

As a postscript to the views on God it is interesting to note a strand of nature mysticism in both men. Voltaire describes his exhilaration on seeing a sunrise, while Russell's feelings are aroused by the sea which, he says, "satisfies all my love of boundlessness and change and vast regularity, and has an extraordinarily exhilarating and yet calming effect on all my thoughts and feelings". Elsewhere he writes of his impression of the Cornish cliffs and in another letter that "My most profound feelings have remained always solitary and have found in human things no companionship. The sea, the stars, the night wind in waste places mean more to me than even the human beings I love best and I am conscious that human affection is to me at bottom an attempt to escape from the vain search for God." Here one recognises a frustrated religious impulse, of which more below.

Voltaire's attitude to dogma is a natural corollary to his views on metaphysics referred to earlier. It seems to him the height of folly and presumption to make categorical statements on matters which can never ultimately be resolved: "All dogma is ridiculous, deadly. All coercion on dogma is abominable. To compel belief is absurd." His viewpoint is that of the rational empiricist, and he is appalled by two of the consequences of dogma, namely *odium theologicum* and religious warfare. He denounces sophistry and castigates theological disputes as "at once the most ridiculous farce and the most terrible scourge on earth". He likens metaphysical battles to balloons which adversaries throw at each other; when they burst, the air escapes and nothing remains. What he finds both exasperating and tragic is that men kill each other for something which is ultimately incomprehensible: "I'm certain I understand nothing about this; no one ever has and that's the reason why people dismember each other."

Russell is equally impatient and scornful of dogma. He realises (in common with Dostoevsky's Grand Inquisitor) that the demand for certainty is natural to humans, but he nevertheless considers it an intellectual vice as it may lead to conviction in instances where it would be more prudent to withhold judgment in the absence of evidence. He defines faith as "a firm belief in something for which there is no evidence" and comments wryly that "It is an odd fact that subjective certainty is in inverse proportion to objective certainty." One way of combating this tendency is through education, which he claims ought to foster the wish for truth, supported by argument as opposed to the conviction that some particular creed represents the truth. However, while asserting that a decay of dogmatic belief can do nothing but good, he is less optimistic about the psychological need for certainty not finding other outlets: "I admit at once that new systems of dogma, such as those of the Nazis and Communists, are even worse than the old systems, but they could never have acquired a hold over men's minds if orthodox dogmatic habits had not been instilled in youth." This raises the whole thorny question of authority and education and its relation to indoctrination. Russell's solution has been hinted at above, but will be treated more fully below in relation to his ethics.

Had he lived in the twentieth century, Voltaire would doubtless have written an enthusiastic review of Aldous Huxley's *Perennial Philosophy*— he stated that deism is a religion spread through all religions and we are all of the same religion without knowing it. His starting point is the insistence that while belief is an accident of birth, morality is universal; we have already seen his impatience with dogma and metaphysics, which might be summed up in his famous slogan "Ecrasez l'infâme"— (crush the infamous). It is notoriously difficult to give a precise formulation of what Voltaire meant by "l'infâme" but it certainly included the Catholic Church of his day, who thought of him as an atheist because he did not agree with their dictates and still less with the consequences of religious faith: "Blood has run in wars and on scaffolds for 500 years on account of theological disputes … because morality has always been sacrificed to dogma." This last tendency exemplifies the tragedy of the Western idealist, who is inclined to sacrifice the individual to an overall plan.

Before dealing with Voltaire's positive views on religion, I shall mention a few of his criticisms. In one of his stories he criticises the spiritual ambition of an ascetic monk who spends his day sticking nails into himself, and claims that, without adopting this procedure, one can only attend the nineteenth heaven while he himself will reach the thirty-fifth; eventually he is persuaded to give up these excesses and is much happier as a result. However, he loses the respect of others and finally "reprend ses clous pour avoir de la considération" (he resumes his nails in order to be respected). The same kind of attitude is expressed in *Candide* when the travellers are astonished at the lack of ceremony. In El Dorado the monk is an unknown species—Voltaire saw them as disputatious parasites sheltering behind the tax exemptions of ecclesiastical law. He felt that priests should be married and set a moral example to their parishioners. In *Candide* he lambasts the hypocrisy of those who advocate charity in their sermons but do not practise it in their everyday lives. Finally, in *Micromegas* he ridicules the anthropocentric presumption found in Aquinas that the universe was created for mankind: when Micromegas finds this opinion prevalent on the ant heap of a globe he bursts into "an inextinguishable laughter which, according to Homer, belongs to the realm of the gods". And in *Plato's Dream* the demiurge is accused of not having taken humans very seriously because they have been given so many enemies and so little defence, so many diseases and so few remedies, "so many passions and so little wisdom". Voltaire urges humans to see themselves in perspective.

In his *Philosophical Letters*, written to describe his visit to England in 1734, Voltaire reports favourably on the English religious scene in general and on the Quakers in particular. He was impressed by the peaceful coexistence of so many different sects in England and remarked that English people go to heaven by the path they choose. He was struck by the Quakers' use of silence, the fact that they have no priests and elaborate ritual, and by their tolerance exemplified in the code of laws drawn up for Pennsylvania, which stated that no one must be mistreated on account of his religion and that all believers should be regarded as brothers. Voltaire's ideal religion is given in an article from his *Philosophical Dictionary* in an answer to the question of what would be the least pernicious form of religion. It would be, says Voltaire, the simplest one, which would teach a lot of morality and very little dogma, which would not demand assent to a series of unbelievable assertions, the one, finally, which would teach the adoration of one God and principles of justice, tolerance, and humanity. What more can one add?

Russell starts as a dissenter from all known religions on the grounds that they are both untrue and harmful. His analysis of falsehood of religion is surprisingly specious at the outset in that he claims as a matter of logic that only one religion can be true, without taking into account the considerable overlaps between the various traditions. He abhors the Inquisition in the same way as Voltaire and attacks the Church for having impeded scientific progress while it could; for instance, in the fields of physics, dissection and geology. He sees the religious spirit as the antithesis of the scientific in that it already has a set of unalterable axioms which must be adhered to, thus minimising intellectual flexibility.

Other harmful effects include attitudes to sex and birth control. On the last point he quite rightly highlights that if papal edicts were carried out to the letter the result would be widespread poverty and starvation. Russell's metaphysical attitude was, as we have already seen, like that of Camus, one founded on agnostic despair. In the face of the hostility of the universe and the human need to create our own values, he finds the courage of Christian resignation useful (which is more than Nietzsche did) but insists that mankind needs a fearless outlook and a free intelligence. We must go beyond fear, conceit, and hatred to knowledge, kindliness, and courage. Russell believed that if these qualities became widespread (and unlike Voltaire he does not posit a God to back them up) humans would solve their social problems and religion would die out. Incidentally, Russell also praised the Quakers for their emphasis on meditation and commented that the proportion between largely futile bustle and silence was wrong, urging that if the silence were longer the bustle might be less futile. Despite his sporadic mystical insight, it seems to me that Russell's attitudes in this field are not very profound and that he ignores the whole area of symbols and the many modern manifestations of gnosis.

The perils of fanaticism

A fanatic, said Churchill, is one who can't change his mind and won't change the subject. Psychologists such as Jung and Victor Frankl have said that fanaticism is one of the collective neuroses of our day (Jung said that fanaticism is overcompensated doubt). It would be rash to argue that fanaticism has not always existed in some form in the West, certainly since the inception of political and religious persecution, but it is certainly true to say that modern techniques, communications, and propaganda methods make it potentially more dangerous than ever [this essay predates the internet]. Its connection to dogma is partly a compensation for the doubt and uncertainty or angst felt by those who support it and derives partly from the doctrine of exclusive salvation with the echo of the dreaded verse "compel them to come in" and the exhortation to cut off your right hand if it offends you.

Voltaire claims that we are each born with a penchant for domination and imposing our will on our fellow humans, and that this factor, combined with the general human tendency towards extremes, drives us to find outlets for our passions. This justification is often couched in pseudo-rational terms and Voltaire blames abstraction for propping up such attitudes: "This creates wars, torture, violence." His recipe for making fanatics is to persuade before you instruct, hence the instruction is by way of an intellectual crutch to the passions. In *Plato's Dream* the demiurge says that it is easy to criticise his work, but does he think it simple to create an animal who is always rational, who is free and yet who never abuses his liberty? The enquirer is reduced to silence. We must simply try not to succumb to the disease, which Voltaire describes as a kind of almost incurable mental gangrene; the only palliative is "l'esprit philosophique".

Russell would probably have agreed with Voltaire's rhetorical statement that fanaticism is to superstition what frenzy is to fever and rage to anger since, if one is unable to persuade by argument one has to resort to force (Dr Johnson famously remarked that "You raise your voice when you should reinforce your argument"). He claims that every emotion distorts the judgment, and lists the activities inspired by moral fervour—human sacrifices, persecution of heretics, witch hunts, et cetera. He suggests that every isolated passion is, in itself, insane and that insanity might be defined as a synthesis of insanities in which no one passion gains the upper hand; if this were to happen on a large scale, the result is the kind of mass hysteria with which our century is only too familiar. Hence his recommendation that believers in all kinds of -isms should hang together, however different their nostrums and that in the welter of conflicting fanaticism one of the few unifying forces is scientific truthfulness—which brings us back to Voltaire's esprit philosophique.

The most familiar manifestation of mass fanaticism is war. In his day Voltaire, while regarding war as an inevitable scourge, was appalled at the wastage of human life and the triviality of the reasons for which war was initiated. For his part, the First World War came as a revelatory shock to Russell and the profound blow to his optimism about human nature. The giant Micromegas, looking down on the earth from a great height, is astonished that men are fighting over what he regards as a piece of mud. The narrator informs him that below there are 100,000 lunatics in hats who are massacring or being massacred by 100,000 lunatics in turbans and that this kind of spectacle is to be found elsewhere as well.

He is on the point of trampling them all underfoot when he is told not to bother in the immortal words "ne vous en donnez pas la peine—ils travaillent assez à leur ruine" (don't bother, they are working hard enough at their own destruction). In *Candide* a battle is described as a "heroic butchery" and the noise on the battlefield is the kind of harmony the like of which has never been heard. Voltaire scorns the so-called art of destroying the countryside and finds that the crusades were "at once the most universal, the most atrocious, the most ridiculous and the most unfortunate folly". For him the last straw is that each side invokes God and has its standards blessed before setting out to exterminate fellow human beings; and, after it is all over, the survivors all sing the *Te Deum*. At this stage, Voltaire ironically comments that "God is always on the side of the big battalions."

Russell's comments on war are no less withering. In an essay he poses the problem very starkly—shall we put an end to the human race or shall mankind renounce war? He was imprisoned during WWI as a conscientious objector and since that time never ceased warning of the follies of war and the danger of nuclear weapons. His first reaction to the war in 1914 was that "Hardly anyone seems to remember common humanity—that war is a mad horror and that deliberately causing the deaths of thousands of men like ourselves is so ghastly that hardly anything can justify it." He was dismayed that the majority of church ministers supported the war although they were pacifists in times of peace, and that in supporting war they gave emphatic assurance to the conviction that God is on their side and lent relative support to the persecution of men who think wholesale slaughter unwise. In order to avoid war Russell proposed that there be "universal and compulsory disarmament with the creation of an international government [a thorny problem in itself] … armies and navies do not make for safety—the only way to be safe in the modern world is to remove the means of fighting."

"The rarest thing is to combine reason with enthusiasm," claims Voltaire. Huxley's Quarles in *Point Counter Point* wrestles with a similar problem. For Voltaire the solution to the problems posed by dogma and fanaticism has already been hinted at in terms of reason, tolerance, and humanity, which, for him, formed the basis of universal morality. He claims that there is only one morality in the same way as there is only one geometry, hence there should be no grounds for dispute. He asserts that humans are not born wicked but may become so in the same way as one can become ill; he finds the contradictions of greatness and baseness inexplicable, but does not lose his faith in reason and tolerance.

Voltaire was one of the first men to put forward the idea of universal brotherhood in the form in which we understand it today. From the fatherhood of God he derived the brotherhood of humanity, not just within one state, and urged people to be constantly aware of this fact. He describes tolerance as the only balm to discord, and forgiveness of each other's foibles as the first law of nature. Virtue is seen in terms of benevolence towards one's neighbour; his whole ethic is contained in the exhortation to be just and benevolent. His true internationalism, as well as the influence of Confucius, can be discerned in the proposition that a just and benevolent Chinaman is more precious than an argumentative and arrogant theologian—the last word of l'esprit philosophique is to remember human dignity.

Russell claims that the cause of our troubles is skill without wisdom: "If the world is to be saved, men must learn to be noble without being cruel, to be filled with faith and yet open to truth"—they must have faith in humanity while maintaining reason, in short they must have a set of rational ideals. Twentieth-century humans, says Jung, are at once the culmination and the disappointment of the hopes and expectations of the ages. Scientific knowledge has, in Sir Julian Huxley's phrase, raised humans to the status of managing directors of evolution—an awesome responsibility.

The good life, asserts Russell, is the one guided by knowledge and inspired by love. The philosophic temper will enable us, he hopes, to conduct a rational search for knowledge and thus reduce the need to fall back on unprovable assertions of dogma. Progress in wisdom must, however, be matched by progress and ethics, understanding must be transformed into compassion. Russell's reaction to seeing the agony of his friend Mrs Whitehead transformed his outlook; he explained how he saw that the loneliness of the human soul was unendurable and that it could only be penetrated by the highest intensity of the sort of love that religious teachers have preached, and that whatever does not spring from that motive is harmful or at best useless. The only antidotes to fanaticism are tolerance and kindness, levers which are, as Schweitzer points out, within the grasp of each individual. I will leave the last word to Arnold Toynbee: "Human dignity can be achieved only in the field of ethics, and ethical achievement is measured by the degree in which our actions are governed by compassion and love, not by greed and aggressiveness."

The Spiritual Perspective and Political Responsibility

O n the day after 9/11, my friend the biologist Professor Brian Goodwin gathered his students at Schumacher College to reflect on the catastrophic events that had taken place in New York. Together, they came up with the idea of alternating but related loops of fear and love. When we are in the fear loop, we react with fear and suspicion, but if we managed to move into the love loop, we can come from a place of trust, moving from a vicious to a virtuous circle. This model has been widely used by colleagues in the International Futures Forum (www.internationalfuturesforum.com).

In a brilliant book entitled The Paradox of Our National Security Complex, subtitled "How secrecy and security diminish our liberty and threaten our democratic republic", Richard Otto suggests that

> In order to continue to justify the infringement of our liberty for security, the government continues to seek enemies to maintain a state of fear in our society to perpetuate this inequality. This is exemplified by the present war on terrorism that has no clear delineated objectives for its conclusion. As a consequence, we have allowed our public schools to flounder in mediocrity and our infrastructure to deteriorate as we continue to build weapons of war.

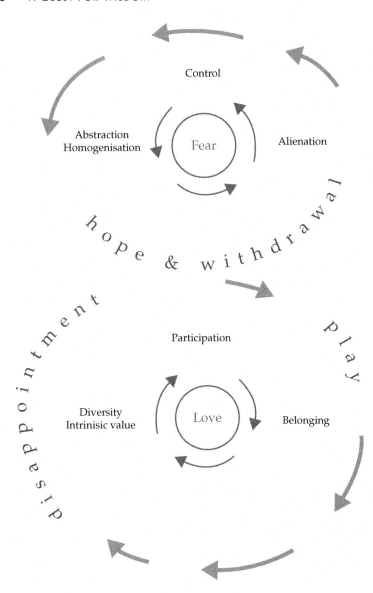

Later, he adds that

> *We claim this colossal war machine is necessary because as a world power we have strategic interests all over the earth. Although this may be true in a superficial sense, the reality is that we are a neo-colonial power that by design enforces our will on the rest of the world by our military presence*

and by clandestine operations sponsored by the CIA that interfere with the internal affairs and sovereignty of many nations.

At the end of the same paragraph, he observes that

As our enemies grow and become bolder, the need for security increases at the expense of our liberty. It is a cannibalistic process in which the hawks in each nation feed off of one another, justifying the diversion of resources to defense while reducing programs that benefit the governed. This is the paradox of our national security complex.

The relevance of these observations will become apparent in the two essays below when the West was dealing with the "Russian threat", which after 9/11 was transmuted into the "Muslim threat", with the "Russian threat" now re-emerging along with the "China threat"—all of which is used as justification for the maintenance of vast military budgets designed to give us "security" but at the same time perpetuating mistrust and keeping us firmly inside the fear loop. And all this at a time when the collapse of ecosystems is the overwhelming security issue that could be addressed with a fraction of the resources expended on the military. The essay dates from 1985 and is published here for the first time. The following essay is from the same year.

Fear is contagious, its chain reaction threatens to annihilate or paralyse us. In bewilderment we reach out for security in power, imagining that our own position can thereby be strengthened and our fears allayed. Our particular group experiences temporary relief, but, correspondingly, the fear of other groups is intensified. A vicious circuit is created, sustained, and perpetuated. The only winner is fear; as Franklin Roosevelt observed: "There is nothing to fear but fear itself."

We feel helpless, swept along by a Gadarene surge. No one seems to know quite where we are heading, and why. As we travel, some veer off to the Left, others to the Right, and still others keep steaming straight ahead. At length, some slow down, stop and begin to ask questions. Has anyone got a compass, do the others know where they are heading? We don't know. After a while we catch sight of a few people retracing their steps back to the spot where we stopped. We question them—why have they returned? Do their former companions have a good sense of direction? It's relative, they reply, but they know they're in the right. In the distance we can hear a great deal of cheering and jeering, mingled with the sound of hackneyed slogans whirring through the air. Even if they stop moving for a moment, the frenzied activity soon continues.

Gradually more and more battle-weary troops struggle into view, all with the same questions in mind. Who are we, where are we going, and how do we get there?

A spiritual compass

We are responding in the belief that rootless, centreless, directionless humans can discover a spiritual compass within themselves which will allow us to take our bearings in the material world. It points to the centre of ourselves, to the centre of our neighbour, then beyond this to the insight that the centre of ourselves *is* the centre of our neighbour. This is expressed in giving, sharing, loving. Fear is melted in the white heat of love. We must not wait to receive, but give in order to receive, the response of responsibility.

Central to our view is the assertion that our society reflects a certain understanding of the human—a predominantly materialist understanding; and that there can be no transformation of society without a transformation of our understanding of the human. Humans are not merely sophisticated material entities, but primary spiritual beings operating in a material world with other spiritual beings like ourselves. Such a shift in perspective will heighten our sense of responsibility, enabling us to perceive the power of ideas in shaping the future and requiring our cooperation in creating such a future in accordance with the vision. Those who thought they were passengers find themselves at the helm.

Philosophical materialism

- Humans have evolved through the interplay of chance and necessity in nature.
- We have no intrinsic purpose or destiny.
- Human consciousness is produced by the brain and perishes with it.
- The physical world is the only dimension of reality.

Social materialism

- Human behaviour and ideas are conditioned and shaped by our environment.
- Fundamental motivations are economic and social.
- Human nature is to pursue selfish or class interests.

- Human value is as a part of the social collective.
- The psychological fulfilment of the individual lies in collective action.
- Individuals may need to be sacrificed in violent revolution in order to attain the peaceful social ideal.

Consumerist materialism

- In the long run the pursuit of selfish interests maximises the benefit of all.
- The individual must make use of economic market forces.
- Humans as consumers and workers are a means towards their own prosperity and that of others.
- Gratification of selfish desires and needs leads to psychological fulfilment.
- Accumulation of possessions, money, and power consolidates the identity and status of the individual.
- Humans can never be content with what they have; they must strive for the latest, largest, or most expensive model which has rendered their current one obsolete.
- If people show any unwillingness to do this, they must be persuaded of their need; it must be pointed out that they risk losing status or the consideration of their neighbours.
- Cultivation of the image through consumption leads to social acceptability and approval.

Materialistic values and features

Although the material dimension is our field of operation, a materialistic climate may well prove destructive if given unbridled sway.

- Con-fusion, literally melting together, resulting in a state of uncertainty, fear, and doubt.
- Lack of vision, direction, perspective, leading to a sense of meaninglessness, hopelessness, and helplessness; culminating in cynical despair and disintegrating relativism.
- Attempts to compensate for these feelings and to acquire a sense of security and identity generate sects claiming absolute truth and demanding unconditional obedience from their members. These are intrinsically divisive, even if they unify their members. Doubt is

overlaid by fanatical certainty; everyone else must be convinced of the rightness of the cause, by inquisition and force if necessary. Those who are not for us, are against us.

- In terms of organisations, human beings are regarded as means, not ends in themselves. They serve the cause, and are individually dispensable. The collective or group is the supreme value.
- Force and coercion are legitimate, either in eliminating dissenters or in saving them from their ignorance. Those outside the group are alleged by propaganda to be not fully human. This means that there is a loss of sensitivity and humanity so far as non-group members are concerned. The negative qualities of one's own group are projected onto the inferior enemy, who hardly deserves to live.
- Pursuit of personal or national self-interest is the only way of maintaining one's status in the jungle hierarchy. This again entails regarding others as means to one's own end. Desires are to be gratified at once, if possible; ambition is encouraged and fostered, so that the next person or country can be put in place or cut down to size. Each works for their own centre without realising the interdependence of the whole. The state is tacitly one of perpetual warfare.
- Accumulation of possessions gives substance, security, and identity. Success in the race can result in pride and arrogance in the face of one's inferior neighbour; lack of success can breed envy, resentment, and even guilt at having "failed".
- Acquisition of power and influence is closely related to material accumulation. Personal or national vanity is satisfied, strutting nationalism is reinforced. Policies are to be decided on expediency in terms of national strategic or economic interest. The individual is encouraged to identify with national triumphs and humiliation; the triumph of one group is the humiliation of another, pride on the one hand with vengeful resentment on the other.
- The cult of the individual is the cult of the hero, the winner, the most successful exploiter in terms of financial, sexual, or physical prowess—the person who *has* most, not people who enrich the lives of others by the radiance of their *being*. The hero is the conquering eagle, the vanquishing lion. He conquers and vanquishes or resolutely defends himself. The noble unicorn is neglected.
- The scramble for power and possessions creates, sustains, and perpetuates divisions in the human race; there are winners and losers in the all-important game.

We cannot "live by bread alone": human needs extend beyond the physical.

Spiritual premises

- The body is an instrument of the spirit, and limits it at present to the three-dimensional world.
- The spirit is free and responsible for its own thoughts and actions, even if subject to various influences and constraints.
- The individual spirit is one with the underlying and transcendent Spirit of Life, Light, and Wisdom. We are one another.
- Everyday physical consciousness is one limited form. Mystics experience other forms which are more real, intense, and unifying. Quality of being, which one *is*, becomes paramount. Fulfilment lies not in divisive exploitation, but in loving self-sacrifice.
- We are all striving for this unity, whether we know it or not. Some seek it in individual relationship, some in political or religious affiliation. These are limited forms of harmony in so far as they separate the individual and prevent him from sensing the all-encompassing cosmic Unity.

Qualities of aspiration

These are qualities towards which we can aspire (literally breathe towards), and which flow from the spiritual understanding of the human being. There will almost certainly be a good many knots to be untied, flows to be unblocked, and surfaces to be cleaned and polished before such qualities can be unfolded and radiated. The process is gradual and lifelong; to the extent that the aspirant reflects these qualities, their relationships, and therefore society in their orbit, will be enriched. The qualities are infused, suffused, and then diffused, communicated.

- The flow of love in gentleness, compassion, sympathy, and sensitivity.
- Awareness and imagination, without which there can be no channel for thoughtfulness and freedom. To be unconscious of needs and drives in oneself and others is a form of blindness and bondage.
- Responsibility (response-ability), the obligation of freedom, and the invitation to participation and involvement; individuals as ends, not as means and functions.

- Tolerance, understanding, and patience stemming from compassionate sensitivity.
- Clear vision growing into courage, resolve, dedication, devotion, energy, fearlessness, and faith in human potential.
- The mind balanced in equanimity, spreading peace, serenity, and tranquillity.
- Spontaneous overflow of sparkling joy.
- Hope and confidence, the cultivation of integrity and honesty in oneself, eliciting the corresponding qualities in others.

The interlink between transformation of values and consciousness, the aim being to create positive flowing relationships in society which are unifying and self-reinforcing rather than self-destructive and divisive; we can then outstretch the warm hand of Love and not the icy fist of power.

Areas of application

Education

- The spiritual nature and qualities of humans need to be taught and fostered—fulfilment lies not in accumulation of possessions and powers, but in self-giving and sharing.
- Each human being should be respected and loved as sacred and unique—this applies to the process and the outcome of education; parents, teachers, and children.
- The senses should be led to appreciate harmony and beauty in art, music, literature, poetry, and nature. The quality of feedback from this will make violence and disruption in these areas less alluring.
- Consciousness should be educated; meditation should be taught in order to enable the individual to contact deeper, more unifying levels of reality and to give people a sense of oneness with their fellow human beings.
- Community and cooperation will flow from these deeper experiences of consciousness. Children will be encouraged to identify with the needs of mankind as a whole, and shown the contribution which they themselves have to make in terms of their relationships.
- Freedom and responsibility will be encouraged. Cooperative participation will make the hierarchical and militaristic model obsolete. Individuals who are neither submissive nor docile will not be manipulated by glib propaganda.

Society

The qualities of aspiration must be cultivated by each individual in their own circle; the above notions of education must be extended to adults as well.

- Materialistic power and possession must be supplanted by spiritual qualities and values.
- Fear, violence, hatred, envy, and suspicion must be defused and the energy positively redirected.
- As a complement to the welfare state, we must give of ourselves in order to relieve the widespread spiritual poverty.
- To the extent that spiritual qualities are embodied and diffused, the need for massive expenditure on law and order will be reduced.
- The stigma of unemployment, a classification based on utilitarian economics and material values, should melt away; it indicates status in terms of having rather than being. The right to *be* is as important as the right to work. As technology limits employment opportunities and frees up more leisure time, values should shift correspondingly from an outer to an inner basis.
- Harmony between humans should correspond with harmony between humans and nature; inner and outer pollution both need attention.
- Health should be promoted by widespread education, so that individuals become aware of their responsibility for the harmony of mind and body, realising their mutual dependence and interaction.
- Recognising the unity and interdependence of humankind, foreign policy should aim to foster trust and cooperation between peoples. National interest, in the long run, cannot afford to work for isolation, supremacy, and the appropriation of maximum material resources for itself. Cultural identity and diversity need not entail cold or hot hostility; each people has a unique contribution to make.
- Fear, threats, and counter threats dominate the current international political scene, while most people cynically and despairingly accept the status quo. Human needs are lost sight of, engulfed in insidious webs of self-interest on the part of those whose living depends directly, or indirectly, on the arms race. When individual nations renounce their eagle- or lion-like aim of dominating the world in the name of their own ideology, the tide of fear can begin to subside

and free cooperation emerge in its place. The discipline and training of the "Services" can be used as a standing army of goodwill, ready to step into the breach when any national or international disaster occurs.

Responsibility and the pneumatocratic vision

The most urgent task facing humankind is to close the "morality gap" between our material power and our spiritual capacity to use it, between our skill and our wisdom. Nothing short of a worldwide spiritual revolution is sufficient, as both Arnold Toynbee and Vaclav Havel have noted. Previous revolutions have shifted the power from one group to another; we must now rethink the whole question of power, so as to use our power productively and creatively rather than destructively and dominatingly. Lust for power and greed for material possessions are fundamentally incompatible with peaceful coexistence; different ideas must spread into practice, ideas embodied in the lives of men and women.

- Faith and confidence in the energies, enthusiasm, and positive creative potential of humankind can actually make the vision self-fulfilling.
- This process starts with YOU and ME. We are transmitters of life. If we do not work to transform ourselves and our relationships, how can we expect society to be transformed? Transformation is powerless without transformers.
- Each positive circuit which we create in our orbit works on the whole. If we each diffuse spiritual qualities, we can create an irresistible tide of goodwill and sympathetic concern, an infusion and trans-fusion of inspiration.
- The clear crystal can draw in and radiate human light and love.

Fear of Freedom

In defending our freedom, we are actually enslaved by fear.

A recent play by Arthur Kopit, encouragingly entitled *The End of the World*, but performed in English under the title of *The Assignment*, brings the psychology of deterrence to a new pitch of crazy sophistication. The second act consists of three interviews: the first with a general, the second with a hard-line strategist, and the third with two zany characters responsible for running computer programmes of possible nuclear scenarios. The general points out that we need nuclear weapons in order to prevent their use: paradox number one. He then goes on to say that what matters is not your intentions, but how your intentions are perceived by the enemy: "For the purpose of deterrence, a bluff taken seriously is far more helpful than a serious threat taken as a bluff." In other words, strategy comes second to psychology, to the moves and counter-moves of propaganda. If one side makes a threat which is just credible, the other side's fear that the threat might be carried out guarantees its effectiveness, whether or not it is a bluff. *The essence of deterrence lies in the fear provoked.*

This idea is elaborated in the following scenes, all of which are based on real conversations that the author had in Washington. The strategist outlines a situation where a first strike could be justified as a defensive measure. It is assumed that the first striker can obtain an almost insuperable advantage by taking the initiative. If both sides know this, they will be anxious not to be struck first. But in order for this not to happen they themselves must strike first. Now what if one side fears that the other side is going to strike first? Well, they must strike first in order not to be pre-empted. Then the other side perceives the possibility of a pre-emptive strike and must therefore pre-pre-empt; this defensive measure is termed "anticipatory retaliation", a mind-boggling contradiction in terms but an inexorable part of the nuclear logic of fear and deterrence.

Once side retaliates (strikes) because it *thinks* that the other side is about to do so, and cannot take the risk of being wrong. The two zany characters, Jim and Pete, now take up the theme of war breaking out precisely because no one wants it to. The starting point is that nuclear war is the last thing either side wants. Suppose that one side moves nuclear weapons into an area as a show of strength—in other words as a bluff. The other side may respond in like manner, which prompts the first side to bring their weapons out of storage as a stronger bluff. This move, however, may be interpreted as readiness to strike, thus engendering widespread fear and panic; and it is just this fear and panic which may bring about a pre-emptive strike, if the political pressure is really on.

We can see that the basis of deterrence is fear, and that fear may lead to its own fulfilment. In the long run, it is an extremely precarious basis for international relations, especially where double bluff psychology is so inextricably complex. In his poem "Knots", the psychiatrist R. D. Laing focuses on the ramifications of mutual fear. A few lines will convey the general confusion and misperception:

> *Jack is frightened because Jill is dangerous*
> *Jill appears dangerous because Jack is frightened*
>
> *The more Jack is frightened not to be frightened*
> *the more frightened he is to appear frightened*
>
> *Jack therefore tries to frighten Jill*
> *by appearing not to be frightened*
> *that she appears not to be frightened*

And Jill tries to frighten Jack
by appearing not to be frightened
that he appears not to be frightened.

If we substitute US for Jack and USSR for Jill (or vice versa) and apply it to the first two lines, the result is:

US is frightened because USSR is dangerous
USSR appears dangerous because US is frightened—

And conversely. The second couplet will lead to a bluff in the form of a show of strength ("It is the only language the B*****s understand"). The rest illustrates the double bluff which could become treble or even quadruple—who could really tell?

In January 1932, Professor John Macmurray gave a series of broadcasts entitled *Freedom in the Modern World*. Many of his remarks struck me as distressingly relevant to the 1980s, distressingly because his insight of over fifty years ago has still not been applied: "We are fear-determined, and our one demand is the fear-demand, the demand for security, for protection. Our dilemma lies in the fact that the more we try to defend ourselves the more we destroy ourselves by isolating ourselves more and more from one another." We conventionally rest our security on weapons of attack and defence: the other side will be afraid to attack us either because of possible reprisal or because our defences are adequate to their offensive. What we fail to appreciate, until we travel to Eastern Europe, is that our own defences are perceived as threatening the security of the other side, who seek reinforcement through a further build-up; so the SDI (Reagan's Strategic Defence Initiative) is perceived as giving the US the possibility of a safe first strike (this is not the place to argue the issue in detail). In sum, our security threatens them, and their security threatens us in an inherently unstable balance of terror; not unstable in the short run, perhaps, but logically so in the long run.

The question now becomes: how can we overcome the fear and suspicion which our present "security" arrangements are supposed to resolve, but which in fact perpetuate a psychological vicious circle? *In defending our freedom, we are actually enslaved by fear.* Only the fearless are truly free, for fear is a form of dependence on an external force. In addressing myself to this dilemma of our time, I want to concentrate on the underlying psychology, rather than on immediate practical proposals, which are only too likely to be based on old, unworkable assumptions. It is clear that a continuation of fear, doubt, suspicion, and the pursuit of power and domination can only lead ultimately to disintegration and destruction: the head is aligned to the will without the participation of the heart; the head calculates, reasons, and plans, while the will carries it all out. The heart is missing, excluded from political matters unless aroused by compassionate appeals. *Nothing short of a revolution in perception and values will remedy our malaise.* Instead of perceiving our interests as separate and exclusive, we will have to recognise our mutual interdependence and the fact that we are all striving for fulfilment as human beings; instead of the value of the survival of the fittest—each person/family/nation/block for themselves—we need to instil the values of service, love, and brotherhood. Such a revolution is no longer an altruistic option for humanity; it is rapidly becoming a necessity, a prerequisite for our long-term cooperative survival. Individuals have a responsibility to realise this and help others arrive at the same conclusion. Only when such realisation is widespread can it have an effect on world opinion. At present, only a handful have reached this stage, but my feeling is that many more are ready to support the logic of the above diagnosis.

St Francis asked to be an instrument of peace, to sow love where there was hatred, faith where there was doubt, and hope where there was despair. He saw that only concentration on and embodiment of positive qualities was an adequate response to the prevalence and influence of negative qualities. In our own day, the Dalai Lama conveys the same message when he insists that anger cannot be overcome by anger and that with anger peace is impossible; likewise, fear cannot be overcome by fear, but only by love—"Perfect love casts out all fear." Fear is divisive, it separates and isolates, makes people withdraw and contract defensively. Love, on the other hand, is expansive, encouraging outgoing trust and confidence, tending towards unity. The Russian sociologist Pitirim Sorokin (1889–1968) wrote reflecting on his own experiences of imprisonment and being condemned to death: "Hate begets hate, violence engenders violence, hypocrisy is answered by hypocrisy, war generates war, and love creates love. Unselfish love has enormous creative and therapeutic potentialities, far greater than most people think. Love is a life-giving force, necessary for physical, mental and moral health."

Let us see how this could work in practice. The first condition is that the love should be genuine; if it is a bluff, confidence and trust are further eroded, fear is reinstated, and we are back to where we started. Love can be expressed as goodwill, trust, compassion, and in many other forms. If A manifests love towards a former enemy B, B's initial reaction will tend to reflect the old pattern of suspicion and hostility, because he cannot imagine that A has really changed: he will interpret the move as a bluff, as a means of gaining a temporary propaganda advantage, and may even say as much. Suppose now that A explains that his move stems from the new values of service and brotherhood referred to above. Once again, B may see this initiative as a bluff. "By their fruits you shall know them," he thinks to himself, "and the only fruits I know of to date taste pretty foul." At this point, A might give up, in which case fear and suspicion are once again the winners. He must, however, persist, because only such persistence will convince B in the long run, changing his perceptions and subsequently his values. It is easy to understand that changing mutual perceptions is more of a process-reinforcing circuit than an event producing an overnight sensation in the media. Without persistence and courage, love/goodwill/compassion does not stand a chance; and because we are always looking for quick results, we wrongly conclude that a policy of goodwill is unrealistic and naïve. Ultimately, it can be effective and, moreover, stable in the long run as it will tend to build up a virtuous rather than a vicious self-reinforcing circuit of relationships.

Our fears limit the scope of our freedom. Fear of God is not now widespread, but fear of public opinion, ridicule, and ostracism is. We are taught to seek the approval of others by a system of rewards and punishments, at the root of which is the pleasure experienced in receiving approval, and the discomfort of censure and disapproval. In each case we place the need for approval outside ourselves, making others the arbiters and standard of judgment; we are therefore dependent and liable to fear of disapproval; and to the extent that we are dependent, we are not free. This trend encourages conformity and obedience at the expense of originality and independence of thought. If we want to make sure of not incurring someone's disapproval, we are careful not to say anything which might offend them, all the more so if they are in an influential position in relation to our own interests.

We conform to others' expectations out of fear, or else because we have no genuine convictions and values of our own. The ideals of service and brotherhood can become inner convictions and standards against which to measure the challenges and responses of life. If public opinion disapproves, so much the worse for public opinion; we can be freed from its grip by aspiration towards a more noble rather than superficial and volatile authority. Public opinion hailed Jesus and then called for the release of Barabbas, manipulated as it was by a small number of powerful people who knew what they wanted and how to achieve it.

Freedom from fear is the starting point for the courage to love and persist in that love unconditionally, regardless of hostile and indifferent opinion. Our ideals are powerless unless they are embedded as inner and unshakeable convictions. In changing our perceptions of others, we help change their perceptions of us; those who are aware of this must make a start. True non-violence (*ahimsa*), maintained Gandhi, should mean a complete freedom from ill will and anger and hate, and an over-powering love for all. May love melt down the chains of fear which bind us to antiquated perceptions and limited values.

Some Aspects of the German Democratic Republic

It is very interesting to reread these reflections from 1983 in the light of subsequent developments. The people I met still believed in the worldwide triumph of communism six years before the collapse of the Berlin Wall. My first visit to Bulgaria was also in the summer of 1989, and I remember hearing of the resignation of their President Zhivkov while driving to a meeting on the Gaia Hypothesis in Cornwall. I spent part of the summer of 1983 in Leipzig, taking a course at the university to improve my German. I visited Goethe's house in Weimar, where I was struck by the contrast between the opulence of his public rooms and the simplicity of his private quarters behind. As related in my introduction above to an article about Viktor Frankl, I also visited Buchenwald on the same day. One other outing of note was to a model farm where we were served a sumptuous tea. I refrained from eating much as there were more flies landing on the food than I had seen before or since …

Suddenly you see the wall behind you, barbed wire and concrete stretching into the distance in both directions, then a look-out post. You have crossed the border and the train trundles into Oebisfelde station for passport and customs control. What are you taking into the country as a gift? No publications apart from the *Morning Star* and *Marxism Today*, I hope, as they are the only reliable sources of information on Britain. Postcards?—Fine. I had visions of trying to explain why I had with me Whitehead's *Process and Reality*, the magnum opus of a well-known bourgeois philosopher, but my cases were not opened. Out of the window the first slogans—white printed on red—"The Protection of the Border Is the Affair of the Whole People", "The Teaching of Marx is Almighty, Because it is True" (Lenin), "Away with NATO Rockets". Further on, affixed to a factory, "Karl Marx Lives in our Lives and Deeds".

Leipzig station is one of those gigantic vaulted constructions, rather larger than King's Cross. The university is five minutes' walk away, one tram stop. Trams and buses are frequent and cheap—about 4p per ride, irrespective of the distance. In the Karl Marx Platz one finds the university, the concert house, the post office, and the opera house. The last two buildings have the respective slogans "In the DDR the Ideas of Karl Marx are Being Realised" and "Everything for the Benefit of the People". By chance I met a fellow Scot who was also looking for accommodation. In turn we came across a landlady who was looking for some lodgers, so we made our own arrangements. Her flat was comfortable and well furnished—we were luckier than those who had to share a bed, as we both had our own rooms.

Society and economics

The population of the DDR is around 17 million. There is no unemployment, indeed, the people can hardly envisage such a state of affairs. Some 88% of women of employable age work. Wages are fixed by the state and provide for a reasonable standard of living, even if the gap between East and West Germany is glaring.

The town centres are generally in good repair, but suburbs tend to be more depressing and dilapidated than Western counterparts; there is less street lighting. There are virtually no parking restrictions in Leipzig, a city of some 500,000 inhabitants, hence no meters and wardens. Naturally, there are far fewer cars: the ones there are—Trabant and Wartburg, for instance—are small, noisy, and smelly although they are meant to be quite reliable. The waiting list for a car is about thirteen years. One has to wait some eight years for a telephone, and up to two years for a washing machine or fridge. These, however, are the worst examples. Clothes and less sophisticated consumer goods, including TVs and other electronic equipment, are readily available.

Basic commodities are very cheap and plentiful—milk, cheese, bread, biscuits, Wurst, beer, etc. Soft drinks and water are ruined by the addition of particularly revolting carbon dioxide. Eating out is cheap. Restaurants are graded and prices fixed accordingly. A main course and beer would cost £1.50. If you drink nothing but beer, you have to beware of going into a restaurant where none is available after 8 pm. Vegetables and fruit are sold at so-called vitamin bazaars. There is a plentiful supply of cauliflower, cabbage, turnips, potatoes, and apples. Cherries were in season. Towards the end of July this year's tomatoes, apples, and pears started to appear. Items which were scarce or unavailable included: mushrooms, peppers, celery, peaches, apricots, bananas, grapes, and oranges.

Ideology and the media

As described above, there are slogans everywhere, many more, by all accounts, than in other Eastern European countries. The main emphasis is on the close alliance with the Soviet Union, the maintenance of socialism, the importance of sport, and the threat of NATO aggression. The newspapers reinforce these messages daily, as does the youth organisation, which has its own journal. A headline might consist of a message of solidarity sent to the Central Committee of another communist country. News of the West features mainly NATO rockets, unemployment, economic collapse, and disasters. Magazine stands have a range of general interest and leisure interest publications, but, conspicuously, no pornography. Bookshops are well stocked with literature, science, economics, and philosophy—also with travel brochures to other communist countries where the people are allowed to go on holiday—depending on availability of foreign currency. Incidentally, the State Bank is very crowded, so that service is cumbersome and slow.

There is a pervasive sense of the historical inevitability of the advent of socialism and communism in the World. Handbooks describe how the process of transition was instigated in the Soviet Union in 1917, and has continued ever since. Capitalism is regarded as doomed by the forces of history. Any attempt to deny this or to hinder revolutionary "progress" is branded as "revisionist" or "reactionary". "Progress" can only be in the communist direction, *by definition*. There is a ready-made answer to all social problems. Slick use of terms covers over any cracks in the system. The words "Imperialists" and "Aggression" can only be predicated of capitalist regimes. Thus it is impossible to argue that the Soviet presence in Afghanistan is an example of imperialist aggression, like the US in Vietnam. Moreover, it is a communist duty to defend any gains for socialism against reactionary forces, as well as to fight for "progress" where the disunity arises: hence foreign intervention is capitalist interference in "internal affairs" or "international solidarity": the guerrilla becomes the heroic freedom fighter. Human rights questions are brushed aside with the accusation that unemployment is a violation of human rights; the Soviet Union is idealised as the harbinger of the New Jerusalem.

Peace

According to socialist ideology, there can be no peace on earth without worldwide communism. There are slogans to go with everything, including sport, peace, and socialism. As already mentioned, there is a close association between the words capitalist, imperialist, and aggression. Any build-up of arms is a reaction to a prior NATO or US threat. This year, with the imminent possibility of the deployment of Pershing and cruise missiles, the fear is intensified; memories of war and devastation are reawakened in a people who have experienced it first-hand. If NATO deploys these weapons, the Warsaw Pact will have no alternative but to respond; they will not be browbeaten by the Americans. The scale of the threat plays straight into the hands of the propagandists, since it is so obvious that the US is trying to gain the upper hand in order to negotiate from strength. One of the most penetrating arguments concerns the profit accruing to those companies who manufacture the arms ...

In class one morning we are discussing these issues and reach a point of loggerheads—we cannot accept that we will be swallowed up by socialism, but they see world domination by socialism as inevitable and as their mission and purpose. I realise that we are missing each other as human beings. I rise and give the greeting of peace to all present, communists and non-communists. The human contact prevents us from entrenching ourselves in dogmatic positions. I am reminded and remind them of Einstein and Russell—"Remember your humanity and forget the rest."

Culture and religion

There were many concerts in Leipzig, some in the open air. Every evening at six in the Thomaskirche, where J. S. Bach was Kantor, there is a short service of two organ pieces, with a psalm and prayer between. Even if there is no trace of The New Age or meditation in the DDR, the Church is in good heart. The meetings organised in various cities this year attracted up to 100,000 people, over half of whom were under twenty-five. There is a substantial training scheme for theological students, even if committed Christians are unlikely to be found in the Central Committee. One pastor remarked that the state had noticed that Christians were good and honest workers ... This year Church and state are cooperating to celebrate the centenary of Luther, seen in some quarters as a Marxist before his time. In the Nikolaikirche there was a horrendous anti-war exhibition, almost as horrific as the smouldering remains of Buchenwald, transformed into a monument against fascism. While visiting the site we heard shots in the distance ...

In the end, brotherhood and sisterhood cannot be founded on atheistic materialism, it can only arise from communion with the transcendent Spirit of Love within each of us.

Towards a Culture of Love—an Ethic of Interconnectedness

*T*his *essay was based on a presentation given to a memorable conference I arranged with Prof Henryk Skolimowski and Dr Leszek Sosnowski at the Jagiellonian University in Krakow in 2007. I develop the notion of an ethic of interconnectedness more fully in the final chapter of my book* Resonant Mind, *and it seems to me more relevant than ever. It was first published in the volume* Towards a New Renaissance—Values, Spirituality and the Future. *Later in the essay I discuss the ideas of Rep. Dennis Kucinich, a former Democratic presidential candidate whose thinking is decades ahead of its time; and also the little known work of the Russian sociologists Pitirim Sorokin (1889–1968), the first professor of sociology at Harvard.*

> *"Three kinds of progress are significant for culture: progress in knowledge and technology; progress in the socialisation of man; progress in spirituality. The last is the most important. Technical progress, extension of knowledge, does indeed represent progress, but not in fundamentals. The essential thing is that we become more finely and deeply human."*
>
> —Albert Schweitzer

Albert Schweitzer is remembered not only for his medical missionary work in tropical Africa, but also for his gifts as an organist and
for his philosophical and theological work. His key ethical principle is "reverence for life" (Ehrfurcht vor dem Leben), an insight
that came to him one afternoon on the river. We are familiar enough
with his first category of progress in knowledge and technology, but,
as he points out, social progress is more important and progress in
spirituality is the most fundamental level. Here he uses the resonant
phrase of becoming "more finely and deeply human", which I take to
represent a refinement of consciousness that is reflected in ethically
informed action. This means closing the gap between knowledge and
wisdom, ensuring that technological and spiritual progress go hand
in hand.

Aldous Huxley expressed a similar concern but more strongly in
his book *Ends and Means*, published during the Second World War in
1941: "In the world in which we find ourselves, technological advance
is rapid. But without progress in charity, technological advance is
useless. Indeed, it is worse than useless. Technological progress has
merely provided us with a more efficient means for going back-
wards." A Machiavellian world based on power politics, acquisition, and use of biological or depleted uranium weapons is a case
in point.

A science of interconnectedness

Before coming more specifically to what I mean by an ethic of interconnectedness, it is useful to highlight the development of a science
of interconnectedness in physics, biology, and psychology, disciplines
that have until recently been dominated by atomistic conceptions of
isolated particles, genes, or individuals which put an emphasis on
separation rather than unity. This sense of isolation in an indifferent
cosmos has led to widespread alienation and loss of meaning. On the
other hand, more holistic concepts in science stress participation and
belonging as ways of overcoming this sense of alienation. And Arthur
Koestler has provided the useful idea of a "holon", which is at once
a whole and a part: cells are individual but form elements of organs;
organs are in turn individual but forms part of the body, just as the
body is part of the earth and the individual a part of society. And the

earth is part of the solar system, which is in turn part of the Milky Way galaxy and so on.

Physicist John Archibald Wheeler has asserted that "The universe does not exist 'out there', independent of us. We are inescapably involved in bringing about that which appears to be happening. We are not only observers. We are participators. In some strange sense this is a participatory universe." The inseparability of observer from the observed has been a standard element in quantum theory since the 1930s even if many physicists do not share the view that consciousness actually "collapses the wave function". The physicist and philosopher David Bohm elaborated a new view whereby unity is prior to separation with his ideas of the "implicate" and "explicate" orders (literally enfolded and unfolded orders). For him, reality is "undivided wholeness in flowing movement" (his best-known book is *Wholeness and the Implicate Order*), so wholeness is primary and part-ness or separation is secondary and derived from this.

Ecology and biology have built on the systems view of the world introduced in the 1940s by Ludwig von Bertalanffy. His key insight is the distinction between open (organic) and closed (mechanistic) systems where the former interact and exchange with the environment in a dynamic way. Life forms and habitats (ecosystems) are both complex open systems. As Fritjof Capra observes, the very principles of ecology are applied in holistic biology: "interdependence, recycling, partnership, flexibility, diversity, and, as a consequence, sustainability". The metaphor of the "web of life" says it all, beautifully expressing both unity and interconnectedness. Other concepts from biology include *symbiosis*—cooperation between organisms for mutual benefit—and *synergy*, where individual elements within a system work together for the good of the whole. Then Jim Lovelock's Gaia hypothesis questions the sharp distinction between organism and environment, arguing that organisms regulate the composition of the atmosphere for their own benefit—this is mutuality in action.

In psychology, Jung's idea of the collective unconscious posits a unity beneath the surface while mystics from all traditions describe an intuitive sense of unity beyond the senses. This mystical or transpersonal insight is also reflected in the near-death experience (NDE) and underlies the experience of life review, where people experience events as if they were another person involved in the same episode. In other words, the event is not relived from their own vantage point but as if they are another. In this sense, each event has as many aspects as there are experiencers.

Metaphysics and ethics

In his book *The Crooked Timber of Humanity*, Sir Isaiah Berlin asserts that "Ethical thought consists of the systematic examination of the relations of human beings to each other, the conceptions, interests and ideals from which human ways of treating each other spring, and the systems of value on which such ends of life are based." These ideas of relation and value rest in turn on a person's world view or metaphysic, thus intrinsically linking metaphysics with ethics. Christian eschatology (or the Last Things) consists of death, judgment, heaven and hell. If death is the end, then there can be no relationship between one's conduct in this life and one's fate in the next. However, to the extent that an afterlife is posited, then the question arises.

I believe that we can gain some insights into this matter from the NDE life review. As already mentioned, this seems to enable people to experience events from another person's angle. This would only be logically possible if there is an underlying unity and connectedness of consciousness, which is also experienced in mystical states. So unity of consciousness implies an ethic of interconnectedness. The experience of the life review takes place within an atmosphere of love emanating from what is usually sensed as a "being of light" who also embodies the spiritual qualities of peace, joy, and compassion. The *Bhagavad Gita* puts it like this:

> The yogi sees himself in the heart of all beings and he sees all beings in his heart. This is the vision of the yogi of harmony, a vision which is ever one. And when he sees me [Krishna] in all and he sees all in me, then I never leave him and he never leaves me. He who is in the oneness of love, loves me in whatever he sees, wherever this man may live, in truth this man lives in me.

The yogi understands the unity of life and consciousness that "we are one another" and it becomes natural to apply the golden rule of doing as you would be done by. For me, the NDE life review is a demonstration of the unity of consciousness and hence of the necessity of an ethic of interconnectedness that is also found in the New Testament. Here Christ encourages us to see him in all people and act accordingly: "For inasmuch as you did it to the least of them, you did it to me." Love of God and your neighbour is the cornerstone of Christian ethics that is reflected in the NDE life review. It points towards a very considerable degree of personal moral responsibility.

The evolution of consciousness

It is a commonplace to argue that the focus of evolution has moved from physical to mental, moral, or, more widely, cultural development. The idea of an evolution of consciousness has been put forward for more than 100 years and is sometimes related to a scheme that includes reincarnation, as with Rudolf Steiner. Oswald Spengler followed Hegel in applying a cyclical analysis to the rise and fall of cultures, and his book *The Decline of the West* struck a somewhat disconcerting chord when it was published during the First World War in 1917. It represented an internal crisis of confidence in the Western project. Arnold Toynbee followed this up with his massive twelve-volume *Study of History* published between 1934 and 1961.

Toynbee was also concerned with the genesis of civilisations, which he attributed to the activities of the "creative minority" within an existing society. Fritjof Capra builds on this idea in his book *The Turning Point*, arguing that the holistic (and transpersonal) movement represents just this creative minority that is the seed of a new culture. The sociologist Pitirim Sorokin offers a model involving an alternation between what he calls sensate (materialistic) and ideational (spiritually based) cultures, arguing that our current sensate culture is giving way to a spiritual renaissance, a hope and aspiration also shared by Toynbee. More recently, systems theorist Ervin Laszlo has offered his own idea of a "macroshift" from "logos" to "holos", citing the same kind of data referred to above that point to an emerging science of interconnectedness. Yet another model is offered by Spiral Dynamics, with its characterisation of phases of conscious development moving from blue (conservative) through orange (scientific and technological materialism) to more integrated levels beyond the green of the ecologically sensitive self.

The Bulgarian sage Beinsa Douno (Peter Deunov, 1864–1944) offers his own model of the evolution of consciousness on the basis of a grand scheme of involution (moving from the One to the many, or oneness to differentiation) and the reverse process of evolution from separation towards unity. He distinguishes five stages:

- Primitive collective consciousness (Lucien Levy-Bruhl's *participation mystique* or Owen Barfield's original participation)
- Individual consciousness (towards differentiation, separation)
- Collective consciousness (socialism, communism)
- Cosmic consciousness (the conscious mystical sense of unity)
- Divine consciousness (even wider and deeper).

Current societies alternate between forms of individual and collective consciousness, while in the transpersonal movement there is growing acknowledgement of the significance of cosmic consciousness (also R. M. Bucke's phrase) as a new phase of development.

Beinsa Douno provides two other parallel schemes of evolution. The first is what he calls Four Degrees of Human Culture:

- Violence—force, domination, power
- Law—threat, control (external)
- Justice—universal, excludes privilege
- Love—life for the whole.

The reader can see here that the end point of Douno's thinking points towards what he calls a Culture of Love beyond violence, law, and justice. Love internalises the universal principle of justice with its principle of dedication to the life of the whole. Likewise, his analysis of four systems runs:

- Clericalism, corresponding to the prevalence of outer ceremony
- Militarism, corresponding to the use of force
- Capitalism, corresponding to exploitation.

The shortcoming of all these systems, in his view, is that they all employ the same methods of violence, constraint, control, and fear. Only with the application of love—the fourth system—are these contradictions overcome and is a virtuous circle established.

Underlying the philosophy of Beinsa Douno are three fundamental principles:

- Love, bringing warmth to the heart
- Wisdom, bringing light to the mind
- Truth, bringing strength and freedom to the will.

In addition, two further principles—justice or equity and virtue—make up the symbolism of the pentagram, which is also danced in Douno's paneurhythmy (literally, universal harmony of movement) for which he also composed the music. The movements of paneurhythmy are replete with symbolism that combines the masculine and feminine principles represented by wisdom and love.

Dennis Kucinich and the politics of interconnectedness (www.kucinich.us)

Some readers will be aware of the remarkable forward-looking campaign by Rep. Dennis Kucinich for the Democratic presidential nomination, which he took all the way to the Convention. Kucinich has been an implacable opponent of the war in Iraq, observing that dichotomous thinking leads to war and a vicious circle of escalating violence. He sees the role of the US president as overcoming divisions through reconciliation and healing, remembering that the motto of the United States— *E pluribus unum*—can be applied on a planetary scale on the basis of the following principles: faith, optimism, hope, renewal, justice, non-violence, cooperation, mutuality, courage, integration, transformation.

Returning to the origins of the US, Kucinich observes: "Whether we look at the first motto of the United States, *E pluribus unum* (out of many, one), which is a spiritual principle, or in the later motto 'In God We Trust,' we have to recognise the Founders were immersed in contemplation of a world beyond our experience, one of spirit, of mysticism, one which saw the potential of the country as unfolding in a multidimensional way, both through the work of our hands and the work of our hearts."

Kucinich calls for an evolutionary politics "of creativity, of vision, of heart, of compassion, of joy; to create a new nation and a new world using the power of love, of community, of participation, to transform our politics, and yes, to transform ourselves", adding "Let us remake

America by reconnecting with a higher purpose to bring peace within and without, to come into harmony with nature, to confirm and to secure the basic rights of our brothers and sisters."

His proposal for a Department of Peace has received over forty votes of support in Congress and has been adopted as policy by a number of local Democratic parties. And in 2004, he received the Gandhi Peace Prize for his efforts. Dennis explains:

> Americans have proven over and over again we're a nation that can rise to the challenges of our times, because our people have that capacity. And so, the concept of a Department of Peace is the vehicle by which we express our belief that we have the capacity to evolve as a people, that someday we could look back at this moment and understand that we took the steps along the way to make war archaic. War is not inevitable. Peace is inevitable!

In a lecture on evolutionary politics, he commented that "We are in a period of chaos, which is driven by fear, by control, by power, by secrecy, mistrust, fragmentation, isolation, and by policies which use the lexicon of unilateralism and of preemption." However, the power of consciousness is to call forth the new:

> The world is multidimensional. The new vision is a holistic one that understands the power of intention and the power of co-operation, of mutuality, of trust, of seeing the world as one. That vision then becomes our outer reality. Ours is the ability, through our consciousness, to create peace, to create love. The organ of transformation is the human heart because there is nothing—no weapon ever made—that is more powerful than a human heart.

This is an inspiring and visionary message that echoes Beinsa Douno's Culture of Love and is way ahead of our current thinking while giving it a sense of direction.

Ethical mysticism — creating the future

It is our duty to remain optimists. The future is open. It is not predetermined and thus cannot be predicted—except by accident. The possibilities that lie in the future are infinite. When I say "It is our duty to remain optimists", this includes not only the openness of the future but also that which all of us contribute to it by everything we do: we are all responsible for what the future holds in store.

—Sir Karl Popper, *The Myth of the Framework*

I believe that this remark by the philosopher Sir Karl Popper contains a profound moral truth. Pessimists paralyse the efficacy of their own actions in a self-fulfilling loop that entails a passive lack of creative impulse. Moreover, as Kucinich points out in the previous section, if positive intention is a key component of activism, then it becomes a tool to be employed.

Albert Schweitzer's ethic of reverence for life is a powerful formula in the way he defines it: "Just as white light consists of coloured rays, so reverence for life contains all the components of ethics: love, kindliness, sympathy, empathy, peacefulness, power to forgive." He adds: "Whenever my life devotes itself in any way to life, my finite will-to-live experiences union with the infinite will in which all life is one, and I enjoy a feeling of refreshment which prevents me from pining away in the desert of life." This is an actual definition of ethical mysticism—the feeling of union with the infinite arising from selfless service. And this is entirely consistent with acting on the golden rule which exemplifies the ethic of interconnectedness already explained. In this way there is an expansion of both consciousness and ethics.

The basic dichotomy of the future is the choice between a path of fear and a path of love. The path of fear is a vicious circle that brings power, control, mistrust, and alienation. While the path of love is a virtuous circle of participation, trust, and belonging. This second path can only be followed through conscious inner intent, while the triumph of fear relies on ignorance and passivity. Let us act with conscious loving intent.

AFTERWORD

Humanity is now too clever to survive without wisdom.

—E. F. Schumacher

Thank you for sharing with me by reading this far! The essays printed here represent many facets of my lifelong quest for wisdom and understanding—the path of *jnana* or *gnosis*, although I have not neglected the paths of action (*karma*) or love (*bhakti*). It is my hope that in reading them you have gleaned some helpful insights and inspirations to illuminate your own path through life and give you courage to live as fully as possible in this beautiful though imperfect and in some ways frustrating world.

I recently reread the profound four studies of Goethe by Albert Schweitzer, and was particularly struck by two passages in the context of this afterword. The first is when Goethe was asked: "What can a man bequeath of his spirit to the world?"—to which he replied, "The only thing that we can leave behind us for the men to come is not systems, but confessions and professions. We can set them forth and say: 'This was my purpose, this was my wish, this was my thought.' And our successors may take from the confession of faith that we place before them whatever seems good to them, whatever is of lasting truth to them."

As T. S. Eliot once remarked, "The meaning of the poem lies somewhere between the poet and the reader"—so it is with this book of essays.

The second passage comes from Schweitzer's Goethe prize address in Frankfurt, delivered on August 28, 1928. Here he writes that Goethe's spirit places a threefold obligation upon us:

> We must wrestle with circumstances, so that those who are imprisoned by them in their exhausting jobs may nevertheless be able to preserve their spiritual lives. We must wrestle with men, so that, distracted as they constantly are by the external things so prominent in our time, they may find the road to inwardness and remain on it. We must wrestle with ourselves and with everyone else, so that, in an age of confusion and inhumanity, we may remain loyal to the great humane ideals of the 18th century, translating them into the thought of our age and attempting to realise them. This is our task, each in his own life, each in his own calling, in the spirit of the great child of Frankfurt.

These prescient themes of wrestling with busyness and distraction in relation to the preservation of inwardness and our spiritual lives are all the more intense today.

Writing in the beginning of 2020, there is a growing sense of collective unease about human prospects during the course of this century. Collapse and extinction are now in the air and major disruption seems inevitable if we simply continue with business as usual. However, we should remember that the outer reflects the inner, so we need to prioritise change on an inner level, applying, as Sandra Ingerman suggests, the alchemy of the soul to transform dense lead consciousness into gold: as she puts it: "It is who we become that changes the world, not what we do. The world changes by how we change."

The tension between old and new, old and young has been exemplified at the World Economic Forum on sustainability in the clash between President Trump and Greta Thunberg. Trump said: "This is not a time for pessimism. This is a time for optimism. Fear and doubt is not a good thought process because this is a time for tremendous hope and joy and optimism and action. But to embrace the possibilities of tomorrow, we must reject the perennial prophets of doom and their predictions of the apocalypse."

Surely it is in fact a time for realism, as Greta insists, but not in the cynical political sense. Rather a refocusing of our efforts away from exploitation towards regeneration, finding ways to live in harmony with nature, as the Prince of Wales has been arguing. We are depleting nature's capital—Earth Overshoot Day now occurs before the end of July—and advanced countries are using the equivalent of over four planets in terms of resources. At the same time, we are increasing our numbers as well as trying to maintain economic growth with its corresponding impact on resources. Like Naomi Klein in her new book *On Fire*, I am wondering if the expansive and extractive mindset of unlimited capitalist consumption is compatible with sustainability, let alone regeneration. Moreover, individualism and free markets are ill-equipped to address "a problem that demands collective action on an unprecedented scale" towards radical system change.

Along with many others, I have been working towards a new ecological and spiritual world view for forty years. This means taking an interconnected systems view of life at all levels and realising we are all collectively responsible for co-creating a sustainable and equitable future for the whole of life. I am convinced that the ultimate direction of human evolution is towards a culture of love and wisdom and therefore cosmic consciousness when we become aware that there is only one life and one consciousness. Hence we are expressions of the whole and are therefore ethically one another and should act accordingly. This is what Riane Eisler calls an ethic of care and compassion based on partnership rather than old-fashioned domination. We may not all live to see the advent of this new culture where we all work for the whole out of love, but we can personally use the principles of love and wisdom to set our compass direction in the knowledge that inner shifts of vision and imagination create and precede outer transformation. As Gandhi expressed it: "Be the change you want to see in the world." We now need to transform ourselves from rapacious caterpillars to butterflies that live more lightly on the earth and beautify the world with their presence.

Postscript

Heresy, Dissidence and Authority

Since I wrote these words in January 2020, we have experienced a major disruption, the likelihood of which I referred to above, and as a consequence of business as usual in our relationships with nature and our pursuit of "gain of function" biological research. We have also experienced a major information war and extensive censorship of non-mainstream views. All this reinforces Albert Schweitzer's contention quoted above that "We must wrestle with ourselves and with everyone else, so that, in an age of confusion and inhumanity, we may remain loyal to the great humane ideals of the 18th century, translating them into the thought of our age and attempting to realise them."

Over the past few months, so-called "conspiracy theorists" have become the new heretics and dissidents. This weaponised and derogatory term was invented by the CIA in the 1960s to discredit and defame those who questioned the truth of the official Warren Commission report on the Kennedy assassination; the same applies to questioning the 9/11 Commission Report, the shortcomings of which have been forensically exposed by Prof David Ray Griffin in his comprehensive analysis laid out in a series of books beginning with *The New Pearl Harbor*. The conspiracy theorist label is used against those who speak truth to power, and many journalists are cowed by the threat of being branded in this way, even if this is entirely unjustified. Judgment is a matter of reason, evidence, and discrimination for each of us to join the dots and draw our own conclusions—the key issue is which dots to join and on what basis.

The Inquisition—an early manifestation of a police state—was created in the thirteenth century to suppress the views of the Cathars of Languedoc. From the mid-sixteenth century, heretical books were placed on the Index of Prohibited Books, only abolished by Pope Paul VI in 1966. Enlightenment figures such as Voltaire promoted tolerance and freedom of speech and expression—he wrote his *Treatise on Tolerance* in 1763. Both the American and French revolutions promoted liberty, although there is a significant difference of emphasis between "life, liberty and the pursuit of happiness" and "liberty, equality and fraternity"—the first implicitly highlighting individualism where the second balances this individualism with social concerns.

In this treatise, Voltaire writes that "There was a time when it was thought necessary to issue decrees against those who taught a doctrine at variance with the categories of Aristotle" (then he lists a number of other items). Further on, he concludes that "The law of intolerance is absurd and barbaric; it is the law of tigers; except that it is even more absurd and horrible, because tigers tear and mangle only to have food, whereas we wipe each other out over paragraphs." Writing on the damage done by intolerance, he states: "What? Is each citizen to be allowed to trust his own reason, and to believe whatever this enlightened or deluded reason shall dictate to him? Yes indeed, provided he does not disturb the public order."

Over the past few months we have witnessed a new episode of Inquisition and the implicit creation of an online Index of Prohibited Material. There has been a steep rise in censorship by social media companies of views at variance with mainstream narratives: dissident content is summarily removed. Heretical and subversive views are not tolerated, open debate is stifled in favour of officially sanctioned orthodoxy, whistle-blowers are abused and demonised. Manipulated by fear and on a flimsy pretext of security, we are in danger of abjectly surrendering the very freedom of thought and expression that our ancestors fought so courageously to secure in the eighteenth century and which constitutes the essence of our Enlightenment legacy—so conspicuously absent in authoritarian China. Yet we are in danger of drifting in the same direction with the introduction of new tracking and tracing surveillance technology further enabled by the roll-out of 5G.

Voltaire's biographer Evelyn Beatrice Hall summarised his outlook in the famous and oft-quoted phrase referring to a passage where he wrote that "Think for yourselves and let others enjoy the privilege of doing so as well: 'I disapprove of what you say, but I will defend to the death your right to say it.'" We forget this Enlightenment message at our peril if we are to continue to uphold freedom of expression and an open exchange of views. In the words drafted by James Madison in the 1791 First Amendment to the US Constitution: "Congress shall make no law prohibiting … or abridging the freedom of speech, or of the press."

For me, this brings me back to the fundamental principles of Beinsa Douno: that we understand and do our best to embody both personally and in our institutions the principles of Love, Wisdom, Truth, Freedom, Justice, Goodness, and Peace. "There is nothing greater than these principles; there is no straighter or surer path."

BIBLIOGRAPHY

Aeschliman, M. D. (1998). *The Restitution of Man*. Grand Rapids, MI: Wm. B. Eerdmans.

Aivanhov, O. M. (1984). *Cosmic Moral Laws*. Frejus, France: Prosveta.

Alexander, E. (2012). *Proof of Heaven*. London: Piatkus.

Alexander, E., & Newell, K. (2017). *Living in a Mindful Universe*. London: Piatkus.

Alexander, E., & Tompkins, P. (2014). *The Map of Heaven*. London: Piatkus.

Alger, W. R. (1871). *A Critical History of the Doctrine of a Future Life*. New York: Middleton.

Amiel, H.-F. (1889). *Journal*. Mrs Humphry Ward (Ed.). London: Macmillan.

Anderson, W. (1996). *The Face of Glory*. London: Bloomsbury.

Appleyard, B. (1992). *Understanding the Present*. London: Picador.

Ariès, P. (1976). *Western Attitudes Towards Death*. London: Marion Boyars.

Ariès, P. (1981). *The Hour of Our Death*. London: Penguin.

Arkle, W. (1974). *A Geography of Consciousness*. London: Neville Spearman.

Assagioli, R. (1975). *Psychosynthesis*. London: Turnstone.

Bache, C. M. (2000). *Dark Night, Early Dawn*. New York, SUNY Press.

Bache, C. M. (2019). *LSD and the Mind of the Universe*. Rochester, VT: Park Street Press.

Badham, P., & Badham, L. (1987). *Death and Immortality in the Religions of the World*. New York: Paragon House.

Baldwin, W. J. (1995). *Spirit Releasement Therapy*. New York: Headline.

Balfour, E. B. (1976). *Living Soil*. London: Faber.

Bamford, C. (Ed.) (1994). *Rediscovering Sacred Science*. Edinburgh, UK: Floris.

Barbour, I. G. (1998). *Religion and Science*. London: SCM.

Baring, A. (2013). *The Dream of the Cosmos*. New York: Archive.

Barrett, Sir W. (1926). *Death-Bed Visions*. London: Psychic.

Barrett, W. (1986). *Death of the Soul*. Oxford: Oxford University Press.

Baruss, I., & Mossbridge, J. (2017). *Transcendent Mind*. Washington, DC: APA.

Bateson, G. (1979). *Mind and Nature*. London: Fontana.

Beard, P. (1966). *Survival of Death*. London: Psychic.

Beard, P. (1980). *Living On*. London: George Allen & Unwin.

Beard, P. (1986). *Hidden Man*. Norwich, UK: Pilgrim.

Beauregard, M. (2012). *Brain Wars*. New York: HarperCollins.

Beckett, S. (1952). *En Attendant Godot*. Paris: Editions Minuit.

Beloff, J. (1993). *Parapsychology: A Concise History*. London: Athlone.

Berdyaev, N. (1937). *The Destiny of Man*. London: Geoffrey Bles.

Berger, P. (1967). *The Social Reality of Religion*. London: Penguin.

Bergson, H. (1919). *L'Energie Spirituelle*. Paris: Presses Universitaires de France.

Bergson, H. (1932). *Matière et Mémoire*. Paris: Presses Universitaires de France.

Bergson, H. (1946). *The Creative Mind*. New York: Citadel.

Berlin, Sir I. (1959). *The Crooked Timber of Humanity*. London: John Murray.

Berman, M. (1984). *The Re-Enchantment of the World*. London: Bantam.

Berry, T. (1999). *The Great Work*. New York: Harmony.

Berry, W. (1991). *Standing on Earth*. Cambridge: Golgonooza.

Bertalanffy, L. von (1952). *Problems of Life*. London: Watts.

Bertalanffy, L. von (1968). *General Systems Theory*. London. Allen Lane.

Beveridge, W. I. B. (1955). *The Art of Scientific Investigation*. London: Science Book Club.

Blackie, J. S. (1874). *Self-culture, a Vade Mecum for Young Men and Students*. London: Edmonston & Douglas.

Blackmore, S. J. (1982). *Beyond the Body*. London: Heinemann.

Blackmore, S. J. (2011). *Consciousness: A Very Short Introduction*. Oxford: Oxford University Press.

Blavatsky, H. P. (1885). *The Secret Doctrine*. London: Theosophical Press.

Blavatsky, H. P. (1889). *The Key to Theosophy*. London: Theosophical Publishing House, 1968.

Bleier, R. (Ed.) (1986). *Feminist Approaches to Science*. New York: Pergamon.

Bocock, R., & Thompson, K. (Eds.) (1985). *Religion and Ideology*. Manchester, UK: Manchester University Press.

Bohm, D. (1980). *Wholeness and the Implicate Order*. London: Routledge & Kegan Paul.

Bohm, D. (1987). *Unfolding Meaning*. London: Ark.

Bohm, D., & Hiley, B. (1994). *The Undivided Universe*. London: Routledge.

Bohm, D., & Krishnamurti, J. (1985). *The Ending of Time*. London: Gollancz.

Bonhoeffer, D. (1951). *Letters and Papers from Prison*. London: Simon & Schuster.

Bortoft, H. (1996). *Goethe's Way of Science*. Edinburgh, UK: Floris.

Bouratinos, E. (2018). *Science, Objectivity, and Consciousness*. Princeton, NJ: ICRL Press.

Brabazon, J. (2000). *Albert Schweitzer: A Biography*. Syracuse, NY: Syracuse University Press.

Brandon, S. G. F. (1962). *Man and His Destiny in the Great World Religions*. Manchester, UK: Manchester University Press.

Brandon, S. G. F. (1967). *The Judgement of the Dead*. London: Weidenfeld & Nicolson.

Broad, C. D. (1935). Normal cognition, clairvoyance and telepathy. *Proceedings of the Society for Psychical Research*, part 142, *XLIII*(3): 397—438.

Broad, C. D. (1962). *Lectures on Psychical Research*. London: Routledge & Kegan Paul.

Brinkley, D. (1994). *Saved by the Light*. New York: Villard.

Broughton, R. S. (1991). *Parapsychology: The Controversial Science*. London: Rider1992.

Brown, H. (1986). *The Wisdom of Science*. Cambridge: Cambridge University Press.

Brown, L. (1991). *Eco-Economy*. New York: W. W. Norton.

Brown, R. (1974). *Immortals at My Elbow*. London: Bachman and Turner.

Brunton, P. (1943). *The Wisdom of the Overself*. London: Rider.

Brunton, P. (1952). *The Spiritual Crisis of Man*. London: Rider.

Brunton, P. (1984). *Essays on the Quest*. London: Rider.

Brunton, P. (1984). *Perspectives*. New York: Larson.

Buber, M. (1937). *I and Thou*. New York: Charles Scribner's Sons.

Burckhardt, T. (1987). *Mirror of the Intellect*. Cambridge: Quinta Essentia.

Burnet, J. (1932). *Early Greek Philosophy*. Edinburgh, UK: A. & C. Black.

Burr, H. S. (1972). *Blueprint for Immortality*. London: Neville Spearman.

Burt, Sir C. (1975). *ESP and Psychology*. A. Gregory (Ed.). London: Weidenfeld & Nicolson.

Burtt, E. A. (1924). *The Metaphysical Foundations of Modern Science*. London: Routledge & Kegan Paul.

Bury, J. B. (1928). *History of the Freedom of Thought*. London: Williams and Norgate.

Butterfield, Sir H. (1949). *The Origins of Modern Science*. London: Bell.

Cadman, D. (2002). *A Sacred Trust*. London: Temenos.

Campbell, J. (Ed.) (1964). *Man and Transformation*. London: Routledge & Kegan Paul.

Camus, A. (1947). *La Peste*. Paris: Gallimard.

Camus, A. (1956). *The Myth of Sisyphus*. London: Penguin.

Capra, F. (1976). *The Tao of Physics*. London: Fontana.

Capra, F. (1982). *The Turning Point*. London: Wildwood House.

Capra, F. (1986). *The Web of Life*. New York: Anchor Doubleday.

Capra, F. (1987). *Uncommon Wisdom*. London: Century.

Capra, F. (2002). *The Hidden Connections*. New York: Doubleday.

Capra, F., & Luisi, P. L. (2014). *The Systems View of Life*. New York: Cambridge University Press.

Cerminara, G. (1967). *Many Mansions*. London: Neville Spearman.

Chandra, A. (2018). *The Scientist and the Saint*. Cambridge: Archetype.

Charles, R. H. (1899). *The Doctrine of a Future Life*. London: A. & C. Black.

Charles, R. H. (1912). *Immortality*. Oxford: Clarendon.

Chopra, D., & Kafatos, M. (2017). *You Are the Universe*. London: Rider.

Chopra, D., & Mlodinow, L. (2001). *War of the Worldviews*. New York: Harmony.

Churton, T. (1987). *The Gnostics*. London: Weidenfeld & Nicolson.

Citro, M. (2011). *The Basic Code of the Universe*. New York: Park Street.

Clarke, C. (2013). *Knowing, Doing and Being*. Exeter, UK: Imprint Academic.

Collingwood, R. G. (1940). *An Essay on Metaphysics*. Oxford: Clarendon.

Collins, C. (2002). *The Vision of the Fool and Other Writings*. Ipswich, UK: Golgonooza.

Comella, P. (2013). *The Collapse of Materialism*. Virginia Beach, VA: Rainbow Bridge.

Conford, P. (1988). *The Organic Tradition*. Bideford, UK: Green Books.

Coomaraswamy, A. K. (1989). *What Is Civilisation?* Ipswich, UK: Golgonooza.

Cornwell, J. (Ed.) (1995). *Nature's Imagination*. New York: Oxford University Press.

Copleston, F. (1980). *Philosophies and Cultures*. New York: Oxford University Press.

Copleston, F. (1982). *Religion and the One*. London: Search.

Cranston, S., & Williams, C. (1984). *Reincarnation: A New Horizon in Science, Religion and Society*. New York: Julian.

Crookall, R. (1960). *The Study and Practice of Astral Projection*. London: Aquarian.

Crookall, R. (1961). *The Supreme Adventure*. Cambridge: James Clarke.

Crookall, R. (1978). *What Happens When You Die*. London: Colin Smythe.

Cummins, G. (1935). *Beyond Human Personality*. London: Ivor Nicholson & Watson.

Dampier-Whetham, Sir W. C. D. (1950). A *History of Science*. Cambridge: Cambridge University Press, 1950.

DeConick, A. D. (2016). *The Gnostic New Age*. New York: Columbia.

Denton, W. (1988). *The Soul of Things*. London: Aquarian.

Deunov, P. (1968). *La Sagesse*. Paris: Le Grain de Ble.

Deunov, P. (1970). *The Master Speaks*. San Francisco, CA: Sunrise.

Deunov, P. (1983). *L'Enseignement deVie Nouvelle*. Paris: Courrier du Livre.

Devall, B., & Sessions, G. (1985). *Deep Ecology*. Salt Lake City, UT: Peregrine Smith.

Dewitt, R. (2004). *Worldviews*. Oxford: Blackwell.

Dossey, L. (1982). *Space, Time and Medicine*. London: Shambhala.

Dossey, L. (1984). *Beyond Illness*. London: Shambhala.

Dossey, L. (1989). *Recovering the Soul*. New York: Bantam.

Dossey, L. (1991). *Meaning and Medicine*. New York: Bantam.

Dossey, L. (1999). *Reinventing Medicine*. San Francisco, CA: Harper.

Dossey, L. (2001). *Healing beyond the Body*. San Francisco, CA: Harper.

Dossey, L. (2016). *One Mind*. London: Hay House.

Dostoevsky, F. (1880). *The Brothers Karamazov* (2 vols.). London: Heinemann, 1975.

Douno, B. (Peter Deunov) (2016). *The Teacher, Volume 1 The Dawning Epoch*. M. Mitovska & H. Carr (Eds.). London: Shining World Press.

Draper, J. W. (1875). *History of the Conflict between Religion and Science*. New York: King.

Dupre, L. (1993). *Passage to Modernity*. New Haven, CT: Yale University Press.

Easwaran, E. (Ed.) (1986). *The Bhagavad Gita*. London: Arkana.

Easwaran, E. (Ed.) (1987). *The Dhammapada*. London: Arkana.

Eccles, Sir J. (1994). *How the Self Controls Its Brain*. Berlin: Springer.

Eccles, Sir J., & Popper, Sir K. (1984). *The Self and Its Brain*. London: Routledge & Kegan Paul.

Eccles, Sir J., & Robinson, D. N. (1985). *The Wonder of Being Human*. London: Shambhala.

Eddington, Sir A. (1928). *The Nature of the Physical World*. Cambridge: Cambridge University Press.

Ehrlich, P., & Ehrlich, A (1990). *The Population Explosion*. London: Hutchinson.

Eisler, R., & Fry, D. P. (2019). *Nurturing Our Humanity*. New York: Oxford University Press.

Eliade, M. (1958). *Rites and Symbols of Initiation*. New York: Harper & Row.

Eliade, M. (1979). *A History of Religious Ideas, Vol. 1*. London: Collins.

Eliade, M. (1982). *A History of Religious Ideas, Vol. 2*. London: Collins.

Eliot, T. S. (1921). *The Waste Land*. London: Faber and Faber.

Eliot, T. S. (1935). *Murder in the Cathedral*. London: Faber and Faber.

Eliot, T. S. (1944). *Four Quartets*. London: Faber and Faber.

Elworthy, S. (2014). *Pioneering the Possible*. Berkeley, CA: North Atlantic.

Emerson, R. W. (1897). *Complete Works*. London: Routledge.

Evans-Wentz, W. Y. (1960). *The Tibetan Book of the Dead*. Oxford: Oxford University Press.

Fawcett, D. (1931). *The Zermatt Dialogues*. London: Macmillan.

Fawcett, D. (1939). *The Oberland Dialogues*. London: Macmillan.

Feng, G.-F., & English, J. (1972). *Tao Te Ching*. London: Wildwood House.

Ferguson, M. (1981). *The Aquarian Conspiracy*. London: Routledge & Kegan Paul.

Fernando, S. (Ed.) (1991). *The Unanimous Tradition*. Colombo, Sri Lanka: Institute of Traditional Studies.

Ferrer, J. N. (2002). *Revisioning Transpersonal Theory*. New York: SUNY Press.

Ferrer, J. N. (2017). *Participation and Mystery*. New York: SUNY Press.

Filoramo, G. (1990). *A History of Gnosticism*. Oxford: Blackwell.

Fiore, E. (1980). *You Have Been Here Before*. London: Sphere.

Fisher, J. (1985). *The Case for Reincarnation*. London: Granada.

Fortune, D. (1987). *Through the Gates of Death*. London: Aquarian.

Foss, L., & Rothenberg, K. (1988). *The Second Medical Revolution*. Boston, MA: Shambhala.

Foss, L. (2001). *The End of Modern Medicine*. New York: SUNY Press.

Frankl, V. (1964). *Man's Search for Meaning*. London: Hodder & Stoughton.

Frankl, V. (1973). *Psychotherapy and Existentialism*. London: Penguin.

Frankl, V. (1973). *The Doctor and the Soul*. New York: Vintage.

Frankl, V. (1975). *The Unconscious God*. London: Hodder & Stoughton.

Frazer, Sir J. G. (1913). *The Belief in Immortality, vol. 1*. London: Macmillan.

Frazer, Sir J. G. (1890). *The Golden Bough*, in 12 vols. London: Macmillan, 1937.

Free John, Da (1983). *Easy Death*. Honolulu, HI: Dawn Horse.

Freud, S. (1927c). *The Future of an Illusion. S. E., 21*. London: Hogarth.

Freud, S. (1912-13). *Totem and Taboo. S. E., 13*. London: Routledge & Kegan Paul, 1950.

Freud, S. (1930a). *Civilisation and Its Discontents. S. E., 21*. New York: W. W. Norton, 1961.

Friedman, H. L., & Hartelius, G. (2015). *The Wiley Blackwell Handbook of Transpersonal Psychology*. Chichester, UK: John Wiley.

Fromm, E. (1942). *The Fear of Freedom*. London: Routledge & Kegan Paul.

Fromm, E. (1949). *Man for Himself*. London: Routledge & Kegan Paul.

Fromm, E. (1950). *Psychoanalysis and Religion*. London: Yale.

Fromm, E. (1956). *The Art of Loving*. New York: Harper.

Fromm, E. (1956). *The Sane Society*. London: Routledge & Kegan Paul.

Fromm, E. (1978). *To Have or to Be*. London: Cape.

Fromm, E. (1980). *Beyond the Chains of Illusion*. London: Abacus.

Fromm, E. (1984). *On Disobedience*. London: Routledge & Kegan Paul.

Gober, M. (2018). *An End to Upside Down Thinking*. Cardiff, CA: Waterside.

Gollwitzer, L. H., Kuhn, K., & Schneider, R. (Eds.) (1958). *Dying We Live*. London: Harper Collins.

Goodwin, B. (1994). *How the Leopard Changed Its Spots*. London: Weidenfeld & Nicolson.

Goodwin, B. (2007). *Nature's Due*. Edinburgh, UK: Floris.

Gore, A. (1992). *Earth in the Balance*. London: Earthscan.

Gore, A. (2016). *The Future*. London: W. H. Allen.

Goswami, A. (1993). *The Self-Aware Universe*. London: Simon & Schuster.

Graham-Smith, Sir F. (Ed.) (1994). *Population: the Complex Reality*. London: Royal Society.

Greaves, H. (1969). *Testimony of Light*. London: Churches' Fellowship for Psychical and Spiritual Studies.

Gregory, R. (Ed.) (1987). *The Oxford Companion to the Mind*. Oxford: Oxford University Press, 1987.

Grey, M. (1985). *Return from Death*. London: Arkana.

Grey of Fallodon, Viscount (1926). *Fallodon Papers*. London: Constable.

Greyson, B., & Flynn, C. P. (1984). *The Near-Death Experience*. Springfield, IL: Charles C. Thomas.

Griffiths, B. (1976). *Return to the Centre*. London: Collins.

Griffiths, B. (1982). *The Marriage of East and West*. London: Collins.

Griffiths, B. (1992). *A New Vision of Reality*. London: Collins.

Grof, S. (1985). *Beyond the Brain*. New York: SUNY Press.

Grof, S. (2019). *The Way of the Psychonaut*. San Francisco, CA: MAPS.

Grof, S., & Halifax, J. (1978). *The Human Encounter with Death*. London: Souvenir.

Grosso, M. (1986). *The Final Choice*. Walpole, NH: Stillpoint.

Guenon, R. (1975). *Crisis of the Modern World*. London: Lukacs.

Gurney, E., Myers, F. W. H., & Podmore, F. (1886). *Phantasms of the Living*. London: Trübner.

Hagger, N. (1992). *The Fire and the Stones*. Shaftesbury, UK: Element.

Hammarskjöld, D. (1964). *Markings*. London: Faber.

Hampe, J. C. (1979). *To Die Is Gain*. London: Darton Longman & Todd.

Hands, J. (2015). *Cosmosapiens*. London: Duckworth.

Happold, F. C. (1963). *Mysticism*. London: Penguin.

Hardy, Sir A. (1979). *The Spiritual Nature of Man*. Oxford: Clarendon.

Harman, P. M. (1983). *The Scientific Revolution*. London: Methuen.

Harman, W. (1988). *Global Mind Change*. New York: Knowledge Systems.

Harman, W. (1992). *A Re-Examination of the Metaphysical Foundations of Modern Science*. San Francisco, CA: Institute of Noetic Sciences.

Harman, W., & Clark, J. (1994). *New Metaphysical Foundations of Modern Science.* San Francisco, CA: Institute of Noetic Sciences.

Hastings, J. (Ed.) (1913). *Encyclopaedia of Religion and Ethics.* In 12 vols. Edinburgh, UK: T. & T. Clark.

Hawkins, D. R. (1995). *Power vs. Force.* London: Hay House, 2012.

Hawkins, D. R. (2003). *I—Reality and Subjectivity.* London: Hay House.

Head, J., & Cranston, S. L. (1977). *Reincarnation: The Phoenix Fire Mystery.* New York: Julian.

Hesse, H. (1922). *Siddhartha.* London: Picador, 1973.

Hesse, H. (1927). *Steppenwolf.* London: Martin Secker, 1929.

Hesse, H. (1930). *Narcissus and Goldmund.* London: Penguin, 1959.

Hesse, H. (1943). *The Glass Bead Game* London: Penguin, 1960.

Heymann, E. (2006). *The Deeper Centre.* London: Darton Longman & Todd.

Hick, J. (1966). *Evil and the God of Love.* London: Macmillan.

Hick, J. (1976). *Death and Eternal Life.* London: Collins.

Hiley, B., & Peat, F. D. (1987). *Quantum Implications: Essays in Honour of David Bohm.* London: Routledge & Kegan Paul.

Hoeller, S. A. (1982). *The Gnostic Jung.* London: Theosophical Publishing House.

Holgate, Sir M. (1996). *From Care to Action.* London: Earthscan.

Holgate, Sir M. (1999). *The Green Web.* London: Earthscan.

Holton, G. J. (1993). *Science and Anti-Science.* Cambridge, MA: Harvard University Press.

Hopkins, G. M. (1953). *Poems and Prose.* London: Penguin.

Hulme, T. E. (1924). *Speculations.* London: Routledge & Kegan Paul.

Huxley, A. (1941). *Ends and Means,* London: Chatto & Windus.

Huxley, A. (1946). *The Perennial Philosophy.* London, Chatto and Windus.

Huxley, A. (1977). *The Human Situation.* London: Chatto & Windus.

Inge, W. R. (1899). *Christian Mysticism.* London: Methuen.

Inge, W. R. (1929). *The Philosophy of Plotinus.* London: Longman.

Jahn, R., & Dunne, B. (1987). *Margins of Reality.* New York: Harcourt, Brace Jovanovich.

James, W. (1899). *Human Immortality.* London: Constable.

James, W. (1903). *The Varieties of Religious Experience.* London: Longman.

James, W. (1921). *Pragmatism.* London: Longman.

Jantsch, E. (1980). *The Self-Organising Universe.* London: Pergamon.

Johnson, R. (1953). *The Imprisoned Splendour.* London: Hodder & Stoughton.

Johnson, R. (1984). *Light of All Life.* Norwich, UK: Pilgrim.

Jung, C. G. (1924). *Psychological Types.* London: Kegan Paul.

Jung, C. G. (1933). *Modern Man in Search of a Soul.* London: Routledge & Kegan Paul.

Jung, C. G. (1963). *Memories, Dreams, Reflections*. A. Jaffe (Ed.). London: Routledge & Kegan Paul.

Jung, C. G. (1968). *Collected Works, vol. 9, part 1, The Archetypes and the Collective Unconscious*. London: Routledge & Kegan Paul.

Jung, C. G. (1969). *Collected Works, vol. 8, The Structure and Dynamics of the Psyche*. London: Routledge & Kegan Paul.

Jung, C. G. (1970). *Collected Works, vol. 10, Civilisation in Transition*. London: Routledge & Kegan Paul.

Jung, C. G. (1970). *Collected Works, vol. 11, Psychology and Religion: East and West*. London: Routledge & Kegan Paul.

Jung, C. G. (1973). *Letters, vol. 1 (1906–50)*. London: Routledge & Kegan Paul.

Jung, C. G. (1977). *C. G. Jung Speaking*. London: Thames & Hudson.

Jung, C. G. (2014). *The Undiscovered Self*. London: Routledge.

Kant, I. (1766). *Dreams of a Spirit Seer*. New York: Swedenborg Foundation, 2003.

Katz, S. T. (Ed.) (1978). *Mysticism and Philosophical Analysis*. London: Sheldon.

Keller, E. F. (1985). *Reflections on Gender and Science*. New Haven, CT: Yale University Press.

Kelly, E. F., Crabtree, A., & Marshall, P. (2015). *Beyond Reductionism*. New York: Rowman & Littlefield.

Kelly, E. F., & Kelly, E. W. (2007). *Irreducible Mind*. New York: Rowman & Littlefield.

Kelsey, M. T. (1988). *Afterlife*. New York: Crossroads.

Khursheed, A. (1987). *Science and Religion: Towards the Restoration of an Ancient Harmony*. London: Oneworld.

King, M. L. (1958). *The Words of Martin Luther King Jr*. New York: Newmarket.

King, A., & Schneider, B. (1991). *The First Global Revolution*. London: Simon & Schuster.

Kingsley, P. (1993). *In the Dark Places of Wisdom*. Inverness, UK: Golden Sufi Center.

Kingsley, P. (2003). *Reality*. Inverness, UK: Golden Sufi Center.

Kingsley, P. (2019). *Catafalque—Jung and the End of Humanity*. London: Catafalque.

Klein, N. (2019). *On Fire*. London: Allen Lane.

Koestler, A. (1945). *The Yogi and the Commissar*. London: Cape.

Koestler, A. (1959). *The Sleepwalkers*. London: Hutchinson.

Koestler, A. (1964). *The Act of Creation*. London: Picador.

Koestler, A. (1978). *Janus*. London: Hutchinson.

Koestler, A., & Smythies, J. R. (1969). *Beyond Reductionism* London: Hutchinson.

Kohlberg, L. (1981). *The Philosophy of Moral Development*. New York: Harper & Row.

Kolakowski, L. (1982). *Religion* London: Fontana.

Kovacs, B. (2003). *The Miracle of Death*. Claremont, CA: Kamlak Center.

Kovacs, B. (2019). *Merchants of Light*. Claremont, CA: Kamlak Center.

Kripal, J. J. (2019). *The Flip*. New York: Bellevue.

Krishnamurti, J. (1954). *The First and Last Freedom*. London: Orion.

Kropotkin, Prince P. A. (1924). *Ethics: Origin and Development*. Dorchester, UK: Prism.

Kubler-Ross, E. (1969). *On Death and Dying*. New York: Macmillan.

Kuhn, Thomas J. (1970). *The Structure of Scientific Revolutions*. Chicago, IL: Chicago University Press.

Küng, H. (1984). *Eternal Life?* London: Collins.

Küng, H., & Kuschel, K.-J. (1993). *Towards a Global Ethic*. London: SCM.

Laszlo, E. (1991). *Macroshift*. San Francisco, CA: Berrett Koehler.

Laszlo, E. (1989). *The Inner Limits of Mankind*. Oxford, UK: OneWorld.

Laszlo, E. (2014). *The Self-Actualizing Cosmos*. Wheaton, IL: Inner Traditions.

Laszlo, E. (2016). *What is Reality?* New York: Select.

Laszlo, E., Dossey, L., & Chopra, D. (2016). *What Is Consciousness?* New York: Select.

Lawrence, D. H. (1964). *The Complete Poems, Volume 2*. V. de Sola Pinto, & W. Roberts (Eds.). London: Heinemann.

Leggett, D. M. A., & Payne, M. (1986). *A Forgotten Truth*. Norwich, UK: Pilgrim.

LeShan, L. (1987). *Science and the Paranormal*. London: Aquarian.

LeShan, L. (2009). *A New Science of the Paranormal*. Wheaton, IL: Quest.

LeShan, L. (2012). *Landscapes of the Mind*. Guilford, CT: Eirini.

Lethbridge, T. C. (1974). *ESP: Beyond Time and Distance*. London: Sidgwick & Jackson.

Lethbridge, T. C. (1980). *The Essential T. C. Lethbridge*. London: Routledge & Kegan Paul.

Lethbridge, T. C. (1989). *The Power of the Pendulum*. London: Arkana.

Lewis, C. S. (1978). *The Abolition of Man*. London: Harper Collins.

Long, M. F. (1954). *The Secret Science behind Miracles*. Marina del Rey, CA: DeVorss.

Lorimer, D. (1984). *Survival? Body, Mind and Death in the Light of Psychic Experience*. London: Routledge & Kegan Paul. (Reprinted as *Death as Transition*. White Crow, Brighton, UK, 2017.)

Lorimer, D. (1990). *Whole in One*. London: Penguin Arkana. (Reprinted as *Resonant Mind*. White Crow, Brighton, UK, 2017.)

Lorimer, D. (1991). *Prophet for Our Times*. Shaftesbury, UK: Element. (New edition, London: Hay House, 2015.)

Lorimer, D. (1991). *The Circle of Sacred Dance*. Shaftesbury, UK: Element.

Lorimer, D. (Ed. & Trans.) (1994). *Gems of Love (Prayers and Formulas of Beinsa Douno)*. London: Grain of Wheat.

Lorimer, D. (Ed.) (1998). *The Spirit of Science*. Edinburgh, UK: Floris.

Lorimer, D. (Ed.) (2001). *Thinking beyond the Brain*. Edinburgh, UK: Floris.

Lorimer, D. (2003). *Radical Prince*. Edinburgh, UK: Floris Books, 2003. (Abridged paperback, 2004.)

Lorimer, D. (Ed.) (2004). *Science, Consciousness and Ultimate Reality*. Exeter, UK: Imprint Academic.

Lorimer, D., & Robinson, O. (Eds.) (2010). *A New Renaissance*. Edinburgh, UK: Floris.

Lorimer, D., & Sosnowki, L. (Eds.) (2008). *Towards a New Renaissance*. Krakow, Poland: Jagiellonian University Press.

Lovejoy, A. O. (1948). *The Great Chain of Being*. Cambridge, MA: Harvard University Press.

Lovelock, J. (1979). *Gaia: A New Look at Life on Earth* Oxford: Oxford University Press.

Lovelock, J. (1988). *The Ages of Gaia*. Oxford: Oxford University Press.

Lovelock, J. (1991). *Gaia: The Practical Science of Planetary Medicine*. London: Gaia.

Lovelock, J. (2000). *Homage to Gaia*. Oxford: Oxford University Press.

Lovin, R. W., & Reynolds, F. E. (1985). *Cosmogony and Ethical Order*. Chicago, IL: University of Chicago Press.

MacIntyre, A. (1967). *A Short History of Ethics*. London: Routledge & Kegan Paul.

MacIntyre, A., & Ricoeur, P. (1969). *The Religious Significance of Atheism*. New York: Columbia University Press.

Macmurray, J. (1933). *Freedom in the Modern World*. London: Faber & Faber.

Macmurray, J. (Ed.) (1933). *Some Makers of the Modern Spirit*. London: Methuen.

Macquarrie, J. (Ed.) (1967). *A Dictionary of Christian Ethics*. London: SCM.

Marcus Aurelius. *Meditations*. London: Collins, 1974.

Margenau, H. (1987). *The Miracle of Existence*. London: Shambhala.

Margulis, L. (1998). *The Symbiotic Planet*. London: Weidenfeld & Nicolson.

Markides, K. C. (1985). *The Magus of Strovolos*. London: Arkana.

Markides, K. C. (1987). *Homage to the Sun*. London: Arkana.

Mascaró, J. (Trans.) (1962). *The Bhagavad Gita*. London: Penguin.

Mascaró, J. (Trans.) (1965). *The Upanishads*. London: Penguin.

Mascaró, J. (Trans.) (1973). *The Dhammapada*. London: Penguin.

Maslow, A. (1954). *Motivation and Personality*. New York: Harper & Row.

Maslow, A. (1964). *Religion, Values and Peak Experiences*. New York: Viking.

Maslow, A. (1971). *The Farther Reaches of Human Nature*. New York: Viking.

Masterson, P. (1973). *Atheism and Alienation*. London: Penguin.

Matthews, W. R. (Ed.) (1920). *King's College Lectures on Immortality*. London: University of London Press.

Maxwell, N. (1987). *From Knowledge to Wisdom*. Oxford: Blackwell.

Maxwell, N. (2017). *Understanding Scientific Progress*. New York: Paragon House.

May, Robert M. (1988). *Physicians of the Soul*. New York: Amity House.

May, Rollo (1969). *Love and Will*. New York: W. W. Norton.

Mayer, E. L. (2007). *Extraordinary Knowing*. New York: Bantam.

McGilchrist, I. (2009). *The Master and His Emissary*. New Haven, CT: Yale University Press.

McTaggart, J. E. M. (1956). *The Nature of Existence*. London: Doubleday.

Medawar, Sir P. (1986). *The Limits of Science*. Oxford: Oxford University Press.

Merchant, C. (1980). *The Death of Nature*. San Francisco, CA: Harper & Row.

Midgley, M. (2016). *Are You an Illusion?* London: Routledge.

Midgley, M. (2018). *What Is Philosophy For?* London: Routledge.

Milgram, S. (1973). *Obedience to Authority*. London: Tavistock.

Miller, J. G. (1970). *Living Systems*. New York: McGraw Hill.

Miller, L. (Ed.) (2012). *The Oxford Handbook of Psychology and Spirituality*. Oxford: Oxford University Press.

Miller, S. A. (2013). *The New Paradigm*. Winchester, UK: O Books.

Minogue, K. (1985). *Alien Powers: The Pure Theory of Ideology*. London: Weidenfeld & Nicolson.

Mitchell, B. (1980). *Morality: Religious and Secular*. Oxford: Clarendon.

Moriarty, J. (1996). *Turtle was Gone a Long Time*. Dublin: Lilliput.

Moriarty, J. (2001). *Nostos*. Dublin: Lilliput.

Moriarty, J. (2007). *Serious Sounds*. Dublin: Lilliput.

Moriarty, J. (2007). *What the Curlew Said*. Dublin: Lilliput.

Monod, Jacques, *Chance and Necessity,* London, Collins, 1974.

Moody, D. E. (2017). *An Uncommon Collaboration—David Bohm and J. Krishnamurti*. Ojai, CA: Alpha Centauri.

Moody, R. (1975). *Life after Life*. New York: Mockingbird.

Moody, R. (1977). *Reflections on Life after Life*. New York: Mockingbird.

Moody, R. (1988). *The Light Beyond*. London: Macmillan.

Moorjani, A. (2012). *Dying to Live*. London: Hay House.

Morse, M. (1992). *Transformed by the Light*. New York: Villard.

Muller, F. M. (1894). *The Vedanta Philosophy*. London: Longman.

Muller, R. (1984). *New Genesis*. New York: Doubleday.

Mullin, G. (1986). *Death and Dying: The Tibetan Tradition*. London: Arkana.

Myers, F. W. H. (1903). *Human Personality and Its Survival of Bodily Death*. London: Longman, 1927.

Nasr, S. H. (1967). *Man and Nature*. London: Allen & Unwin.

Nasr, S. H. (1986). *The Essential Writings of Fritjhof Schuon*. Warwick, NY: Amity House.

Nasr, S. H. (1989). *Knowledge and the Sacred*. New York: SUNY Press.

Nasr, S. H. (1993). *The Need for a Sacred Science*. New York: SUNY Press.

Nasr, S. H. (1996). *Religion and the Order of Nature*. New York: Oxford University Press.

Nasr, S. H. (1999). *The Spiritual and Religius Dimensions of the Environmental Crisis*. London: Temenos Academy.

Naydler, J. (1996). *Goethe on Science*. Edinburgh, UK: Floris.

Naydler, J. (2018). *In the Shadow of the Machine*. Forest Row, UK: Temple Lodge.

Needleman, J.acob (1986). *The Sword of Gnosis*. London: Arkana.

Needleman, J.acob (1990). *Lost Christianity*. Shaftesbury, UK: Element.

Needleman, J.acob (1993). *The Way of the Physician*. London: Arkana.

Needleman, J.acob (1996). *On Love*. London: Arkana.

Needleman, J.acob (2003). *The American Soul*. New York: Tarcher.

Needleman, J.acob (2003). *Time and the Soul*. Oakland, CA: Berrett-Koehler.

Needleman, J.acob (2011). *An Unknown World*. New York: Tarcher.

Needleman, J.acob (2013). *What is God?* New York: Tarcher.

Neumann, E. (1954). *The Origins and History of Consciousness*. London: Routledge & Kegan Paul.

Neumann, E. (1969). *Depth Psychology and a New Ethic*. London: Hodder & Stoughton.

Nicol, D. (2015). *Subtle Activism*. New York: SUNY Press.

Niebuhr, R. (1936). *An Interpretation of Christian Ethics*. London: SCM.

Niebuhr, R. (1936). *Moral Man and Immoral Society*. New York: Charles Scribner's Sons.

O'Brien, E. (Ed.) (1964). *The Essential Plotinus*. Indianapolis, IN: Hackett.

O'Donohue, J. (1997). *Anam Cara*. London: Bantam.

O'Donohue, J. (2007). *Benedictus*. London: Bantam.

Oerman, N. O. (2017). *Albert Schweitzer, a Biography*. Oxford: Oxford University Press.

O'Grady, J. (1985). *Heresy*. Shaftesbury, UK: Element.

Oldroyd, D. (1986). *The Arch of Knowledge*. London: Methuen.

Ornstein, R. E. (1975). *The Psychology of Consciousness*. London: Penguin.

Ornstein, R. E. (1988). *Multimind*. London: Macmillan.

Ornstein, R. E., & Sobel, D. (1988). *The Healing Brain*. London: Macmillan.

Osborne, A. (1954). *Ramana Maharshi and the Path of Self-Knowledge*. London: Rider.

Osty, E. (1923). *Supernormal Faculties in Man*. London: Methuen.

Otto, R. (2017). *The Paradox of Our National Security Complex*. Winchester, UK: Chronos.

Otto, R. (1923). *The Idea of the Holy*. London: Oxford University Press.

Pagels, E. (1982). *The Gnostic Gospels*. London: Penguin.

Palumbi, S. (2001). *The Evolution Explosion*. New York: W. W. Norton.

Parnia, S., & Young, J. (2014). *Erasing Death*. New York: HarperOne.

Parti, R., & Perry, P. (2014). *Dying to Wake Up*. London: Hay House.

Pascal, B. (1925). *Pensées*. Paris: Hachette.

Paulsen, F. (1899). *A System of Ethics*. New York: Charles Scribner's Sons.

Peacocke, A., & Gillett, G. (1987). *Persons and Personality*. Oxford: Blackwell.

Peck, M. S. (1983). *The Road Less Travelled*. London: Century.

Penfield, W. (1975). *The Mysteries of Mind*. Princeton, NJ: Princeton University Press.

Perry, W. N. (1971). *A Treasury of Traditional Wisdom*. Allen & Unwin.

Plato. *Phaedrus*. R. Hackforth (Ed.). Cambridge: Cambridge University Press, 1952.

Plato. *Protagoras and Meno*. W. K. C. Guthrie (Ed.). London: Penguin, 1956.

Plato. *The Last Days of Socrates*. H. Tredinnick (Ed.). London: Penguin, 1954.

Plato. *The Laws*. T. J. Saunders (Ed.). London: Penguin, 1970.

Plato. *The Republic*. Sir Desmond Lee (Ed.). London: Penguin, 1955.

Plotinus. *The Enneads*. S. Mackenna (Ed.). London: Faber & Faber, 1962.

Polanyi, Sir M. (1923). *Personal Knowledge*. London: Routledge & Kegan Paul.

Polanyi, Sir M. (1959). *The Study of Man*. London: Routledge.

Popper, Sir K. (1962). *The Open Society and Its Enemies*. London: Routledge.

Popper, Sir K. (1995). *The Myth of the Framework*. London: Routledge.

Popper, Sir K., & Eccles, Sir J. (1977). *The Self and Its Brain*. London: Routledge & Kegan Paul, 1984.

Porritt, J. (2005). *Capitalism as if the World Matters*. London: Earthscan.

Potter, K. H. (1965). *Presuppositions of India's Philosophies*. Delhi: Prentice-Hall.

Presti, D. E. (2018). *Mind beyond Brain*. New York: Columbia.

Prigogine, I. (1996). *The End of Certainty*. London: Dover.

Price, H. H. (1953). *Survival and the Idea of Another World*. London: Proceedings of the SPR, vol. 50, part 180.

Pringle-Pattison, A. S. (1922). *The Idea of Immortality*. Oxford: Clarendon.

Radhakrishnan, Sir S. (1932). *An Idealist View of Life*. London: Allen & Unwin.

Radhakrishnan, Sir S. (1939). *Eastern Religions and Western Thought*. Oxford: Oxford University Press.

Radhakrishnan, Sir S. (1947). *Religion and Society*. London: Allen & Unwin.

Radhakrishnan, Sir S. (Ed.) (1948). *The Bhagavad Gita*. London: Allen & Unwin.

Radhakrishnan, Sir S. (Ed.) (1950). *The Dhammapada*. London: Oxford University Press.

Radhakrishnan, Sir S. (Ed.) (1952). *History of Philosophy, Eastern and Western. 2 vols.* London: Allen & Unwin.

Radhakrishnan, Sir S. (Ed.) (1953). *The Principal Upanishads.* London: Allen & Unwin.

Radhakrishnan, Sir S. (Ed.) (1960). *The Brahma Sutra.* London: Allen & Unwin.

Radhakrishnan, Sir S. (1970). *The Present Crisis of Faith.* Delhi: Orient.

Radin, D. (1997). *The Conscious Universe.* London: Harper.

Radin, D. (2006). *Entangled Minds.* New York: Paraview Pocket Books.

Radin, D. (2013). *Supernormal.* New York: Random House.

Radin, D. (2018). *Real Magic.* New York: Harmony.

Rashdall, H. (1924). *The Theory of Good and Evil.* London: Oxford University Press.

Ratsch, D. (1986). *Philosophy of Science.* Downers Grove, IL: Inter-VarsityPress.

Ravindra, R. (2000). *Science and the Sacred.* Adyar, India: Theosophical Society.

Ravindra, R. (Ed.). (2006). *The Inner Journey, Views from the Christian Tradition.* Sandpoint, ID: Morning Light Press.

Ray, P. H., & Anderson, S. R. (2000). *The Cultural Creatives.* New York: Harmony.

Richards, S. (1987). *Philosophy and Sociology of Science: An Introduction.* Oxford: Blackwell.

Ring, K. (1980). *Life at Death.* New York: Coward, McCann & Geoghagan.

Ring, K. (1984). *Heading toward Omega.* New York: Morrow.

Rivas, T., Dirvan, A., & Smit, R. H. (2016). *The Self Does Not Die.* Durham, NC: IANDS.

Ritchie, G. (1978). *Return from Tomorrow.* London: Kingsway.

Robinson, O. (2018). *Paths between Head and Heart.* Winchester, UK: O Books.

Rose, S. (1997). *Lifelines.* London: Allen Lane.

Russell, B. (1931). *The Scientific Outlook.* London: Allen & Unwin.

Russell, B. (1946). *History of Western Philosophy* London: Allen & Unwin.

Russell, B. (1954). *Human Society in Ethics and Politics.* London: Allen & Unwin.

Russell, B. (1957). *Why I Am Not a Christian.* London: Allen & Unwin.

Russell, B. (1958). *Voltaire's Influence on Me.* Geneva: Institut et Musée Voltaire.

Russell, B. (1969). *Autobiography.* London: Allen & Unwin.

Russell, W. (1926). *The Universal One.* Waynesboro, VA: University of Science and Philosophy, 1974.

Sabom, M. (1982). *Recollections of Death.* London: Harper & Row.

Sahtouris, E., & Harman, W. (1998). *Biology Revisioned.* Berkeley, CA: North Atlantic.

Sartori, P., & Walsh, K. (2017). *The Transformative Power of Near-Death Experiences*. London: Watkins.

Sartre, J.-P. (1943). *Being and Nothingness*. London: Routledge, 1956.

Sartre, J.-P. (1946). *L'Existentialisme est un Humanisme*. Paris: Gallimard.

Schacker, M. (2013). *Global Awakening*. New York: Park Street.

Scheler, M. (1954). *The Nature of Sympathy*. London: Routledge & Kegan Paul.

Schiller, F. C. S. (1891). *Riddles of the Sphinx*. London: Swan Sonnenschein.

Schiller, F. C. S. (1903). *Humanism*. London: Macmillan.

Schopenhauer, A. (1851). *Essays and Aphorisms*. London: Penguin, 1970.

Schroedinger, E. (1944). *What Is Life?* with *Matter and Mind* (1958). New York: Cambridge University Press, 1967.

Schroedinger, E. (1954). *Nature and the Greeks*. Cambridge: Cambridge University Press, 1997.

Schumacher, E. F. (1973). *Small Is Beautiful*. London: Jonathan Cape.

Schumacher, E. F. (1977). *A Guide for the Perplexed*. London: Jonathan Cape.

Schweitzer, A. (1906). *Quest for the Historical Jesus*. London: A. & C. Black.

Schweitzer, A. (1923). *Christianity and the Religions of the World*. London: Allen & Unwin.

Schweitzer, A. (1924). *Memoirs of Childhood and Youth*. London: Allen & Unwin.

Schweitzer, A. (1931). *The Mysticism of Paul the Apostle*. London: A. & C. Black.

Schweitzer, A. (1933). *My Life and Thought*. London: Allen & Unwin.

Schweitzer, A. (1936). *Indian Thought and Its Development*. London: Hodder & Stoughton.

Schweitzer, A. (1947). *J. S. Bach*. London: A. & C. Black.

Schweitzer, A. (1947). *The Decay and Restoration of Civilisation*. London: A. & C. Black.

Schweitzer, A. (1949). *Civilisation and Ethics*. London: A. & C. Black.

Schweitzer, A. (1949). *Goethe—Four Studies*. Boston, MA: Beacon.

Schweitzer, A. *The Problem of Peace in the World Today—Nobel Peace Prize Address*. London: A. & C. Black.

Schweitzer, A. (1966). *The Teaching of Reverence for Life*. London: Peter Owen.

Schweitzer, A. (1970). *Reverence for Life*. London: SPCK.

Seamon, D., & Zajonc, A. (Eds.). (1988). *Goethe's Way of Science*. New York: SUNY Press.

Searle, J. R. (1992). *The Rediscovery of the Mind*. Cambridge, MA: MIT Press.

Serrano, M. (1966). *C. G. Jung and Hermann Hesse: A Record of Two Friendships*. London: Routledge & Kegan Paul.

Sharma, I. C. (1965). *Ethical Philosophies of India*. London: Allen & Unwin.

Sharma, I. C. (1975). *Cayce, Karma and Reincarnation*. London: Theosophical Publishing House.

Sheldrake, R. (1981). *A New Science of Life*. London: Blond & Briggs.

Sheldrake, R. (1988). *The Presence of the Past*. London: Collins.

Sheldrake, R. (1990). *The Rebirth of Nature*. London: Century.

Sheldrake, R. (2012). *The Science Delusion*. London: Coronet.

Sherrard, P. (1987). *The Rape of Man and Nature*. Ipswich, UK: Golgonooza.

Sherrard, P. (1990). *The Sacred in Life and Art*. Ipswich, UK: Golgonooza.

Sherrard, P. (1992). *Human Image, World Image*. Ipswich, UK: Golgonooza.

Sherrington, Sir C. (1942). *Man on His Nature*. Cambridge: Cambridge University Press.

Sherwood, J. (1964). *Post-Mortem Journal of T. E. Lawrence*. London: Neville Spearman.

Sherwood, J. (1969). *The Country Beyond*. London: Neville Spearman.

Sidgwick, H. (1886). *History of Ethics*. London: Macmillan.

Siegel, B. (1986). *Love, Medicine and Miracles*. London: Rider.

Skolimowski, H. (1981). *Eco-Philosophy*. London: Boyars.

Skolimowski, H. (1994). *The Participatory Mind*. London: Arkana.

Skrbina, D. (2015). *The Metaphysics of Technology*. London: Routledge.

Smart, N. (1971). *The Religious Experience of Mankind*. London: Fontana.

Smart, N. (1981). *Beyond Ideology*. London: Collins.

Smart, N. (1987). *Religion and the Western Mind*. London: Macmillan.

Smith, C. H. (1991). *Alfred Russel Wallace. An Anthology of his Shorter Writings*. Oxford: Oxford University Press.

Smith, H. (1976). *Forgotten Truth*. New York: Harper & Row.

Smith, H. (2001). *Why Religion Matters*. San Francisco, CA: Harper.

Sorell, T. (1991). *Scientism*. London: Routledge.

Sorokin, P. (1992). *The Crisis of our Age*. Oxford: OneWorld.

Sorokin, P. (2004). *The Ways and Power of Love*. Philadelphia, PA: Templeton.

Spengler, O. (1934). *The Decline of the West*. London: Allen & Unwin.

Sperry, R. (1983). *Science and Moral Priority*. Oxford: Blackwell.

Stace, W. T. (1953). *Religion and the Modern Mind*. London: Macmillan.

Stace, W. T. (1961). *Mysticism and Philosophy*. London: Macmillan.

Steiner, R. (1922). *Theosophy*. London: Rudolf Steiner Press.

Steiner, R. (1955). *Karmic Relationships, 5 vols*. London: Anthroposophical Publishing.

Steiner, R. (1959). *Cosmic Memory*. Englewood, NJB: Rudolf Steiner Publications.

Steiner, R. (1960). *Reincarnation and Karma: Their Significance in Modern Culture*. London: Anthroposophic Press.

Steiner, R. (1962). *Reincarnation and Karma: How Karma Works*. New York: Anthroposophic Press.

Steiner, R. (1963). *Knowledge of the Higher Worlds*. London: Rudolf Steiner Press.

Steiner, R. (1963). *Occult Science*. London: Rudolf Steiner Press.

Steiner, R. (1966). *Theosophy of the Rosicrucians*. London: Rudolf Steiner Press.

Steiner, R. (1968). *Life between Death and Rebirth*. New York: Anthroposophic Press.

Steindl-Rast, D. (2006). Learning to die. In: *The Inner Journey, Views from the Christian Tradition*. L. Kisly (Ed.). New York: Parabola.

Stenmark, M. (2001). *Scientism*. Aldershot, UK: Ashgate.

Stevenson, I. (1966). *Twenty Cases Suggestive of Reincarnation*. New York: American Society for Psychical Research.

Stevenson, I. (1987). *Children Who Remember Previous Lives*. Charlottesville, VA: University of Virginia Press.

Stevenson, I. (1997). *Reincarnation and Biology*. New York: Praeger.

Stevenson, I. (1997). *Where Reincarnation and Biology Intersect*. New York: Praeger.

Streeter, B. H. (Ed.). (1917). *Immortality*. London: Macmillan.

Swedenborg, E. (1756). *Arcana Coelestia. 12 vols*. London: Swedenborg Society, 1909.

Swedenborg, E. (1758). *Heaven and Hell*. London: Swedenborg Society, 1958.

Swedenborg, E. (1758). *Last Judgment*. London: Swedenborg Society, 1961.

Swedenborg, E. (1769). *The Soul and Its Intercourse with the Body*. London: Swedenborg Society, 1947.

Swedenborg, E. (1771). *The True Christian Religion*. London: Swedenborg Society, 1950.

Swinburne, R. (2019). *Are We Bodies or Souls?* Oxford: Oxford University Press.

Tagore, Sir R. (1914). *Sadhana*. London: Macmillan.

Tarnas, R. (1991). *The Passion of the Western Mind*. New York: Ballantine.

Tarnas, R. (2006). *Cosmos and Psyche*. New York: Viking.

Tart, C. T. (2009). *The End of Materialism*. Oakland, CA: New Harbinger.

Tawney, R. H. (1926). *Religion and the Rise of Capitalism*. London: John Murray.

Taylor, A. E. (1924). *Elements of Metaphysics*. London: Methuen.

Taylor, A. E. (1926). *Plato*. London: Methuen.

Taylor, A. E. (1937). *The Faith of a Moralist*. London: Macmillan.

Taylor, S. (2018). *Spiritual Science*. London: Watkins.

Teilhard de Chardin, P. (1955). *The Phenomenon of Man*. London: Fontana, 1965.

Teilhard de Chardin, P. (1966). *Let Me Explain*. London: Fontana, 1974.

Tenhaeff, W. H. C. (1972). *Telepathy and Clairvoyance*. Springfield, IL: Charles C. Thomas.

Thomas, Sir K. (1971). *Religion and the Decline of Magic.* London: Penguin, 1973.

Thomson, A. (1987). *Tradition and Authority in Science and Theology.* Edinburgh, UK: Scottish Academic Press.

Tischner, R. (1925). *Telepathy and Clairvoyance.* London: Kegan Paul.

Toynbee, A. (1956). *An Historian's Approach to Religion.* Oxford: Oxford University Press.

Toynbee, A. (1961). *A Study of History, vol. 12.* Oxford: Oxford University Press.

Toynbee, A. (Ed.) (1968). *Man's Concern with Death.* London: Hodder & Stoughton.

Toynbee, A. (1971). *Surviving the Future.* Oxford: Oxford University Press.

Toynbee, A. (Ed.) (1976). *Life after Death.* London: Weidenfeld & Nicolson.

Toynbee, A., & Ikeda, D. (1976). *Choose Life.* Oxford: Oxford University Press.

Trevelyan, Sir G. (1980). *Magic Casements.* London: Coventure.

Tylor, Sir E.B. (1903). *Primitive Culture. 2 vols.* London: John Murray.

Tyrrell, G. N. M. (1947). *Grades of Significance.* London: Rider.

Tyrrell, G. N. M. (1953). *Apparitions.* London: Duckworth.

Underhill, E. (1911). *Mysticism.* London: Methuen.

Van der Walle, A. (1984). *From Darkness to Light.* London: SCM.

Van Gennep, A. (1960). *Rites of Passage.* London: Routledge & Kegan Paul.

Van Lommel, P. (2010). *Consciousness beyond Life.* London: HarperCollins.

Voltaire (1733). *Lettres Philosophiques.* Paris: Garnier Flammarion, 1966.

Voltaire (1778). *Romans et Contes.* Paris: Garnier Flammarion, 1966.

Von Franz, M.-L. (1984). *On Dreams and Death.* London: Shambhala.

Von Rad, G. (1972). *Wisdom in Israel.* London: SCM.

Walach, H. (2016). *Secular Spirituality.* Berlin: Springer.

Wales, HRH The Prince of, Skelly, I., & Juniper, T. (2010). *Harmony.* London: Blue Door.

Wallace, B. A. (2000). *The Taboo of Subjectivity.* New York: Oxford University Press.

Wallis Budge, Sir E. A. (1969). *The Egyptian Book of the Dead.* London: Routledge & Kegan Paul.

Wambach, H. (1979). *Life before Life.* London: Bantam.

Wambach, H. (1979). *Reliving Past Lives.* London: Hutchinson.

Ward, K. (1987). *Images of Eternity.* London: Darton Longman & Todd.

Warnock, M. (1967). *Existentialist Ethics.* London: Macmillan.

Watts, A. (1951).*The Wisdom of Insecurity.* London: Penguin, 2011.

Watts, A. (1975). *Tao, The Watercourse Way.* London: Penguin, 1977.

Weber, R. (1986). *Dialogues with Scientists and Sages: The Search for Unity.* London: Routledge & Kegan Paul.

Weil, S. (1947). *Gravity and Grace.* London: Routledge, 1963.

Weil, S. (1949). *The Need for Roots*. London: Ark, 1987.

Weil, S. (1950). *Waiting on God*. London: Fontana, 1959.

Weil, S. (1952). *Intimations of Christianity among the Ancient Greeks*. London: Ark, 1987.

Weil, S. (1952). *Selected Essays, 1934-1943*. London: Oxford University Press.

Werbach, M. R. (1986). *Third Line Medicine*. London: Arkana.

Werner, K. (1977). *Yoga and Indian Philosophy*. Delhi: Banasidass.

Whitehead, A. N. (1928). *Science and the Modern World*. Cambridge: Cambridge University Press.

Whitehead, A. N. (1929). *Process and Reality*. London: Macmillan.

Whitehead, A. N. (1933). *Adventures of Ideas*. New York: Collier Macmillan, 1967.

Whiteman, J. H. M. (1986). *The Meaning of Life*. London: Colin Smythe.

Whitmont, E. C. (1983). *Return of the Goddess*. London: Routledge & Kegan Paul.

Whitton, J. L., & Fisher, J. (1986). *Life between Life*. London: Collins.

Wickes, F. (1965). *The Inner World of Choice*. New York: Harper.

Wilber, K. (1979). *No Boundary*. London, Shambhala.

Wilber, K. (1980). *The Atman Project*. New York: Theosophical Publishing House.

Wilber, K. (Ed.) (1982). *The Holographic Paradigm*. London: Shambhala.

Wilber, K. (Ed.) (1984). *Quantum Questions*. London: Shambhala.

Wilber, K. (1995). *Sex, Ecology, Spirituality*. New York: Shambhala.

Wilber, K. (1997). *A Short History of Everything*. New York: Shambhala.

Wilber, K. (1998). *The Marriage of Sense and Soul*. Dublin: Gill & Macmillan.

Wilber, K. (1999). *Integral Psychology*. New York: Shambhala.

Wilber, K. (2000). *A Theory of Everything*, New York: Shambhala.

Wilber, K., Engler, J., & Brown, D. P. (Eds.) (1986). *Transformations of Consciousness*. New York: Shambhala.

Willey, B. (1986). *The Seventeenth Century Background*. London: Ark.

Wilson, C. (1979). *Mysteries*. London: Granada.

Wilson, E. O. (1998). *Consilience*. London: Little, Brown.

Woodhouse, M. (1996). *Paradigm Wars*. Berkeley, CA: North Atlantic.

Woollacott, M. H. (2015). *Infinite Awareness*. New York: Rowman & Littlefield.

Yates, F. (1975). *The Rosicrucian Enlightenment*. London: Paladin.

Young, J. Z. (1987). *Philosophy and the Brain*. Oxford: Oxford University Press.

Zaehner, R. C. (1961). *Mysticism Sacred and Profane*. Oxford: Oxford University Press.

Zaleski, C. (1986). *Otherworld Journeys*. New York: Oxford University Press.

INDEX

Printed by Printforce, United Kingdom